Prophetic Wisdom

SUNY series in Religious Studies
———————
Harold Coward, editor

Prophetic Wisdom

Engaged Buddhism's Struggle for
Social Justice and Complete Liberation

CHARLES R. STRAIN

Published by State University of New York Press, Albany

© 2024 State University of New York

All rights reserved

Printed in the United States of America

No part of this book may be used or reproduced in any manner whatsoever without written permission. No part of this book may be stored in a retrieval system or transmitted in any form or by any means including electronic, electrostatic, magnetic tape, mechanical, photocopying, recording, or otherwise without the prior permission in writing of the publisher.

For information, contact State University of New York Press, Albany, NY
www.sunypress.edu

Library of Congress Cataloging-in-Publication Data

Name: Strain, Charles R., author.
Title: Prophetic wisdom : engaged Buddhism's struggle for social justice and complete liberation / Charles R. Strain.
Description: Albany : State University of New York Press, [2024]. | Includes bibliographical references and index.
Identifiers: LCCN 2023045138 | ISBN 9781438498010 (hardcover : alk. paper) | ISBN 9781438498027 (ebook) | ISBN 9781438498003 (pbk. : alk. paper)
Subjects: LCSH: Social justice—Religious aspects—Buddhism. | Buddhism—Social aspects. | Nonviolence—Religious aspects—Buddhism.
Classification: LCC HN40.B8 S77 2024 | DDC 294.3/376—dc23/eng/20240221
LC record available at https://lccn.loc.gov/2023045138

10 9 8 7 6 5 4 3 2 1

For my brothers and sisters

Paul Farrell Strain
Dennis Ward Strain
Bonnie Ann Doremus

and in memory of

Mary Ruth Erickson

Contents

Acknowledgments ix

Introduction 1

Part One: The Prophetic Wisdom of Elders

Chapter One Like a Fire in the Bones: The Prophetic Voice 13

Buddhist Reflections in a Prophetic Key #1: Cries of the Crows: A Buddhist Take on the Prophetic Voice 31

Chapter Two Crossing Boundaries: Rita Gross and the Transformation of Patriarchal Buddhism 33

Buddhist Reflections in a Prophetic Key #2: Reading a Buddhist Classic of Mother's Grief against the Grain 47

Chapter Three Thich Nhat Hanh: A Buddhist Monk in the Conflagration of War 49

Buddhist Reflections in a Prophetic Key #3: Sea Pirates, Nazis, and the Need for Moral Judgment 65

Chapter Four Joanna Macy and the Work That Reconnects 69

viii | Contents

Buddhist Reflections in a Prophetic Key # 4: Bearing Witness to
the Suffering of Our Time   83

Chapter Five   B. R. Ambedkar: The Annihilation of Caste and
                  the Liberation of the Dalits   87

Buddhist Reflections in a Prophetic Key # 5: Gautama's Leave-Taking   105

Part Two:
Liberation in the American Context

Chapter Six   The American Jeremiad: Creating the City upon
                  a Hill   111

Chapter Seven   Dr. Martin Luther King Jr: America's Jeremiah   127

Buddhist Reflections in a Prophetic Key #6: Reinventing Buddhism
in a Hostile Society   141

Part Three:
From Prophecy to Praxis:
Strategic Action and Social Liberation

Chapter Eight   Nonviolent Action: The Dynamics of Love, Power,
                  and Justice   147

Chapter Nine   From Prophecy to Praxis: Thinking Strategically
                  about Action   165

Chapter Ten   Facing Up to Evil, Abolishing Our Racial
                  Caste System   185

Conclusion   211

Notes   219

Works Cited   259

Index   275

Acknowledgments

Excerpts from the poetry of Thich Nhat Hanh are taken from *Call Me by My True Names: The Collected Poems of Thich Nhat Hanh* (Berkeley, CA: Parallax Press, 1999). They are used with permission. Portions of chapters 1 and 2 appeared in Charles R. Strain, "Borrowing a Prophetic Voice, Actualizing the Prophetic Dimension: Rita Gross and Engaged Buddhism," *Journal of Buddhist Ethics* 25 (2018): 1–30. Early versions of chapter 9 appeared in Charles R. Strain, "Is a Buddhist Praxis Possible?" *Journal of Buddhist Ethics* 25 (2018): 71–97.

Thanks to Roy and Frida Furman for their comments on an early version of chapter 1, and to Frida for comments on chapters 2 and 10. Thank you to Chris Tirres for his comments on an early version of chapter 9. My thanks to Katie Van Heest for her editorial suggestions on the first draft of the book. Matthew Pearson and Kat Keating provided technical help at critical stages in completing the manuscript. I deeply appreciate the comments of the anonymous readers for SUNY Press that helped me to clarify key points.

I appreciated the opportunity to present key theoretical points to the Critical and Constructive Buddhism section of the American Academy of Religion. Discussions with fellow students in the Northwestern University chapter of the Osher Lifelong Learning Institute helped me to clarify my analysis of the African American Jeremiad and especially Frederick Douglass. I deeply appreciate discussions with members of the Chicago Chapter of the Buddhist Peace Fellowship and collaborations with them on actions that embody a prophetic Buddhist ethos. Special thanks to Alex Bernstein, Kevin Havener, Dean Kaufer, Jack Lawlor, and Taigen Dan Leighton. Jim Block has been a fellow team teacher, an intellectual challenger, and a good friend for more than three decades. Thanks to James Peltz and the team at

SUNY Press. Thanks to my sons, Aaron Bobrow Strain and Daniel Strain, for inspiring me to become a better writer. My failings in this regard are my own responsibility. My gratitude to Dianne Hanau-Strain always.

Introduction

Engaged Buddhism at a Crossroads

> So we are now at a point unlike any other in our story. I suspect that we have, in some way, chosen to be here at this culminating chapter or turning point. We have opted to be alive when the stakes are high, to test everything we have learned about interconnectedness, about courage—to test it now when Gaia is ailing and her children are ill. We are alive right now when it could be curtains for conscious life on this beautiful water planet hanging there like a jewel in space.
>
> —Joanna Macy, "Our Life as Gaia"[1]

At the Lakeside Buddha Sangha in Evanston, Illinois, where I practice, we frequently chant the "Discourse on Love," Thich Nhat Hanh's translation of the *Metta Sutta*. We vow to cultivate boundless love for all living beings, "beings who are frail or strong, tall or short, big or small, visible or invisible, already born or yet to be born. May they all live in peace and security."[2] Loving-kindness coupled with equally boundless compassion are of the essence of Buddhist engagement. They are also an endless task and they are not enough.

A simple story will illustrate this point. Two persons walking by a river see a baby floating downstream. They wade in and rescue the baby, but as they reach the shore, they see another, and then another, and another. Each time they rush in to rescue the baby. Then as the next baby floats into view, one person heads upstream. "Where are you going?" asks the remaining person. "I need help." "I am going to find out who is throwing babies into the river," the other responds." The traditional story ends here, and my activist students love it. They, too, are ready to head up the river, but in my version, there is a different ending. The person heading upstream discovers not one or two evildoers but a factory that dumps babies into the river and an interlocking complex of social institutions—economic, political, religious—coupled with social practices, laws, and customs, all undergirded by ideology. In short, not evildoers but an unjust social system. The workers in the town's factory have only a dim idea of the consequences of their actions, and besides, they have babies at home needing to be fed. The stockholders of the factory are you and me through our retirement investments. Dismantling the system will take more than a single generation. Meanwhile, the "waste" continues to be dumped into the river. We should be glad that someone remained behind to rescue and care for the infants. But that is not enough. At some level Engaged Buddhists recognize this as a compelling insight. They (we) struggle, however, to lay out just what sorts of strategic actions are necessary to reconstruct an unjust system.

Engaged Buddhism is an international movement of Buddhists who seek both personal and collective liberation from suffering.[3] Sallie King defines Engaged Buddhism as "a contemporary form of Buddhism that engages actively yet nonviolently with the social, economic, political . . . and ecological problems of society."[4] Christopher Queen, another pioneer in the study of this movement, sees it as "the application of the Dharma . . . to the resolution of social problems . . . in the context of a global conversation on human rights, distributive justice and social progress. . . . It may be seen as a new paradigm of Buddhist liberation."[5] Founders of a new paradigm of Buddhism though they may be, Engaged Buddhists have had to think in a new language, using terms such as "oppression" and "social justice" and to revise their understanding of the meaning of liberation.

Classical Buddhism, like virtually all premodern religious traditions, lacked an understanding of systemic injustice baked into social institutions as structural violence.[6] Despite the teaching of impermanence, classical Buddhist schools viewed social institutions as given and sought world renunciation not world transformation.[7] So Rita Gross, a practicing Buddhist, history of religions scholar, and feminist, boldly affirmed, "I am taking permission, as a Buddhist, to use a prophetic voice."[8] Gross was caught by a boundary-transgressing spirit. Putting the prophetic voice to use, she pioneered a new and deeper form of social engagement for Buddhist practitioners.

Writing in the *Guardian* in the wake of Thich Nhat Hanh's death in January 2022, the Buddhist practitioner, essayist, and social critic Rebecca Solnit brought to consciousness the impact of Buddhism in the West. Buddhism, like a tributary within a watershed that includes feminist, antiracist, and ecological movements, emphasizes equality and nonviolence. It joins others in criticizing the rampant exploitation of the earth and its peoples. Thich Nhat Hanh affected millions, Solnit argued, through his ideas, retreats, books, and practices in ways that are hard to measure. He personified a stream "flowing through the West from which many have drunk without knowing quite where the waters came from."[9]

Prophetic Wisdom explores a complementary narrative, namely, how Engaged Buddhism has been shaped and reshaped by those who have drunk from the waters of the prophetic ethos. Without quite knowing, to parrot Solnit, where these waters came from. Thich Nhat Hanh, our elders, and a new generation of Engaged Buddhists have refreshed their body, speech, and mind through these waters. Multiple streams constitute our cultural watershed. Western Buddhists practicing today—and, to an increasing extent, all Buddhists—are the heirs of multiple religious and secular streams, including those stemming from the Hebrew prophets. It is no longer possible for Buddhists to hold themselves aloof from the "prophetic call for judgment, criticism and responsibility."[10] To recognize our multiple sources of wisdom and the ways in which specific streams nourish us is to invigorate our continuing struggle for social justice and complete liberation. The prophetic ethos, as a religious-ethical mode of being, is accessible to all whose search for the common good opens them to transformation.

In a previous comparative study, *The Prophet and the Bodhisattva: Daniel Berrigan, Thich Nhat Hanh, and the Ethics of Peace and Justice*, I celebrated Christian theologian Paul Knitter's approach to interreligious dialogue as mutual transformation in his book *Without Buddha I Could Not Be a Christian*. He followed the lead of Notre Dame theologian John Dunne by adopting a threefold method: (1) stating a problem or struggle that he has with a particular Christian teaching or practice; (2) "passing over" to examine a related Buddhist teaching or practice; and (3) "passing back" to affirm his commitment as a Christian but now in a transformed way of thinking and acting.[11] I suggested that, in my case, the figures of the prophet and the bodhisattva each constituted one pole of an ellipse and that I found myself in the magnetic field generated by these two classic forms of religious and moral agency. Instead of passing over and back, I saw myself passing back and forth, back and forth.[12]

Now the idea of Buddhists borrowing a prophetic voice has opened a different horizon. Why wouldn't Buddhists embrace the idea that Buddhist teachings and practice might be amplified by incorporating aspects of the prophetic ethos? Doesn't that reflect the truth of interdependent coarising?

Thich Nhat Hanh pointedly said that Buddhism is made up of non-Buddhist elements.[13] The new possibility is to see the prophetic ethos as an integral element in Engaged Buddhism. So, playing upon Knitter's title, I suggest that without Jeremiah I could not be a Buddhist.

The prophetic tradition offers a socially and religiously powerful concept—the concept of justice—that reconfigures the Buddhist dharma. Unjust systems stigmatize certain groups. They also warp all who are shaped by them in ways that affect our relationships, our practices, and even our personalities while imposing more oppression on some than on others. Given the prevalence of oppressive forces within political and economic structures, gender roles, and culturally imposed psychological formations, Rita Gross argues, "it is hard to imagine being serious about liberation or the bodhisattva path without being involved in social action at some level."[14]

Prophetic Wisdom argues that tapping into the prophetic ethos will enhance Buddhism's understanding of and commitment to collective liberation, its commitment to ending collective suffering. There is a vast literature on liberation from oppression, and the term "liberation" has been used in widely different ways. What these ways hold in common is a commitment to the removal of barriers to the self-realization of persons and communities. *Prophetic Wisdom* will focus on liberation from socially constructed barriers, that is, institutionalized forms of oppression. In Buddhist terms, complete liberation requires overcoming collective dukkha.[15] Underlying this particular focus are several assumptions:

- Oppression as the thwarting of the self-realization of persons and communities operates through social structures that empower some and disempower others. It expresses and maintains itself through direct violence but primarily through structural violence.

- Social structures are constructed. Human beings are socialized into these structures from birth. Human beings are as they are because of cultural conditioning and institutionally shaped barriers and supports.

- Social constructions are impermanent. They can be deconstructed and reconstructed.

- Human beings, more or less consciously, reenforce these barriers or work to remove them. They can become agents of liberation.

- Engaged Buddhists agree that an existential revolution, a transformation of the self, must accompany the transformation of ideologies, social institutions, and cultural values and practices. Most Buddhists have emphasized this mode of liberation. This book, however, will focus on systemic change, the transformation of collective dukkha for which we need prophetic wisdom.

Here is a now obvious example of socially constructed structural violence. When I was growing up, curbs on sidewalks were part of the built environment. They were taken for granted. They did not slope down at the intersections. Growing up, it never occurred to me that these curbs thwarted the mobility of people with certain disabilities, and consequently created a barrier to their self-realization. I remain astounded at how long it took before the Americans with Disabilities Act (1990) made me and many others aware of this very tangible form of oppression. So I ask myself what forms of oppression am I totally unaware of right now?

In mid-March 1965, in the aftermath of one of the bloodiest attacks by police on nonviolent civil rights demonstrators in Selma, Alabama, I found myself in a Montgomery jail. Like significant numbers of Northern college students, I had heeded a call from John Lewis and the Student Nonviolent Coordinating Committee to come to Montgomery to keep the pressure up until the march from Selma to Montgomery could be completed. During an initial march on the capitol shortly after I arrived, deputy sheriffs on horseback galloped into our ranks, slashing back and forth with their long clubs. Within a day I was committing civil disobedience protesting this indiscriminate violence. I was part of the student groups packing Montgomery jails.

A naive Northerner, I was feeling, if only in a minor way, the lash of a terrorist state. Lying in jail, isolated, my head throbbing from a police-inflicted scalp wound, I heard a woman wailing, pleading to be let go. At that moment I could think of no reason on earth why she should not be freed from that jail. In the Hebrew Bible, God orders the prophet Jeremiah to call for the women "keeners" whose dirges will wake a somnolent people to the crisis that has come upon them (Jer 9:17–20).[16] I know nothing of the keening woman in Montgomery jail or her fate. I do know that her voice revealed to me what Rabbi Abraham Heschel called "the monstrosity of injustice."[17] Whatever her offense, some solution other than imprisonment seemed imperative. The echo of her voice has never faded. Taking refuge in Jeremiah and thousands of hidden and manifest prophets, I offer this book in honor of her suffering.

Plan of the Book

PART ONE: THE PROPHETIC WISDOM OF ELDERS

As I write, Thich Nhat Hanh, who first coined the term "Engaged Buddhism," has died in Hue near his ancestral home in central Vietnam. Many others who were the first generation to develop an Engaged Buddhism, including B. R. Ambedkar and Rita Gross, have died as well. Engaged Buddhists face a generational passage. New and diverse voices are articulating and living different forms of Engaged Buddhism. They deserve our deep listening. At the same time, it is important to take stock of the visions and actions of those who first blazed a trail for new generations to follow. These elders developed ways of thinking and acting that bear a "family resemblance" to those of the Hebrew prophets. Four such elders will exemplify Engaged Buddhism's ability to tap into the prophetic dimension.

Chapter One: Like a Fire in the Bones: The Prophetic Voice

But first we examine the prophetic texts in the Hebrew Bible to develop a more detailed understanding of the prophetic ethos. Classics speak to us across boundaries of time and space. A genuine classic has the power to transform our ways of thinking and acting. Chapter 1 argues that the prophetic texts of the Hebrew Bible still retain the power of classics. The prophets did not predict the future; they were not soothsayers. Rather they read the signs of the times. But they did much more than this. Amid the collective trauma brought on by the crushing force of imperial invasions, they charted a way out of despair. In the process they became a wellspring sending forth a stream that has surfaced at times and coursed underground at others. It has been and can be tapped into by anyone who cares about justice.

Chapter Two: Crossing Boundaries: Rita Gross and the Transformation of Patriarchal Buddhism

While Rita Gross was the youngest of the four Buddhist elders whose internalization of a prophetic voice we will study, she is also the most explicit in her borrowing. She deserves to go first. Chapter 2 looks at that borrowing. Using the prophetic voice in her case meant uncovering the pervasive ambiguity of the Buddhist tradition in its portrayal of women, its estimation of their religious potential, and its gender-based hierarchical institutional arrangements. Gross's appropriation of the prophetic voice entailed (a) a willingness to engage in social criticism and self-criticism, (b) protest against the abuse of power, (c) a vision of an alternative social order, and (d) a commitment to social activism.[18] While this formulation is true as far as it goes, it does not go far enough. It does not get at the mode of being religious at the core of the prophetic ethos. By referring to what she calls the "prophetic dimension" in Buddhism, Gross suggests that a prophetic stance and mode of being in the world is intrinsic to, but perhaps concealed within, Buddhist teachings and practices.[19]

Chapter Three: Thich Nhat Hanh: A Buddhist Monk in the Conflagration of War

Chapter 3 studies the poetry of the Vietnamese Buddhist monk Thich Nhat Hanh, who first coined the term "Engaged Buddhism." At a superficial level Thich Nhat Hanh would seem to be the last Buddhist to assume a prophetic voice. Not, I hasten to add, because of any deficiency in his way of "being peace" or in his steadfast exemplification of loving speech but because he so deeply incarnates the ethos of a bodhisattva. However, if we steep ourselves in Thich Nhat Hanh's antiwar poetry, we can indeed see the bodhisattva catch fire with the spirit of a prophet.

Chapter Four: Joanna Macy and the Work That Reconnects

Joanna Macy is the visionary elder whose "work that reconnects" we will examine in chapter 4. As we see in the myth that opens this introduction, Joanna Macy has called on Engaged Buddhists and their many allies rooted in other traditions to take part in the Great Turning. If the millions of living species that we, as Buddhists, seek to liberate are not to perish in a sixth great extinction, the human species will need to put the brakes on its blind rush to a cliff's edge and turn in a new direction. In seeking how to combat the psychic numbness that is our default response to the twin threats of a nuclear holocaust and climate change, Joanna Macy also has offered to Buddhists a new understanding of the role of emotions—even ones that Buddhists have labeled as negative—in reconnecting ourselves to our living planet.

Chapter Five: B. R. Ambedkar: The Annihilation of Caste and the Liberation of the Dalits

Except for key essays written by Christopher Queen, Western scholars of Engaged Buddhism have neglected B. R. Ambedkar. A younger contemporary of Gandhi, Ambedkar, a Dalit (Untouchable), was a fierce opponent of the caste system. His unrelenting battle frequently placed him at odds with the Mahatma himself. We learn how any prophetic vision must itself be subject to a prophetic critique. But Ambedkar is even more important because his boldly revisionist form of Buddhism became a source of hope culminating in a mass conversion of his fellow Dalits shortly before his death.

PART TWO: LIBERATION IN THE AMERICAN CONTEXT

Prophetic Wisdom focuses upon the struggle for social justice and collective liberation in the American context. Scholars have pointed to the "American Jeremiad" as a distinctive rhetorical strategy developed by those engaged in this struggle. Engaged Buddhists need to learn this language if they are to communicate beyond their denominational boundaries.

Chapter Six: The American Jeremiad: Creating the City upon a Hill

Chapter 6 argues that the American Jeremiad was a rhetorical strategy designed for a people on a mission, called by God to be a City upon a Hill. Tailored to New World circumstances, it was a goad to world transformation. In the nineteenth century it was appropriated by African Americans who challenged the nation to cure itself of the cancer of slavery. In succeeding generations, it became the idiom through which reformers sought to move the nation to live up to its ideals. Repeatedly it challenged the brutality of the status quo and awakened the conscience of a nation drifting into complacency.

Chapter Seven: Dr. Martin Luther King Jr: America's Jeremiah

"The whole future of America will depend upon the impact and influence of Dr. King," insisted Rabbi Abraham Heschel, a civil rights and peace activist and a prophet himself.[20] Dr. Martin Luther King Jr. was America's Jeremiah of the twentieth century. More than any other leader, he articulated and embodied the prophetic ethos. It is hard to imagine how any group committed to nonviolent action, such as Engaged Buddhists, could seek liberation from collective suffering without coming to terms with Dr. King's mark on the twentieth century. So Dr. King's immense contribution to the jeremiad's call for fundamental social change is the topic for chapter 7.

Introduction | 9

PART THREE: FROM PROPHECY TO PRAXIS: STRATEGIC ACTION AND SOCIAL LIBERATION

Compassion without insight/wisdom, Buddhists insist, is blind. Wisdom uncovers and nurtures seeds of liberation. It holds fast to concrete reality and therefore depends upon knowledge and analysis. The next three chapters challenge Engaged Buddhists to draw upon several disciplines to expand their knowledge of the causes of collective suffering and to develop more consciously their understanding of the means and ends of social transformation.

Chapter Eight: Nonviolent Action: The Dynamics of Love, Power, and Justice

A commitment to use only nonviolent means to create social change is a hallmark of Engaged Buddhism as an international movement. But nonviolent action is an exercise of power. Buddhists are wary of exercising power because it is easily infected by dualistic thinking, group egoism, and patterns of domination. To enter the sphere of politics seeking social change is to wade into swamps of ambiguity. What sort of power can Engaged Buddhists justify exercising? Chapter 8 grapples with this dilemma.

Chapter Nine: From Prophecy to Praxis: Thinking Strategically about Action

Chapter 9 is the most theoretical in the book. It asks how we move from a diagnosis of the pervasive sickness of American society to an analysis of its causes and conditions, how we proceed from there to a constructive vision of an alternative future and, ultimately, to strategically directed action to bring about social transformation and healing. The blinding insights of the prophet become practical guidance through the contributions of a critical social theory and of a Buddhist constructive imagination. We move from prophecy to praxis.

Chapter Ten: Facing Up to Evil, Abolishing Our Racial Caste System

Today numerous issues demand a prophetic critique. Dr. King's version of the three (collective) poisons included militarism, economic exploitation/poverty, and racism. *Prophetic Wisdom* focuses on racism in the American context because it preceded the founding of the country by more than 150 years but also because its venom poisons every aspect of American life. A serpent is entwined around the legs of Lady Liberty. In chapter 10 we will examine systemic racism, account for its persistence in American life, and treat the recent argument by Isabel Wilkerson that it can best be understood as a caste system. *Prophetic Wisdom* must face up to this poison's presence in the American bloodstream and offer a vision of an alternative future. Chapter 10 focuses on one aspect of systemic racism—mass incarceration—and argues that Engaged Buddhists have something distinctive to offer to overcome it.

Buddhist Reflections in a Prophetic Key

Special features of this book are the Buddhist Reflections in a Prophetic Key that appear at the end of the first five chapters and that are tied to the issues raised in their respective chapters. They offer a glimpse of prophetic wisdom giving new twists to old stories, challenging sacrosanct assumptions, and pushing forms of social engagement toward more radical actions. They are intended as spurs to your own imagination.

At one point in their trek through the wilderness, Moses and the elders of the Israelites had gathered outside the main camp in the presence of YHWH when a young man arrived bearing the news that two men had begun to prophesy. Joshua urged Moses to squelch this unauthorized manifestation of the spirit of God. But Moses refused, saying "Would that all the Lord's people were prophets, and that the Lord would put his spirit upon them" (Num 11: 24–29). In fact, the spirit of the Hebrew prophets, or what I call the "prophetic ethos," has become contagious. Increasingly this ethos has spread beyond the boundaries of Western religious traditions. Numerous aspects of the thoughts, speech, and actions of Engaged Buddhists bear a family resemblance to the key traits that characterize the prophetic ethos.

"So, we are now at a point unlike any other in our story." "Would that all engaged people were prophets." Aren't Joanna Macy and Moses (slightly amended) strange collaborators? Maybe not. To choose to be here, actively doing our best to shape our world in a time of unprecedented peril, requires creative hybrid visions of all sorts, drawing on multiple pasts, projecting alternative futures. Engaged Buddhists at a crossroads are challenged to internalize a prophetic ethos. We need prophetic wisdom.[21]

Part One
The Prophetic Wisdom of Elders

Chapter One

Like a Fire in the Bones

The Prophetic Voice

> For whenever I speak, I must cry out, I must shout, "Violence and destruction! . . . . If I say, "I will not . . . speak any more in his name," then within me there is something like a burning fire shut up in my bones; I am weary with holding it in, and I cannot.
>
> —Jer 20:8–9

> History will attest that the Hebrew prophets belong to all people. . . . Today we particularly need the Hebrew prophets because they taught that to love God was to love justice, that each human being has an inescapable obligation to denounce evil where he sees it. . . . The Hebrew prophets are needed today because the thunder of their fearless voices is the only sound stronger than the blasts of bombs and the clamor of war hysteria.
>
> —Martin Luther King Jr., "My Jewish Brother"[1]

Part 1 of this book focuses on listening to the voices of the Hebrew prophets, and then listening to the voices of earlier generations of Engaged Buddhists. In the process we will learn a great deal about the prophetic ethos as a mode of being religious manlifested in living a socially engaged life.

The Hebrew prophets *are* their voice. They claim to make God audible. At moments of crisis their prophetic voices and God's become indistinguishable. God roars like a lion and so does Amos (3:8).[2] To borrow a voice, as Rita Gross does in her critical analysis of patriarchal Buddhism, is to inhabit the spirit that breathes forth the sound. However, assuming a prophetic voice is not as straightforward as it may seem. It is much more complicated than simply engaging in social criticism. Even those of us who situate ourselves within the tradition inaugurated by the Hebrew prophets confront an alien and alienating world when we grapple with those texts in contrast to simply picking a few electric quotations.[3]

The prophets' voices have been inscribed in the texts that bear their names. We have nothing like a full biography of any of these religious radicals. They are agents in a social drama that has been revised, amended, and edited—in some cases over centuries. The prophets are composite personae, nodes where multiple theological and ideological strands intersect. We can find common themes or tropes, the prophets' DNA as it were, but few prophets have the complete set of traits. There are significant differences in their visions and practices. They are cousins, not siblings. One common theme or trope is the Reluctant Prophet:

> MOSES: "O My Lord, I have never been eloquent. . . . I am slow of speech and slow of tongue." (Exod 4:10)
>
> ISAIAH: "Woe is me. I am lost for I am a man of unclean lips." (Isa 6:5)
>
> JEREMIAH: "I do not know how to speak for I am only a boy." (Jer 1:6)
>
> MARTIN LUTHER KING JR.: "With my head in my hands, I bowed over the kitchen table and prayed aloud. . . . "I am here taking a stand for what I believe is right. But now I am afraid. . . . I am at the end of my powers. . . . I can't face it alone."[4]

From the beginning we are introduced to the prophet as a flawed human being. In each of these cases the reluctant prophet's plea is met with a divine assurance of constant support, and these prophets accept their calling.

The Hebrew prophets, including men, women, and prophetic guilds, proclaim or perform the divine message in words, songs, and symbolic actions.[5] They do not employ the discourse of moral deliberation moving from core principles, justified rationally, to applications, a process that is open to public debate.[6] Their voices ring with passion. Their method is not didactic. They do not offer sage advice; rather they present shocking images that depict a cosmos in disarray.

The prophets seek to move their audience to a dramatic change. Raw and crude language strips away the veneer of politeness that insulates elite society from the horrors of a violent world—a world that these powerful leaders have, in no small part, made. Lamentations, pleas for repentance, arguments with God, and oracles that anticipate disaster falling on the northern kingdom of Israel and, later, the southern kingdom of Judah and the surrounding countries are a few of the ways in which the Hebrew prophets voice their messages. Each of these forms of speech is intended to destabilize its audience.[7]

Communication also occurs through dramatic actions, through the body, and not merely through the mouth. Symbolic actions such as Jeremiah's wearing a yoke (Jer 27:1–2; 28:10–11) and Isaiah's walking naked through the streets of Jerusalem for three years (Isa 20:2–6). underscore the oral message. Numerous scholars interpret prophetic performances as "street theater."[8] Louis Stulman summarizes the meaning of these symbolic acts by suggesting that they "serve as witness, liturgy, reparation, provocation, re-enactment, and protest as well as disaster and survival theater."[9]

The prophets' raw speech and provocative action, which scholars describe as "disruptive, fragmentary, jarring," can be seen as skillful means for breaking through the obliviousness of the power elite to the corrosive effects of injustice and the collective numbness enforced through the ideology of a divinely secured state.[10] "Peace, peace," the smooth-talking, false prophets proclaim, "when there is no peace" (Jer 6:14).

Uttered under the cloud of a Babylonian invasion of Judah, Jeremiah's words resonate long after both that empire and Judah became dust in the wind. Dr. King, standing in a long line of prophets, testified to the urgent need for a prophetic voice even as he himself magnified it. His words and actions are a testimony to the endurance of what I call the prophetic ethos.

Louis Stulman and Hyun Chul Paul Kim point out that it is relatively rare that the stories of those who were crushed by imperial conquest are preserved and, indeed, play an ongoing role in transforming future societies. The period inscribed in the prophetic texts includes the invasion of the northern kingdom of Israel by the Assyrians (722 BCE), the conquest of the southern kingdom of Judah by the Babylonians (587 BCE), and the conquest of the Babylonians by the Persians in the later part of the sixth century BCE. These books are the "survival literature" of peoples undergoing cultural collapse as well as social destruction:[11]

> How does literature so laden with loss operate as an artistic expression of hope? In the first place, it translates lived chaos into language and so creates a bearable distance between traumatic events and their symbolic representations. It refuses to indulge in denials about the nation's monstrous losses, generating space for the work of grief, a prerequisite to the work of hope. This trauma corpus puts virtually every facet of community life under a microscope and calls for action, transforming victims of violence into active meaning makers. It creates alternatives to the old world, alternatives that contour a future for a people seemingly without one. Moreover, it makes a stunning claim that raw historical power is subservient to the power and purposes of God. This polyphonic corpus speaks with clarion voice that God's purposes are not thwarted by geopolitics or cosmic forces.[12]

Stulman's quotation takes us into the religious heart of the tradition anchored by the Hebrew prophets:

- Employing symbolic representations of "lived chaos," the prophetic imagination overcomes denial and opens a space for the practice of grief.

- Using the microscope of justice, it critically investigates every facet of social life.

- Operating from a different understanding of power, it unveils geopolitics as an exercise in delusion and, in so doing, it creates an alternative narrative to those that glorify the empire du jour.

- Committing itself to the practice of hope, it imagines an alternative future.

- Performing a call to action, it seeks to transform victims into "meaning-making agents."

- Creating polyphonic texts, it invites, rather it demands, an ethically driven interpretation.

What's missing from this analysis of the prophetic DNA are two traits widely emphasized in popular as well as scholarly interpretations of the Hebrew prophets:

- Appealing to the subversive memory of Exodus, prophets bear witness to a liberating God who acts in the present crisis.

- Criticizing the idolatry of the power elite, the prophets undermine the ideology that upholds an unjust social order.

Each of these traits of the prophetic ethos amplifies what Dr. King frequently called "the fierce urgency of now."[13]

Prophetic Texts as Classics

The wager of this chapter and, indeed, of the whole book is that the prophetic texts of the Hebrew scriptures still retain the power of genuine classics to spark our religious and ethical imagination and that Engaged Buddhism can articulate its commitment to the liberation of all beings more deeply by borrowing a prophetic voice. "If the text is a genuinely classic one, my present horizon of understanding should always be provoked, challenged, transformed," argues theologian David Tracy.[14] Rhetorician Margaret Zulick adds that such classics offer a "flash of sublimity." "We are jolted into a new order of magnitude," she writes.[15] "Certain expressions of the human spirit so disclose a compelling truth about our lives that we cannot deny them some kind of normative status," Tracy concludes. "Thus do we name these expressions, and these alone 'classics.'"[16] A classic does not yield its meaning apart from my act of allowing this provocation to work in an unforeseen way. I am compelled to go beyond my confined self-understanding. This description should not be taken to mean that the constitution of a work as a classic is a purely subjective event. In Tracy's understanding, classics represent a form of public communication that is an alternative to rational argumentation. They compel reflection over many generations and across the boundaries of cultures.[17]

Redacted over centuries, prophetic texts present difficult challenges to any interpreter. If we take the book of Jeremiah as our model of a prophetic classic, we are confronted with a multiplicity of genres, including poetry, prose, and a "biography" of the prophet. The text speaks with a plurality of voices and presents several disparate endings. In this "polyphonic" text incompatible ideological positions are placed in dialogue with one another. Sheer juxtaposition forces the reader or hearer to become an active meaning maker. For those who experienced the chaos of a culture in ruins and forced exile, this text offered both an honest recognition of a traumatic past and a way to transcend victimhood.[18]

The power of the prophetic texts of the Hebrew Bible to generate new interpretations is dramatically presented in the Dead Sea Scrolls. The Qumran community's wrestling with the prophetic texts took two forms: Pesharim and expanded prophetic narratives. The Pesharim were commentaries on the prophetic texts that clearly distinguished between the verses of the biblical texts and the commentary that excavated their hidden, eschatological meaning. The Pesharim assume that the original prophetic books have a hidden meaning that refers to the present moment in the life of the community. The expanded prophetic narratives, in contrast, blurred the line between verses and commentary. Their authors appropriated the prophetic voice by both alluding to and rewriting the text. They repackaged the original message. In this regard the community was only doing what Deutero-Isaiah did in appropriating the voice of Isaiah and expanding the prophet's message. So, one Qumran text rewrites Ezekiel's vision of the dry bones (Ezek 37) to explicitly affirm "the bodily resurrection of the righteous of Israel." Both approaches, Alex Jassen concludes, "reflect the belief that the interpretation of prophetic scripture is itself a prophetic experience. . . . Inspired . . . exegetes become partners with the ancient prophets in the process of discerning the full meaning of their words."[19]

Deconstructing the Prophetic Voice

It is hard to get past the anger of the God expressed in the prophetic texts. By Elizabeth Van Volde's calculation, in the Hebrew Bible YHWH explodes in fury "more than five hundred times."[20] She adds that no woman in the Hebrew Bible expresses anger. Anger is a gendered emotion.[21] We must not quickly skate past the blatant power dynamics revealed in Van Volde's troubling analysis.

However, God's actions are never seen as an exercise of raw power. They are included within a frame of justice: "The Lord rises to argue his case; he stands to judge the peoples. The Lord enters into judgment with the elders and princes of his people. . . . What do you mean by crushing my people, by grinding the face of the poor?" (Isa 3:13–15). They invoke the language of the courts to level indictments, judgment, and punishment. YHWH becomes the prosecuting attorney, the judge, and the one who executes judgment.

The difficulty here is that it is *retributive* justice that characterizes this frame. In what scholars call the Deuteronomic theology the victims of a powerful empire crushing Israel or Judah must be portrayed as deserving their fate in order that YHWH might still be seen as in control.[22] Divine punishment, however violent, restores a cosmic order that has been disrupted by those who broke their covenant with God. In this logic the place to break the chain is not with God's anger but with vengeance or retribution. A different model of justice is needed that will challenge the power imbalance that is expressed in the metaphor of an angry God.

One way to come to terms with the recurrent images of an angry God is to place prophetic discourse within a helpful frame that Cathleen Kaveny calls "moral chemotherapy," a treatment appropriate for a social body riddled with the cancer of injustice.[23] Like chemotherapy, prophetic indictments are extreme measures to be used only when the violation of core values threatens the soul of a society. Under normal circumstances public discourse should employ practical reason, that is, moral deliberation that weighs competing values and social goals, formulates reasonable arguments, and suggests possible courses of action. However, where injustice has been normalized, where moral apathy prevails, where social evil has become entrenched, and where religious practices have become exercises in hypocrisy, rhetoric that shatters complacency is justified. Care, however, must be taken. Such discourse can also poison social relationships by fomenting "culture wars." As with chemotherapy, the prophetic indictment must be precisely targeted to avoid destroying healthy social tissue.[24]

While we may grant Kaveny's argument that leveling a prophetic indictment is appropriate only in extreme situations, it is important to recognize that denunciation is only one part of the prophetic task. Recalling Exodus, redefining the justice framework, engaging in ideology critique, the practice of grief, the practice of hope, and a call to action are also integral to the prophetic ethos. These elements function as spiritual disciplines within that ethos.

Throughout her analysis of patriarchal Buddhism, Rita Gross applies a "prophetic method" to deconstructing Buddhism, uncovering a true kernel by stripping away layer upon layer of androcentric denigrations of women's spiritual capacities.[25] We will see how she does this in the next chapter. For now, I will apply that prophetic method to a deconstruction of the prophetic texts themselves. The prophets deserve to be tested with the same level of scrutiny that they themselves applied to the dominant ideology.

Feminist biblical scholars have argued convincingly that the prophets' misogynistic words and images, too, need a moral chemotherapy. Among the shocking images are those depicting God and God's relationship with Israel and Judah. Throughout the prophetic corpus sinful Israel and Judah are each portrayed as an unfaithful wife or a whore. Hosea's depiction of God fits the pattern of an abusive husband (Hos 1–2).[26] God's retribution for Judah's failure to uphold its covenantal obligations is imagined as an act of sexual violence that is seen as justified because of the nation's profligacy (Jer 13:21–22, 13:25–27). Julia M. O'Brien argues that metaphors always invoke a "frame." Prophetic texts "remain fully ensconced within their culture's most enduring ideology, that of patriarchy."[27] Put bluntly, how can we acknowledge the prophetic texts as creating a radical breakout of the ideological prison of an unjust system when their metaphors are so deeply entrenched in the violence of their patriarchal culture?

It is impossible to avoid a critical reading of the prophets. They require an ethical exegesis. Different texts offer strikingly different readings of divine commands. Isaiah's famous proclamation that at the day of judgment the nations will turn swords into plowshares and spears into pruning hooks (2:4) is directly contradicted by the prophet Joel, who sees exactly the reverse taking place (plowshares into swords) leading to a bloody climax (3:9–10). Readers are faced, as Stulman puts it, with "the formidable task of distinguishing true from false prophecy."[28] An ethical exegesis works from the history of prophetic criticism of ideologies that justify domination to examine its own ambiguous texts. So, Gross sees the prophets' misogyny as reflecting a "cultural bias," not their core vision. Modern feminism, as heir to the prophetic ethos, has stripped away that husk.[29]

Juliana Claassens looks for alternative, countervailing images in the cracks and fissures of the text. A metaphor, for example, God as abusive husband, may predominate, but that does not mean that it imposes a monolithic framework. Claassens excavates the metaphor of God as mother to countermand the dominance of misogynistic metaphors. This image disrupts the dominant image of a God whose sovereignty is communicated through the image and actions of a Divine Warrior whose robes are soaked with the blood of Judah's enemies (Isa 63:1–4).[30] The God whose tears mingle with those of her prophet and those of God's people is not omnipotent but vulnerable, suffering with a suffering people (Jer 8:18–9:1).[31] Warrior gods do not weep. Isaiah juxtaposes God as a woman in labor to God as warrior (42:13–14).[32] Warriors have power only to take life; women in labor have the power to bring forth life. Such alternative images limn a countervailing narrative that liberates God from the honor/shame framework that demands retribution for any act that offends God's glory.[33] Ultimately it is this framework that offends contemporary readers.

The deconstruction of any religious tradition is a necessary component of retrieving its message. Traditions arise and consolidate themselves within cultures that are not just, that are cancerous. Applying a prophetic method to reading the prophetic texts of the Hebrew Bible is a necessary part of the process of selective borrowing. Next, we will uncover the ways in which the prophetic ethos functions as a spiritual discipline, ways that might be adopted and adapted by Engaged Buddhists. Following our earlier summation of Louis Stulman's definition of that ethos, we will examine five key themes: the practice of justice, the subversive memory of Exodus, the critique of the royal consciousness, the practice of grief, and the practice of hope.[34] All of these practices working in tandem constitute the prophetic ethos.

The Praxis of Justice

Justice, justice shall you pursue.

—Deut 16:20

The pursuit of justice is what we expect of the Hebrew prophets. Isaiah minces no words: "Seek justice, defend the orphan, plead for the widow." YHWH has an allergic reaction to those who perform religious services with blood on their hands: "I have had enough" (Isa 1:11–15; cf. Amos 5:21–24). We misconstrue the prophets' understanding of justice, however, if we think of it only in juridical terms. To seek justice is to seek God because justice is an attribute of God.[35] Seeking justice is a spiritual practice, not simply an ethical imperative (Isa 1:10–17).

Singling out the widow, the orphan, and the alien pushes the notion of justice to encompass those who in a patriarchal society are outside the borders of moral consideration. They inhabit a no-man's-land because they lack the requisite male guardian or have no clan affiliation. Having no place in the social structure, they are nobodies. YHWH's demand that they be included challenges the way borders are drawn. The prophets' defense of the widow, the orphan, and the stranger morphs into an uncompromising condemnation of the injustice of the power elite.[36] Revealing just how strident the prophetic voice can be, Micah compares the power elite of

Judah to cannibals "who tear the skin off my people and the flesh off their bones, who . . . break their bones in pieces and chop them up like meat in a kettle" (Mic 3:2–3). The prophets do not ground their condemnations in some utopian ideal of justice; rather, as Rabbi Abraham Heschel puts it, they confront "the monstrosity of injustice."[37]

There is a short stanza buried in one of Amos's oracles that illustrates this monstrous injustice. YHWH proclaims an indictment of Israel: "Because they sell the righteous/for silver and the needy for a pair of sandals—they who trample the head of the poor into the dust of earth and push the afflicted out of the way" (Amos 2:6–7). Selling humans for private gain is a familiar charge, but what is striking are the flimsy sandals for which the needy are sold. It is not sufficient that the poor are condemned to be exploited, indentured to the powerful. They must be humiliated, robbed of whatever threadbare dignity they have clung to, treated like dirt.[38]

The Subversive Memory of Exodus

> I brought you up out of the land of Egypt and led you forty years in the wilderness, to possess the land of the Amorite. And I raised up some of your children to be prophets . . .
>
> —Amos 2:10–11

Remember, the book of Deuteronomy proclaims, above all, remember who you are and who brought you to the land where you prosper (Deut 8:1–20).[39] The Hebrew prophets, Michael Walzer explains, "cast their arguments in a style appropriate to the linearity of Exodus politics: they look back to the deliverance and the covenant and forward to the promises."[40] The prophets are unanimous in their appeals to the God of Exodus, a God who is moved by the plight of the marginalized and oppressed. From Moses and Miriam (Exod 15) to Amos (2:10, 3:1) and Micah (6:3–4), from Jeremiah (32:20–23, 32:36–41) to all three Isaiahs (10:24–26; 11:15–16; 48:20–21; 52:4; 63:7–14), the prophets frame the crisis of the present and their hope for deliverance in terms of this originating myth.[41] To forget is to return to Egypt. To remember is "to break every yoke," to actualize the " 'ineradicable subversion' of the Exodus story."[42]

In *The Liberating Path of the Hebrew Prophets: Then and Now*, Rabbi Nahum Ward-Lev offers a fresh twist on the tasks and accomplishments of the Hebrew prophets. They not only leveled their critique of the imperialist worldviews of their age, and the injustice perpetrated by both the northern kingdom of Israel and the southern kingdom of Judah. They not only brought to the surface the subversive memory of Exodus. In the midst of the catastrophic destruction of the central institutions of their society, they "brought forth a radical reworking of the Israelite tradition, reimagining the people's communal life as an ongoing liberation journey with God." "The key to this new way," Ward-Lev continues, "is a reconceptualization of the exodus from event in the past to an ever-present process."[43] So, Jeremiah voices God's new liberation for the people by saying they will no longer refer to Exodus in the past tense but will soon refer to a new exodus from exile in Babylon (Jer 16:14–15). At each crisis, each liminal moment, the people will refer to Exodus in the present tense. Exodus ceases to be only a subversive memory and becomes a liberating consciousness operating across a vast expanse of time.[44]

In so doing the prophets' main contribution was to inaugurate what Ward-Lev calls the "prophetic stream." Michael Walzer documents how the stream leapt over its religious channels, spreading into movements for radical, political change: "Since late medieval or early modern times, there has existed in the West a characteristic way of thinking about political change . . . , a story we repeat to one another. The story has roughly this form: oppression, liberation, social contract, political struggle, new society. . . . We call the whole process revolutionary."[45] Oppression and liberation have become reflexive categories for making sense of many different chains of events. After the end of World War II, the prophetic stream leapt its Western channels to become an intrinsic element in a spate of national liberation movements struggling to break the chains of colonial subjugation. The Exodus narrative evaporated, but the underlying structure of oppression/liberation remained. Simultaneously, these categories have been taken up by many groups *within* nations seeking liberation from a whole panoply of oppressive domestic forces.

The Critique of the Royal Consciousness

> It is the vocation of the prophet to keep alive the ministry of the imagination, to keep on . . . proposing futures alternative to the single one the king wants to urge as the only thinkable one. Indeed, the poetic imagination is the last way left to challenge . . . the dominant reality.
>
> —Brueggemann, *Prophetic Imagination*[46]

Clearly Exodus lies at the bedrock of Judah's consciousness and the prophets recall Exodus in order to contradict the prevailing ideology and the unjust structures that it enshrines. Walter Brueggemann sees the prophets' messages as attacks on what he calls Judah's "royal consciousness." That consciousness cemented, seemingly in perpetuity, a cosmic order anchored in the holy city of Jerusalem where God dwelled and kings and priests ruled seemingly forever. God had been yoked to the will to power of the political and religious establishment. YHWH was, as it were, "on call."[47]

A series of invasions by successive imperial powers erased the northern kingdom of Israel in 722/1 BCE and in 587 BCE left the southern kingdom of Judah in ruins. The destruction of Jerusalem in 587 BCE not only overthrew political and economic institutions, it rent the sacred canopy that the royal ideology claimed would shelter the people of Judah forever.[48] In the wake of this collective trauma, the prophets inaugurated a process of transformative learning. They challenged the prevailing frame of reference.[49] More precisely, they saw God's hand at work in the shattering of that frame. They demanded a new understanding of God and history.

Wherever it is found, Brueggemann argues, the royal consciousness forecloses any future inconsistent with its assumption of permanence. It anesthetizes the moral imagination. Having a god on permanent retainer means no transgressing the hierarchical boundaries glued in place by this ideology. By calling into question the royal consciousness, the prophets opened a space for the religious imagination. They also broke the yoke that would harness God: "A truly free God is essential to marginal peoples if they are to have a legitimate standing ground against the oppressive orders of the day."[50] For Brueggemann, a transcendent deity constitutes "a court of appeal against the highest courts and orders of society."[51]

The Practice of Grief

> My joy is gone, grief is upon me, my heart is sick. . . . For the hurt of my poor people I am hurt, I mourn, and dismay has taken hold of me. Is there no balm in Gilead?
>
> —Jer 8:18, 21

Trauma and longing are intimately related to the prophetic persona. The spiritual work of the prophet transforms them into grief and hope. Louis

Stulman captures both aspects as central to the intentionality of the prophetic texts. "Written prophecy invites its readers to imagine the unthinkable . . . the end of culture and the return to primeval chaos. . . . Written prophecy shifts the wreckage of war from ground zero to the symbolic world of language, affording readers the opportunity to name their ordeal, mourn it, and survive it. Equally remarkable . . . , prophecy seeks to generate hope in people whose worlds have collapsed, and whose cherished forms of faith and culture have been broken seemingly beyond repair."[52]

Walter Brueggemann argues that the stereotype of the angry prophet screaming in righteous indignation is overblown. Giving voice to anger is one rhetorical strategy among many employed by the prophets. Far more central is what Brueggemann calls "the practice of grief," signifying a performance, a spiritual discipline to which one is called.[53] As many others have done, Brueggemann follows the lead of Rabbi Abraham Heschel, who argued that the prophets participated in the "divine pathos" and thereby disclosed a God who suffers and mourns for her people.[54] In some passages in Jeremiah it is difficult to find a line between YHWH's grief and Jeremiah's (Jer 8:18–9:3).[55] If the prophet gives voice to the divine pathos, the prophet also stands in solidarity with a suffering people against a God who chastises them (Jer 8:21).[56] Sounding the depths of the prophets' grief, we grasp their deep well of compassion, compassion strong enough to resist an angry god.

Grief cuts through denial, the delusion of the Jerusalem elite that the state would remain secure forever. Those who chanted "The Temple of the Lord, the Temple of the Lord, the Temple of the Lord" assumed that God would never allow the violation of His dwelling place (Jer 7:4).[57] While those elites still slept soundly, Jeremiah is instructed by YHWH to call out the "keeners," a women's guild whose social role was to perform a family's—or, here, a nation's—grief. In this case the lamentations of these women performed a prophetic function: All is not well (Jer 9:17–18).[58] If the practice of grief is not embraced, Brueggemann insists, sorrow finds an outlet in anger, in blaming others, even in collective violence. So, the Jerusalem elite responded to Jeremiah's wake-up call, his call to action, not by joining in lamentation but by clamoring for his execution (Jer 26:10–11, 38:4–6).[59]

In Lamentations grieving reaches its apogee. A narrator articulates the Deuteronomic theology that the destruction of Judah and the exile of her people is the result of YHWH's righteous judgment over Daughter Zion. But she will have none of it. "Is it nothing to you, all you who pass by? Look and see if there is any sorrow like my sorrow" (Lam 1:12). In a series of litanies, she lays before God in concrete detail the painful results of His fierce anger: "You have not forgiven. . . . You have made us filth and rubbish. . . . You have seen the wrong done to me. . . . Why have you forgotten us completely?" (Lam 3:42, 3:45, 3:59, 5:20).

"To lament," Kathleen O'Connor concludes, "is to pray in a spirit of resistance." Daughter Zion calls God to account. Unlike in the book of Job, her voice is not drowned out in a roaring theophany. In Lamentations, the Deuteronomic theology is repudiated but a new one is not yet born.[60] Jeremiah also challenges the Deuteronomic frame. When physically beaten by his opponents in the royal court, he declares his innocence and accuses God of seducing and overpowering him. I did not deserve this, he claims (Jer 20:1–18). Here we catch a glimpse of an entirely different understanding of suffering not as punishment for sin but as part and parcel of the struggle to serve God and to awaken the people (Jer 12:1).[61]

The Practice of Hope

> The days are surely coming, says the Lord, when I will make a new covenant with the house of Israel and the house of Judah. It will not be like the covenant that I made with their ancestors which they broke. . . . I will put my law within them and I will write it on their hearts.
>
> —Jer 31:31–33

The prophetic texts that were written or redacted in the wake of the cultural collapse of the sixth century BCE transform the longing that accompanies trauma into the practice of hope. The loss of an entire way of life is unthinkable but it is grievable. With the destruction of Jerusalem and the devastation of the surrounding countryside looming, Jeremiah, who has practiced grief with unmatched intensity, is instructed by YHWH to purchase a plot of land from a relative (Jer 32). This action symbolically counters despair as the final word in a world in which all bearings have been erased. "See today I appoint you over nations and over kingdoms to pluck up and to pull down . . . to build and to plant (Jer 1:10).

"The task of the prophetic imagination," argues Brueggemann, "is to bring to public expression those very hopes and yearnings that have been denied so long and suppressed so deeply that we no longer know they are there."[62] The wisdom of the status quo declares "there is nothing new under the sun" (Ecc 9). The world of the imperial powers is closed, insular, that of the exiles in Babylon is shattered. In either case the key question is not whether an alternative world is feasible but is it imaginable?[63] Brueggemann sees "radical hope" as a prison break from the world of Ecclesiastes "What has been is what will be . . . ; there is nothing new under the sun" (1:9). Such hope is "committed to the bare idea that something good will emerge" even when one is in the midst of the despair voiced in Lamentations. In Jeremiah's case his prophecy that the people would receive a new heart with God's law written in it constituted a radical hope, for there would be no need in that society for priest or king or any other authority standing between the people and their God. It would be Moses's hope come true.

Michael Walzer pushes further, arguing that Exodus in the West has catalyzed, again and again, a radical politics grounded in hope:

> The strength of the [Exodus] narrative is given by the end though it is also crucial that the end be present at the beginning, as an aspiration, a hope, a promise. What is promised is radically different from what is. . . . Exodus is a journey forward—not only in time and space. It is a march toward a goal, a moral progress, a transformation. . . . Canaan is a promised land because Egypt is a house of bondage. Beginning and end stand in a necessary relation. . . . Egypt is not just left behind; it is rejected, it is judged and condemned. The crucial terms of that judgment are *oppression and corruption*. God's promise generates a sense of possibility. . . . The world is not all Egypt.[64]

Several points need to be underscored: Oppression is both a willed and a systemic imposition of suffering on others. To call something oppressive is to level a moral judgment. Egypt is not just abandoned; it is condemned. Without hope, oppression becomes fate, bad weather. The end must be grasped in the beginning. The end is radically different from the beginning. The world is not all Egypt. Those who reach the end are morally and politically different than they were in Egypt.

This form of hope is not wishful thinking. It is fully engaged in a now that dynamically includes past and future. Rebecca Solnit offers a redefinition of hope that can be read as a riff on Jeremiah's performance in the midst of an enemy's siege: "Hope is not like a lottery ticket you can . . . clutch feeling lucky. . . . Hope is an ax you can break down doors with in an emergency; because hope should shove you out the door, because it will take everything you have to steer the future away from endless war, from the annihilation of the earth's treasures and the grinding down of the poor."[65] Action—Jeremiah buying the field, and, we can imagine plowing and planting it—validates hope as it transforms both the self and its communities.

Conclusion

So where does this elaboration of the prophetic ethos leave us? It is important to note that the prophets were not world-transforming radicals.[66] They were not agents of democracy. Nor did they call for a revolution. They did not engage in policy debates and they certainly did not engage in the pragmatic art of political compromise.[67] Frequently their spiritual descendants surpassed them in engaging in some or all of these transformative practices. That granted, we have seen how the prophetic ethos functions as a spiritual discipline:

- Prophets are their voice. Their frequently harsh rhetoric functions as a moral chemotherapy that is appropriate for a society that is sick unto death.

- The prophetic texts of the Hebrew Bible are frequently polyphonic. Their conflicting theologies call forth an ethically grounded act of interpretation.

- Application of a "prophetic method" to the prophetic texts themselves, criticizing their ideological frame, is necessary in order to salvage meaning from these texts.

- Prophets confront the "monstrosity of injustice." They test all aspects of society in light of God's preferential option for the widow, the orphan, and the alien.

- Prophets tap into a subversive memory of Exodus as the model for collective life.

- The prophets transform Exodus from a past event into an ongoing process of liberation.

- The prophets denounce the "royal consciousness," its deluded understanding of power, and its practice of geopolitics.

- Prophets participate in the divine pathos. Grieving, they stand in solidarity with their people even when the people have violated their covenantal obligations.

- The prophets offer a radical hope to the people in exile whose sacred canopy has been destroyed. The world is not all Egypt.

- The prophetic performance, in all of its aspects, is a call to action.

Certainly, Buddhists will hesitate to embrace all of these traits of the prophetic ethos. Each trait offers its own challenge to Buddhist thought and practice. If Buddhists are serious about "borrowing a prophetic voice," they (we) should not evade those challenges. To be sure, Buddhists do not see themselves as an explicit continuance of the "prophetic stream." While the prophetic ethos may be a stream that surfaces episodically in both religious and secular forms, it nevertheless remains an enduring underground aquifer that Buddhists can tap into selectively. A fusion of perspectives that open to different horizons is not easily accomplished. This deep immersion in the prophetic tradition as its own classic form of being religious and acting ethically establishes a prelude to any such fusion.

Buddhist Reflections in a Prophetic Key #1

Cries of the Crows:
A Buddhist Take on the Prophetic Voice

On the face of it, the prophets' raw speech and their frontal attack on those who ruled Israel and Judah seem the antithesis of what Buddhism commends as right speech, one trail along the Eightfold Path. The *Aṅguttara Nikāya* offers the prevailing understanding of right speech: "Monks, when speech possesses five factors, it is well spoken, not badly spoken, and it is blameless and irreproachable among the wise. What five? It is spoken at the proper time; what is said is true; it is spoken gently; what is said is beneficial; it is spoken with a mind of loving-kindness" (*Aṅguttara Nikāya* 5:236).[1] What, then, are we to make of all those Zen masters whose shouts can hardly be called gentle?

My favorite example of a koan that challenges both social and religious authority is Zen master Zhaozhou's encounter with an old woman hoeing a field. "What would you do if you suddenly met a fierce tiger," he chides her. "Nothing in this world frightens me," she replies and returns to her hoeing. If Zhaozhou were truly wise, he would have recognized that hoeing is her spiritual practice and left her to it. Instead, he roars like a tiger. Without batting an eyelash, the old woman roars back. No civil dialogue here, instead a wealth of meaning. Zhaozhou, seems to be saying "Why are you, a woman, and an old woman at that, out here all alone? I'll show you how to be properly afraid." The woman's roar establishes her ineradicable equality. Zhaozhou's gender bias and his male superciliousness are but one more weed to be hoed away. Even enlightened masters can play the fool. Not to be outdone, Zhaozhou concludes enigmatically, "There is still this." The woman, we can be sure, continues to hoe the field.[2]

In a number of Buddhist schools verbal combat clearly is one form of right speech. Sharp-tongued women discomfiting Zen masters are hardly the norm but neither are they rarely to be found. Another case features Ziyong, a seventeenth-century woman and a Chinese Zen master. A monk takes up verbal combat by shouting. Ziyong replies, "What is the point of reckless shouting like that? If I take up the challenge of speaking, I must borrow the light and the dark, the form and the emptiness of the mountains and hills and the great earth, the call of magpies and the cries of the crows."[3] Quite evidently, there is shouting and then there is shouting. Gentle speech may be the default setting, but Zen teachers, like the Hebrew prophets, use a full range of skillful speech—even the crow's raucous caw.

The *Aṅguttara Nikāya* quotes the Buddha as saying that a monk, "having investigated and scrutinized, . . . speaks dispraise of one who deserves dispraise" as well as praises those who deserve praise (*Aṅguttara Nikāya* 5:236). Sallie King comments that not only are monks to speak forcefully when the situation warrants it but that "they have a moral duty to do so."[4] This can include calling to account those who harm the community. When hate speech, fearmongering, and egregious lies become normalized through their endless reiteration, gentle speech will not do. To be sure, other texts in the Pali canon counsel one who "dispraises" to focus on the bad action and not on the bad actor, or, as some Buddhist advocates put it, borrowing language from Christians, right speech should denounce the "sin" but not the "sinner."[5]

In short, there is no hard-and-fast rule. In the case of harsh speech, the Buddha offers a set of criteria to distinguish sharp speech from vituperative speech. It must be "true, correct, and beneficial"; moreover, it must be uttered at a propitious time (*Majjhima Nikāya* 139).[6] Such careful as well as forceful speech accords with Kaveny's understanding of the prophetic task as employing a "moral chemotherapy." In this light, personal invective is simply poisonous. King amplifies Kaveny's argument. She suggests that public critical speech, wisely performed, can change "the power dynamic in the country." It can curtail the would-be despot's attempt to commandeer and monopolize power. It challenges us to resist oppression *and* the oppressor. "This is indeed," King concludes, "a major benefit to be gained by overt, sharp speech uttered at the right time."[7] For the Hebrew prophets the right time was the present.

Chapter Two

Crossing Boundaries

Rita Gross and the Transformation of Patriarchal Buddhism

> THE BUDDHA: Yet still there are these fools who doubt
> that women too can grasp the truth.
> Gotami, show miracles,
> That they might give up their false views.
>
> NARRATOR: Gotami bowed to the Lord
> then leaped into the sky.
> Permitted by the Buddha, she
> displayed her special powers.
>
> —Jonathan Walters, "Gotami's Story"[1]
>
> How could a religion that has such a clear understanding of non-duality, such a strong realization that gender is illusory and unreal, get things so completely wrong on the ground, in the everyday world, and in its institutional life?
>
> —Rita Gross, "Is the Glass Half-Empty or Half-Full?"[2]

The story of Gotami's spiritual attainment comes from the Pali canon. Gotami is the clan name for the Buddha's foster mother. It is used throughout the following story to indicate a basic parallelism between Gautama the Buddha and Maha Pajapati. "Well-gone-one, I am your mother," Gotami chants; "you're my father. . . ./ I suckled you with mother's milk/ which quenched thirst for a moment./ From you I drank the dharma-milk,/ perpetually tranquil."³ Gotami enters *parinirvana* before the Buddha along with five hundred of her fellow nuns. "The Buddha's great nirvana, good,/ but not as good as this one:/ Gotami's great going out/ was positively stellar."⁴ Gotami is presented in this canonical document as a "Buddha for women."⁵ As we will see, this story is one example of what Buddhist scholar Rita Gross calls an "indigenous Buddhist feminism."⁶ The recovery of long-silenced voices that challenge the hegemony of male-centered discourses is one aspect of Gross's adoption of a prophetic persona.

Crossing Boundaries

In the introduction, I acknowledged Rita Gross's explicit borrowing of a prophetic voice as the inspiration for this book and I examined briefly how Gross applied a "prophetic method." Gross consciously situated herself as a feminist within the prophetic stream. While she is the youngest of our four forbearers, it is fitting that we begin with her.

Rita Gross was born in 1943. She grew up living with her parents on a Wisconsin farm and in a house that lacked indoor plumbing but, more importantly, without books. As she grew up, the kinds of things that interested her—books, learning—seemed restricted to males. Subsistence farming and adherence to the strictures of a conservative Christian sect offered no escape from the prison of gender roles. So, it seemed all too unlikely that she would go to college, let alone apply to and be accepted into a graduate program at the Divinity School of the University of Chicago in1965. Gross had forged ahead despite the discouraging words of an undergraduate professor who thought a scholarship would be wasted on her because she would marry and that would be the end of her academic aspirations. She was one of only a dozen or so women in a school that enrolled four hundred students.⁷ Surmounting hurdles became the story of her life. Gross bucked the androcentric bias of her field, the history of religions, to produce one of the first dissertations to employ feminist methods to uncover women's hidden religious lives—a study of the roles of women in Australian aboriginal cultures. After completing her graduate studies, Gross taught for many years at the University of Wisconsin–Eau Claire.

Gross's passionate exploration of women's religious experiences and creativity led her to pioneering efforts to transform the discipline of the history of religions through leadership in the American Academy of Religion. In 1980 she coedited with Nancy Falk *Unspoken Worlds: Women's*

Lives in Nonwestern Cultures, a work that both played an important role in establishing a new paradigm for the history of religions and broadened the focus of feminist studies of religion to include non-Western traditions.[8] Other very important books followed. For our purposes the classic text *Buddhism after Patriarchy: A Feminist History, Analysis and Reconstruction of Buddhism* (1993) and the collection of essays on Engaged Buddhism *Soaring and Settling: Buddhist Perspectives on Contemporary Social and Religious Issues* (1998) deserve the closest attention.

In her thirties, Gross became a Buddhist. As always, her boundary crossings challenged friends and critics alike. In this case her feminist colleagues wondered why she would affiliate herself with another patriarchal religion after suffering so long in a fundamentalist Christian sect. One answer, perhaps, arose out of a transformative religious experience. Walking across campus on a beautiful autumn day, preparing her class in her head as she walked, yet deeply grieving the impending death of a lover to brain cancer, she suddenly blurted out, "The Four Noble Truths are true." The stunning clarity of this experience permanently shaped her life.[9] She practiced for many years in the Tibetan Buddhist tradition and in 2005 became a senior teacher at Jetsun Khandro Rimpoche's Lotus Garden Center in Virginia. Rita Gross died in 2015.

Acknowledging the improbability of a Wisconsin farm girl becoming an internationally regarded scholar and a Buddhist practitioner, Rita Gross had to find a path across several minefields as a historian of religion using a feminist approach to her discipline, a Buddhist scholar who was also a Buddhist practitioner, and a feminist who was willing to practice within a patriarchal religion. Each of these approaches, she insists, was looked upon with suspicion by other scholars. The three approaches were not sealed into different compartments of her brain and being. She particularly saw an urgent need for feminist insights to transform academic business as usual and to spark the Buddhist community into social action. Feminism, she argued, "is one of the great contemporary manifestations of the prophetic voice shorn of outmoded and outdated cultural biases."[10]

Gross confronted the objection that using symbols and concepts from different traditions in her own world construction is inappropriate. A mature, reflective person, she countered, will continuously incorporate symbols and ideas to reconstitute one's worldview and to redirect one's actions. Those symbols and ideas need not be confined to the culture of her birth—in her case that of a Wisconsin farm girl raised in a patriarchal, fundamentalist Christian sect.[11] That would truly be a sentence to a life in prison.

The danger in any appropriation, Gross suggests, is that one becomes a mindless shopper in "the great spiritual supermarket." The danger can be obviated by a commitment to the "cross-cultural descriptive study of religion" in which any tradition studied is examined with both objectivity and empathy.[12] The next step is more controversial. Given a world in which conflicts among religious traditions are both possible and actual, there is an ethical imperative to go beyond careful, empathic description to foster the full flourishing of all human beings through embracing cultural and religious pluralism in which both respect and mutual transformation are the norm. This, in turn, entails a third step: one must not only describe but also expose and challenge patriarchy, militarism, fundamentalism, and other destructive ideologies no matter how sincerely they are held.[13] These multiple steps resulted in a distinctive combination of cross-cultural history of religion, feminism, and critical and constructive Buddhist "theology," a combination frowned upon by those invested in any one of these approaches.[14] Together they describe what Gross means by applying a prophetic method.

Classical Buddhism, like virtually all premodern religious traditions, lacked an understanding of structural violence. Despite the teaching of impermanence, it viewed social institutions as given and offered no vision of a postpatriarchal world.[15] Liberation "was not the result of justice and righteousness but of mindful awareness, detachment and tranquility." Western Buddhists practicing today—and, to an increasing extent, all Buddhists—are the heirs of multiple religious and secular strands, including those stemming from the Hebrew prophets. Buddhism's reluctance to apply its sublime understanding of compassion to oppressive social and political institutions remains a major issue confronting Buddhist practice. Buddhists must heed the "prophetic call for judgment, criticism and responsibility."[16] Gross charges Engaged Buddhists with failing to apply a critical eye to the Buddhist traditions themselves. They focus largely on the larger society, on globalization, on Western models of development, and on undemocratic institutions. They are less likely to focus on the systemic warping of Buddhist teachings, practices, and institutions.[17]

While Gross speaks of borrowing a prophetic voice in numerous places in both *Buddhism after Patriarchy* and *Soaring and Settling*, in one place she refers to "the need for Buddhism to develop its prophetic dimension."[18] This formulation suggests that a prophetic stance and mode of being-in-the-world is not alien to but concealed within Buddhist teachings and practices. The prophetic voice is not entirely a graft of a different way of being religious. Gross points to the bodhisattva ethic of compassion as the seed of prophetic social action. Given the prevalence of oppressive forces within political and economic structures, gender roles, and culturally imposed psychological formations, she argues, "it is hard to imagine being serious about liberation or the bodhisattva path without being involved in social action at some level."[19] Elsewhere she sees compassion and justice as mutually transformative. Each, she claims, can correct what is lacking in the other.[20] Here it seems that compassion with a critical edge arises from viewing the realm of collective dukkha with a clear eye.

Trauma and Longing

Challenged by Christian theologian John Cobb to acknowledge that her borrowing of a prophetic voice was a legacy of her graduate studies in Judaism and Christianity, Gross begged to differ. Her prophetic stance emerged much earlier, she insisted; its roots plunged much deeper. Gross credited two experiences in her teenage years for setting her course. The first experience focused on her frustration at being born in a female body before the second wave of feminism. She felt boxed in, not with a glass ceiling but rather with solid concrete above, below, and around. Milking cows one day, she experienced a liberating illumination. From out of the blue, she suddenly blurted out, "It's not me. I'm not what's wrong. There is nothing wrong with my female body. It's the system—the system."[21] The moment quickly passed but her experience of self-acceptance persisted. The concrete box—the system—remained. Only with time would she find the tools to break out of what she repeatedly calls "the prison of gender roles."[22] The recognition that there is an oppressive system that systematically warps our lives catapulted her onto the plane that all modern liberation movements take as given. It also meant that she would never "willingly accept having [her] reality named for [her] by others."[23]

The second experience was deeply traumatic. Gross was raised within a very conservative, fundamentalist Christian sect that was explicitly patriarchal. "I was given systematic training in hatred parading as religious conviction and faith," she said. When, as a teenager, she mildly suggested that other religions might worship the same God under different names, she was publicly condemned at her mother's funeral and soon thereafter excommunicated. This experience left her traumatized but also longing for some positive experience of Christianity.[24] Trauma and longing, as we have seen, are gateways into the prophet's experience of pathos.

A Feminist Reading of the Buddhist Tradition

Despite these multiple boundaries that she had to cross, Rita Gross herself viewed the simultaneous emergence of a new wave of feminism and Buddhism's encounter with the West as an auspicious moment, a moment to be seized.[25] Her application of a prophetic method is developed in all her writings but most significantly in *Buddhism after Patriarchy*. Although it was published three decades ago, *Buddhism after Patriarchy* remains an indispensable model of a fruitful critique of Buddhism in the service of its transformation.[26] Gross's reading against the grain begins with a reluctant Buddha. The story of the Buddha's negative response to repeated requests by his foster mother, Prajapati, and his disciple, Ananda, to include women as renunciants is well known. What is important, Gross suggests, is that the Buddha changed his mind. Enlightenment did not confer freedom from cultural bias. The Buddha, too, had to overcome imprisoning preconceptions about gender. The more important threads in the early literature for Gross are examples of the Buddha directly teaching nuns, indicating his conviction that they could achieve enlightenment. While the Buddha's terms of acceptance of women into the monastic sangha dictated "institutional subordination," they did not imply "spiritual subordination": "[Women and men] lived the same lifestyle, did the same practices, and even looked alike, both having shaved heads and identical robes."[27]

The all-too-human Buddha that Gross underlines is but one example of her search for a usable past. Communities, she insists, are constituted by memory, remembering a past that is not dead and gone but present and defining. We saw in the case of the prophets how the subversive memory of Exodus was refashioned into an ongoing journey of liberation. What happens when the past is erased or if some groups in the society are rendered invisible? It becomes repressive and dismissive of the contributions of those groups in the present. Recovering women's voices and experiences restores a subversive memory. The search for a usable past must be a search for an accurate past. A feminist approach assumes "quite reasonably that a recounted past that ignores data about the female half of the population cannot be accurate." To say that Buddhism is androcentric in its worldview and patriarchal in its institutions is simply an accurate interpretation of its past.[28]

Gross digs through the layers of the tradition excavating what she calls Buddhism's "quadruple androcentrism": in the oldest layer, stories of men and their experiences were more likely to be recorded than those of women; when recorded, stories of women tended to be ignored as the tradition evolved; Western scholars compounded the problem by ignoring or ridiculing the few extant records of Buddhist women; and, finally, contemporary Buddhists have followed suit in perpetuating this androcentric bias. Across the length and breadth of the Buddhist tradition, views of women and, most especially, statements about their capacity to attain enlightenment are inherently contradictory.[29] Such conflicting judgments require critical attention and an argument for the dharmic centrality of one stream over the other. Gross does not hesitate to make this critical judgment. Despite the presence, even the prevalence, of texts that denigrate women, "a feminist interpreter of Buddhism can make a strong case that the core of the tradition is without gender bias . . . and that sexist practices are in contradiction with the essential core teachings of the tradition."[30] In such a case, judgment is not simply a weighing of conflicting evidence. It is a moral act, a commitment to move the tradition beyond androcentrism as inimical to the flourishing of women and men. While the majority opinion across traditions is that there is some problem with female birth, the minority opinion that gender is irrelevant to practice, Gross argues, is the one most consistent with core Buddhist teachings.[31] This contradiction requires explanation.

Patriarchy, Gross insists, is a historical phenomenon not a reflection of human biology. It is a product of causes and conditions. Emerging within a patriarchal culture, early Buddhism saw withdrawal into a countercultural community as its most viable social expression. Renunciation, not reform, was the core spiritual action.[32] Those who withdrew from society carried its androcentric worldview and patriarchal structures with them. The permeation of patriarchal structures and practices throughout the tradition is itself a reflex of cultural biases.

Moving beyond uncovering the two streams that course through the length and breadth of Buddhist history, Gross also deconstructs the widespread teaching that birth as a woman is due to negative karma. Karma is not fate; it is the product of causes and conditions. To assume that women alone generate those causes and conditions is to blame the victim. One who acts compassionately "would not be willing to support, passively or actively, fundamentally cruel and oppressive institutions or situations such as gender privilege, militarism or economic exploitation."[33] Gross explicitly uses the term "oppression" to characterize patriarchal Buddhism. To name oppression as oppression and not something else is to take a leap forward. Dukkha is not only existential in character but social and systemic as well. Karma, reinterpreted, attunes us to the ways in which the actions of many solidify and become a systemic burden. Gross recognizes that the concept of "oppression" is borrowed from prophetic traditions, in her case, one result of the mutual transformation of Buddhism and feminism. It signifies the fixated patterns of those who exercise power *over* others out of self-interest and self-delusion. As the product of causes and conditions, collective dukkha can and must be undone.[34]

When we talk about how power is claimed, legitimated, and exercised, we are adopting a justice discourse, which focuses on structures, institutions, and collective norms that either support or undermine the attempts of individuals to flourish. Gross rejects any model of gendered equality, that is, any form of "separate but equal" roles for women and men. Any prescribed gender roles will overtly oppress some and at some level imprison all. "Every feminist agenda for the future really derives from an unstated assumption that sex is not a relevant criterion for awarding roles or value."[35]

The descendants of the Hebrew prophets found an emancipatory kernel in the prophetic texts despite their misogynistic narratives. Beyond her diagnosis of Buddhism's profoundly ambiguous record in its views about women and its persisting history of domination through patriarchal institutions, Gross is similarly intent on retrieving an emancipatory kernel, in her case within the Buddhist dharma. The Mahāyāna teachings of emptiness and dependent coarising express that emancipatory potential.[36] Because all phenomena are empty of any permanent "nature" but rather are products of causes and conditions, there are no such things as fixed gender-based traits. Reified understandings of male and female traits are themselves products of particular historical conditions and can be altered by reshaping their causes and conditions.[37]

Equally important for Gross is the Mahāyāna teaching of *tathāgatagarbha*. While usually translated as "Buddha Nature," Gross prefers its more literal translation as "Buddha-womb" or "Buddha-embryo." The potential of all living beings to actualize their *tathāgatagarbha* makes institutional restrictions on the practice of a whole class of human beings and the tradition's androcentric denigration of women's capacity for enlightenment violations of Buddhism's liberatory intent. "Taken together the concepts of emptiness and Buddha Nature provide a very firm basis to argue that gender equality is a normative, rather than an optional position, for Buddhists. If gender equality is normative, then actively working to undercut gender hierarchy and privilege is *a required ethical norm for all Buddhists*, not merely a marginal position for a few feminists"[38] (Italics added). The Mahāyāna teaching, a corollary to the concept of dependent coarising, that the liberation of each is contingent on the liberation of all also supports this required ethical norm.

It calls for active resistance to and reconstruction of patriarchal Buddhism that impedes the emancipation of both women and men.

Indigenous Buddhist Feminism

In *Buddhism after Patriarchy*, Gross unearths the neglected narratives of women in the early Pali canon, especially as represented in the *Therīgāthā*, an early collection of poems by Buddhist nuns. Many, if not most, of these poems express enlightenment experiences, stories of women who "split open the mass of mental darkness."[39] This focus on women's proven capacity to become enlightened in this life must be read as a counternarrative to patriarchal Buddhism's denigration of birth in a female body.

In *Buddhism beyond Gender*, published posthumously, Gross takes her search for alternative narratives of Buddhist women to a new level. She counters the charge that the Buddhist feminism that she espouses is a Western (read alien) import and that its imposition is a form of neo-colonialism. Instead of defending her borrowing of a prophetic voice, she uncovers that voice from within multiple strands of Buddhism, from what she calls "indigenous Buddhist feminism."[40] At the beginning of this chapter we examined "Gotami's Story," which was included in the early Pali canon. That Gotami brought along five hundred nuns to reach enlightenment is a testimony to her power. Only "fools," the Buddha says, fail to acknowledge her accomplishments. Stories of the Buddha's wife, Yasodhara, in later folk poetry counter the predominant narrative line by emphasizing her partnership with the Buddha-to-be over the course of many lifetimes. She rightly calls Buddha to task for neglecting to even inform her about his plans to follow the path of renunciation without her. In a Sanskrit text, the *Mūlasarvāstivāda Vinaya* partnership becomes permanently cemented: Gautama and Yasodhara conceive a child on the night that he leaves. While Gautama follows an arduous path of spiritual searching for six years, Yasodhara also follows an equally challenging path. She remains pregnant for this entire time, giving birth on the very night that Gautama becomes enlightened.[41] Throughout the centuries of Buddhist expansion, new stories have been invented to convey women's experiences. In a Thai Buddhist story, Yasodhara (here called "Bimba") gives way to her grief. During a visit by the Buddha to his hometown after many years absence, Yasodhara/Bimba, like Daughter Zion, laments her treatment by her husband. Lamentation escalates to become indictment: "You abandoned me and our child without any compassion."[42] "It is quite refreshing," Gross concludes, "to learn that a radical criticism of the Buddha's behavior could be inserted into narratives about his life" even after the traditional hagiography had been well established in Thai Buddhism.[43]

These examples of "indigenous Buddhist feminism" criticize the tradition's androcentric version of the Buddha's leave-taking that implicitly denigrates the role of women in the Buddha's life. In true prophetic mode these stories rescue those important women from the silence and passivity to which the main lines of the tradition confine them. They recover a subversive memory; they bring those confined to the margins into the spotlight; and they level a judgment on the "fools" who disregard the importance of women to the whole process of liberation.[44]

Transforming Trauma and Longing

Soaring and Settling represents Gross's most constructive effort. She makes it clear that the exploration of her own "generative experiences" and "recurring formative events" is typical of feminist theologies. Moving from autobiography to religious reflection, Gross argues, is a way of avoiding a false universalism. Moreover, her approach reflects the feminist principle that "the personal *is* the political." Gross's approach to transcendence and immanence is a case in point. The temptation for a Buddhist is to dismiss the Hebrew prophets' commitment to a transcendent God as expressing an extreme version of a dualistic ideology. Gross follows a more challenging path. "Constructing theology as a Buddhist non-theist," she argues, "encourages one to ask different questions of immanence and transcendence."[45] Rather than seeing both concepts as traits of the divine, Gross sees their roots in modes of religious experience. Religious experiences are primary; theistic or nontheistic concepts are secondary, useful or not as they may be. What Gross calls the "spiritual impulse" of transcendence is fundamentally tied to the experience of "longing and vision, and to the remaking of worlds" that concretely connects with a prophetic mode of being religious, especially in offering hope for an alternative world. Transcendence in Gross's case involved a break with an authoritarian and repressive religious upbringing and with the "prison of gender." Experiences of transcendence, she writes, "took me quite literally into another world of feeling. . . . In that world longing to see clearly and to experience reality was appropriate and satisfying. Thus, transcendence," she concludes, "was literally my salvation."[46] The experience of immanence, on the other hand, has to do with peace and tranquility, with being at home in one's body and in this rich and wondrous world that we share. This appreciation,

Gross believes, "has everything to do with *being* rather than *doing*." Both modes are necessary, and Gross seeks a middle path to avoid falling into a self-righteous renunciation of the world or a crusading mentality on the one hand and a deadening spiritual complacency on the other.[47] Mindfulness in action becomes a process of "soaring and settling," transcendence and immanence. In effect, Gross's constructive suggestion establishes a common ground on which Engaged Buddhists and those embodying the prophetic tradition might meet and share their differing visions of religious experience.

The Practice of Grief and Leaning into Anger

The very title of her book, *Buddhism after Patriarchy*, represents a claim on all Buddhists to imagine an alternative future and then to undertake a moral journey. As we have seen, Gross views the traumatic experience of an abusive religious community as what led her to adopt a prophetic stance. I have interpreted this stance as "the practice of grief." The longing that accompanies trauma is transformed by the Hebrew prophets into the "practice of hope." The world is not all Egypt. And Buddhism is more and other than its reified patriarchal institutions or its androcentric teachings.

Gross speaks of two deaths, both of someone deeply loved who might have become a lifelong partner. Contrary to those Buddhists who see grief as a symptom of clinging, she sees the grief that accompanied these losses as having taught and transformed her more than thousands of hours of meditation: "What is counterintuitive is that the anguish of grieving which no one would ever choose could be so productive. . . . Through leaning into grief I learned . . . that fighting impermanence only brings suffering, while dancing with impermanence launches one into the immediacy of nowness."[48]

It is easier to explain what "leaning into grief" is not—not self-pity, not fearful flight, and not stoic repression or resignation—than what it is. In one essay Gross speaks of "touch and go" as how one relates to the present moment with its emotional undertones. "Leaning in" sounds more like full immersion, and certainly Gross means to fully engage the present. "Dancing with impermanence" implies a choreographed set of movements. With each emotion there is a different partner with different steps. No escape from grief's minor chords. No spontaneous resolution. And yet Gross insists that learning this dance was more transformative than thousands of hours of meditation.

What Gross argues about leaning into grief applies just as well to the anger that, at times, seems to engulf the Hebrew prophets. Politics, she argues, is a realm of practice. Caring about a cause in the midst of conflict provides an unending opportunity to grapple with the three poisons: aversion/anger, attachment/clinging, and delusion/ideological fixation. "Like any unenlightened energy," she insists "each of the three poisons includes the potential for its transmuted form. Aversion contains muted clarity; attachment contains unrealized compassion; and ignorance contains complete all-inclusive spaciousness."[49] But what can Gross possibly mean by the *clarity* in anger? Like burning wet wood, anger's smoke stings our eyes and blurs our vision. Clarity might be the last thing we would expect to distill from anger. Aggressively expressed, an angry response to a perception of injustice results in mutual entrenchment more often than not.

Before she developed a solid spiritual discipline, Gross admits that she periodically vented her anger and frustration at sexist comments and behaviors, giving her a momentary satisfaction but alienating her audience. Anger, too, must be danced with, not sharply and angrily repressed. Critical intelligence buried in the anger must be retained lest tamed anger lead to apathy. Instead, Gross works with the "great passion" involved in her feminist commitment. Passion must be tempered with compassion for those on all sides of an issue lest it breed ideological fixation and contempt for the other.[50]

Virtually all causes contain a germ of truth that is obscured by anger. Only when the smoke is blown away can we see that germ. To be sure, this obligates a Buddhist activist to take up the difficult task of pursuing a just cause while acknowledging the germ of truth in one's opponent's position. "Being correct is the easy part," Gross concludes. "How does one express righteousness nondualistically?"[51] From this perspective the prophetic voice at its most strident has not fully undergone this transformation. Righteous anger calls out the monstrosity of injustice but obscures its roots in one's own life. However, only "leaning in," not a simple repudiation of prophetic discourse, will suffice.

Conclusion

> "Ultimately, I wrote *Buddhism after Patriarchy* because it was the most useful and helpful thing that I could imagine ever doing in my life," Gross insists. "It is . . . what I can do to fulfill my bodhisattva vows, what I can do to alleviate the suffering inherent in imprisonment in patriarchy and gender roles. I have often thought of it as an offering born of my own suffering to try to chip away at samsara, at pain-laced conventional life. . . . It is what prophetic message I have to offer."
>
> —Rita Gross, *Soaring and Settling*[52]

Rita Gross's prophetic voice arose in her teenage years and was expressed in her resistance to systemic gender oppression and abusive religious training. As a scholar she employed a prophetic method to Buddhist texts, practices, and institutional arrangements. Her interpretation of Buddhist thought and practice included elements that bear a "family resemblance" to a prophetic way of being religious. In the introduction I argued that Gross's borrowing includes but goes deeper than the four traits that she herself pointed out: a willingness to engage in social criticism and self-criticism, a protest against the abuse of power, a vision of an alternative social order, and a commitment to social activism. Key points developed in this chapter indicate her tapping into a fuller understanding of the prophetic *dimension*.

- Rita Gross saw the borrowing of a prophetic voice as a fulfillment of her Bodhisattva vows.

- As with the prophetic texts, Gross's critique emerges from a particular social context. Rooted in her personal experience of trauma and longing, Gross dramatizes what it means to be confined to the prison of gender roles much as Jeremiah did for Judah's collective trauma by bearing the yoke.

- Buddhism is historically ambiguous in its treatment of women and its understanding of their spiritual potential. Androcentric views infect all Buddhist traditions. They equate full humanity with men, their attitudes and dispositions. They validate men's claims to power while shoving to the margins texts that affirm the full spiritual equality of women. Indra's Net is systemically warped.

- Systemic ambiguity requires an ethical interpretation that is incumbent on all Buddhists. Patriarchy and its oppressive impact are not a "women's issue." They are a justice issue.

- Gross uncovers an emancipatory kernel within the Buddhist dharma, specifically in the teaching of Buddha-Nature that is the antithesis of androcentric teachings.

- In her final work, Gross recovers an "indigenous Buddhist feminism" that constitutes a subversive and empowering memory, as was the case with the Hebrew prophets revivifying the Exodus story. Finding a "usable past" both within the Buddhist canon and in later Buddhist cultures subverts the androcentric accounts of the Buddha's life.

- Gross's "leaning into grief" as a spiritual discipline mirrors Jeremiah and the women keeners who engaged in the practice of grief.

- Although she interprets hope as a flight from the present moment and, therefore, as a spiritual obstacle, Gross shares feminism's pursuit of an alternative social order. She also calls for the transformation of Buddhist sanghas in ways that reflect the full humanity of women and men and that respond more fully to our common need for community.[53]

"All I have tried to do in my scholarship and my thinking," Gross insisted, "is to tell the truth."[54] As with the Hebrew prophets, truth telling came with a price. Gross found herself buffeted again and again by forces within Buddhist and academic communities that were resistant to the painful process of reexamining and recasting venerable traditions and modern variants. Nevertheless, over a long and fruitful career, Rita Gross persisted.

Buddhist Reflections in a Prophetic Key #2

Reading a Buddhist Classic of Mother's Grief against the Grain

In Buddhist stories, grief is frequently seen as a form of clinging and an obstacle to enlightenment. In one classic story, a mother, Kisa Gotami, has lost her only child. Crazed with grief, she carries her dead child from person to person seeking medicine. Finally, someone sends her to the Buddha, who promises that he will heal her child if she brings him a pinch of mustard seed from a household that has not known death. Kisa Gotami goes forth, but her quest, predictably, fails. However, she sees into the impermanence of existence, gives up her child's corpse, and returns to the Buddha. Recognizing her level of insight, he accepts her request to become a nun, whereupon she quickly reaches enlightenment.[1]

While traditional commentaries emphasize the Buddha's skillful means in leading Kisa Gotami to awareness, Rita Gross emphasizes the Buddha's recognition that Kisa Gotami has the capacity as a woman to become enlightened and that she has made rapid progress along the path to enlightenment.[2] However, Reiko Ohnuma explores the ambiguity of the tradition toward mother love/mother grief. When considered in the abstract, mother love is held aloft as the ideal to be actualized on behalf of all living beings. Yet mother love expressed in grief over a lost child is most often presented as "a potent manifestation of desire, attachment and clinging—all negative emotions in Buddhism that keep one bound within the realm of samsara." Kisa Gotami must not only lay her child to rest; the trajectory of the story leads to her renouncing her role as a mother.[3] Traditional interpretations see Kisa Gotami's grief not as a practice but as a form of delusion that in extreme cases manifests itself as insanity. If mother love, *as a symbol*, represents the ideal, mother grief *in actuality* is the opposite of detached wisdom.[4]

Prophetic social criticism, however, will want to uncover what has been left unsaid in the story. What happened in the village? We know only that Kisa Gotami failed in her quest for the mustard seed and a deep transformation occurred. But how long was her quest? An afternoon? A week? A year? Were her encounters perfunctory: "Do you have mustard seeds?" "Yes." "Has someone in your household died?" "Yes." "I am sorry to have bothered you." Or, as perhaps the Buddha foresaw, was she welcomed by the women of the village into their homes and over cups of tea stories were shared and grief was performed and resolved? Was there, in short, a *practice* of grief? Prophetic wisdom listens for the voices of the women in the village.

We must imagine Kisa Gotami at some point in her visits experiencing *bodhicitta,* the point where one sees one's life as intertwined with all other lives.[5] One cares about them. "In this caring," Gross insists, "emotions are cultivated and trained, not repressed or endured. It is assumed that properly developed and cultivated emotions are as fundamental to a sane, healthy person as a trained and cultivated intellect."[6] We saw how *leaning into grief,* in Gross's dealing with her own losses, became a practice more potent even than hours of meditation. It is this cultivation, this leaning into grief, that is cloaked in silence in the traditional story of Kisa Gotami.

In the *Therīgāthā,* a collection of stories in the Pali canon that record the liberation of nuns, there are numerous stories of women whose grief over a lost child is healed by the Buddha. One of these women, Patachara, goes on to become an important teacher. In one poem Patachara pulls the arrow of grief from five hundred women, all of whom had lost a child.[7] This example is crucial. Here the healer is one who has known grief, has leaned into it, learned from it, and is thereby able to heal others.

Prophetic wisdom requires a further step. We have not truly internalized a prophetic voice until we listen to those who are destitute, whose grief is a product of an unjust society. So, Haitians, living in extreme poverty, would want to know whether Kisa Gotami's child died what they call a "stupid death," a death that was easily preventable if only the most basic of health measures (clean water) and treatments (vaccinations) were made available. A death, in short, imposed by structural violence.[8] We must grieve those stupid deaths. True compassion for grieving mothers might then take on a prophetic edge, becoming a skillful means in challenging systemic injustice. As Walter Brueggemann puts it, "Real criticism begins in the capacity to grieve because that is the most visceral announcement that things are not right."[9]

Chapter Three

Thich Nhat Hanh

A Buddhist Monk in the Conflagration of War

> The war has destroyed not only human lives but all human values as well. It undermines all government structures and systems of society, destroys the very foundations of democracy, freedom, and all human systems of values. Its shame is not just the shame of the Vietnamese, but of the whole world.
>
> —Thich Nhat Hanh, *Vietnam: Lotus in a Sea of Fire*[1]

> Liberate us from your liberation
>
> —Thich Nhat Hanh, *Call Me by My True Names*[2]

Thich Nhat Hanh might well seem to be the least likely person to bear a family resemblance to the Hebrew prophets. The calmness and equanimity in the midst of storm clouds that shine throughout his many writings, such as *Being Peace* and *Peace Is Every Step,* seem utterly free of the anguish and heartfelt cries of the prophets. In "Twenty-Four Brand New Hours," his words breathe peace:

> I join my hands in thanks
> For the many wonders of life;
> For having twenty-four brand new hours before me.[3]

Thich Nhat Hanh's vision of a modern Engaged Buddhism was formed amid the conflagration of the war in Vietnam and was expressed in poems written during that period. While most of his postwar, prolific writings breathe "being peace," the war poems strike a different chord. They do bear a family resemblance to prophetic modes of discourse. Even his classic expression of Engaged Buddhism, *Being Peace,* was intended as a challenge to American peace activists whose speech and actions were frequently anything but peaceful. Treating Thich Nhat Hanh as an exemplar of prophetic wisdom is one concrete way of explaining what he might mean when he says that Buddhism is "made of non-Buddhist elements."[4]

The Role of a Monk in a Time of War

We must not ignore Thich Nhat Hanh's formation as a young monk in the midst of the French Indochina War (1946–54) nor forget how his life was altered dramatically in the midst of the American phase of the war. War, in fact, was the crucible that forged the steely determination of the young bodhisattva who was forced to take on the mantle of a prophet. Thich Nhat Hanh was born on October 11, 1926, in a small village in the middle of Vietnam. At the age of nine he saw a picture of a serene Buddha and decided that he wanted to be like that person. So, at the age of sixteen he followed in the footsteps of an older brother in becoming a novice monk. In many ways the life of this novice was idyllic, tending cattle while memorizing the manual of monastic rules, learning from the quiet discipline—beginning with not slamming doors—of the older monks, earnestly discussing the future of Buddhism in Vietnam with other novices.

The idyll was not to last. At the end of World War II the French sought to reestablish their colonial rule over Vietnam. They were met with fierce resistance by the independence-seeking Viet Minh. Around Thich Nhat Hanh's temple the rattle of gunfire could be heard, and, for a time, the monks had to evacuate. "We had been invaded," Thich Nhat Hanh remembers, "by society and the times."[5] "We have no choice," the young monks believed, "but to bring Buddhism back into everyday life. War has waged disaster. . . . There are so many agonizing cries of death, hunger, and imprisonment. How can anybody feel peace of mind by dwelling undisturbed in a monastery?" Filled with the aspiration to create a new "Engaged Buddhism," yet apprehensive ("Will we really be able to do something?"), the young monks took their message into the urban chaos of Saigon.[6]

In 1954 the French were defeated, and the country was partitioned in anticipation of national elections. The South reneged on this provision of the Geneva Accords, and hostilities broke out between South Vietnamese government forces and the Viet Cong and later with North Vietnam. Thich Nhat Hanh began to teach a socially engaged form of Buddhism between 1957 and 1961 in a series of temples, but his efforts were dismissed by the Vietnamese Buddhist hierarchy as "rabble-rousing." Expelled from one temple after another, the young monks would retreat to a forest hermitage, Phuong Boi (Fragrant Palm Leaves). There they regrouped and developed a spiritual practice that could withstand not only rejection but also the agony of renewed war about to descend upon them.[7]

While the Buddhist hierarchy did not support these early efforts, Thich Nhat Hanh developed a following of young people. One young woman, Cao Ngoc Phoung, captures the idealism of these followers. Deeply involved in working with the poor in Saigon, she had been turned off Buddhism by an older monk who had counseled her to first seek enlightenment as a prerequisite for becoming rightly engaged. Seeking a second opinion, she turned to Thich Nhat Hanh, who encouraged her not to be dualistic. Enlightenment could be achieved in the midst of her everyday engagement.[8]

Besides attracting the young, the monks' activities drew the hostile attention of South Vietnam's security apparatus. Thich Nhat Hanh was particularly under their scrutiny for publishing articles calling for a peaceful resolution of the renewed violent conflict over the fate of Vietnam. These writings particularly attacked the South Vietnamese regime of President Ngo Dinh Diem for refusing to hold nationwide elections.[9] A collection of Thich Nhat Hanh's poetry, *Prayers for the White Dove of Peace to Appear*, was banned by both the North and the South, yet it was circulated widely. Thich Nhat Hanh's clear advocacy for a peaceful resolution of the conflict put his life in jeopardy. At the urging of friends concerned about his safety, he accepted a scholarship to study at Princeton University and left for the United States in autumn of 1961. Later he would teach at Columbia University.

After the coup that ousted President Diem in November 1963, Thich Tri Quang, a member of the hierarchy of the Unified Buddhist Church and a former adversary, urged Thich Nhat Hanh to return to Vietnam. Thich Nhat Hanh, in turn, challenged the UBC to demand a cessation of hostilities, establish a Buddhist university to train a new generation of leaders, and create a center for training social workers. The UBC agreed only to support the second proposal, but by September 1965 Thich Nhat Hanh had established the School of Youth for Social Service (SYSS) within the new Buddhist university.[10] As Thich Nhat Hanh taught at Van Hanh University and worked with young activists, the war and the suffering of the people turned apocalyptic with a major escalation of the United States' involvement in the conflict. During this period many of Thich Nhat Hanh's antiwar poems were written and published in a weekly, *Hai Treu Am* (The Sound of the Rising Tide). One such poem, "Peace" (1964), defied the authorities for whom uttering the very word "peace" was a traitorous act:

> They woke me this morning
> to tell me that my brother had been killed in battle,
> Yet in the garden
> a new rose, with moist petals uncurling
> blooms on the bush
> and I am alive.
> When can I speak the unuttered words that are choking me?[11]

At great cost to the young monk, the words were uttered. Thich Nhat Hanh published a number of books crying out for a cessation of violence. These included the Vietnamese original of *Vietnam: Lotus in a Sea of Fire*. "We also used literature and the arts," he later said, as "'weapons' to challenge the oppression." This was done at considerable risk. Colleagues were arrested for passing out Thich Nhat Hanh's books of poetry.[12]

Once the SYSS was established, young people fanned out into the countryside working alongside villagers to repair their homes, roads, and bridges destroyed by floods or by the United States' relentless bombing campaigns.[13] On February 5, 1966, Thich Nhat Hanh ordained six lay persons as members of the Tiep Hien Order (in the West, this later became known as the Order of Interbeing) based on fourteen precepts.[14]

In the spring of 1966, Thich Nhat Hanh was invited to lead a seminar on the context of the war in Vietnam at Cornell University that was expanded into a lecture tour under the auspices of the Fellowship for Reconciliation, a religiously based peace organization. Recognizing that the United States held the key to any stable resolution of the conflict, Thich Nhat Hanh went with a five-point peace proposal: The United States should declare the right of the Vietnamese people to choose their own government, cease bombing, unilaterally impose a cease-fire except for defense, gradually withdraw American troops, and support the signing of a peace treaty and aid in the rebuilding of the country.[15] Thich Nhat Hanh's outspoken demand for a cessation of hostilities led to his being condemned by both sides of the conflict. Thus began an exile from his home country that was to last for almost forty years.

A Lotus in a Sea of Fire

During his lecture tour across the United States and parts of Europe, Thich Nhat Hanh discussed the Buddhist view of the conflict in visits with key US officials, including Secretary of Defense Robert McNamara; with prominent advocates for peace, including Dr. Martin Luther King Jr.; and with Pope Paul VI. In tandem with these efforts, an English edition of *Vietnam: Lotus in a Sea of Fire* appeared in early 1967. For those of us who were part of the religious wing of the American peace movement, *Lotus* was an oracle, prophecy embedded in a historical analysis that spanned eighteen centuries from Buddhism's early presence in Vietnam, its role in nation building, colonization by the French, and the war for independence to the present resurgence of war. This contextualization put the lie to the Cold War framing of the conflict. Instead, Thich Nhat Hanh offered a "third way," one that accorded with the wishes of most Vietnamese peasants. Being forced to take one side or the other in the conflict was tantamount to destroying the Vietnamese people.[16] The notoriety that Thich Nhat Hanh's third way manifesto gained unfortunately meant that returning to Vietnam would surely lead to imprisonment or even assassination.

How was it that a dispassionate recitation of the historical roots of the violent tsunami breaking upon a small country could be what Thomas Merton, an engaged Catholic monk and pacifist, called "this explosive little book?" Merton himself got to the root of the question when he argued that the masses of Vietnamese people were outside the frame of America's concern. They were not like us, not wanting to become like us, and, therefore, invisible. "These are the views and claims of masses of people," Merton sadly concluded, "whom we do not know, whom we have never tried to understand . . . and whose interests we now believe ourselves uniquely competent to defend with armed power on a massive scale."[17]

"Liberate us from your liberation," Thich Nhat Hanh demanded at one of the many forums in the West where he laid out his peace proposal. This Buddhist monk challenged both the concept and the practice of "liberation" as the dominant manifestation of the prophetic ethos revealing its profound ambiguity. Those who impose liberation on others by force—that is, all sides of the conflict in Vietnam and their Cold War masters—had twisted that prophetic tradition into a demonic parody of itself.

The war would grind on for another eight years with horrendous loss of life. Throughout that time America would continue to blunder in the dark. The Cold War itself burned on for another two decades and nothing was learned about the way America treats invisible people. Yet Thich Nhat Hanh held fast to a glimmer of light—the possibility of a new Engaged Buddhism: "If Buddhism in the future can contribute to the ideology of the [post–Vietnam War, post–Cold War] world, it will have been because of the sufferings that Buddhism is enduring in these days."[18]

In the summer of 1969, Thich Nhat Hanh became the leader of the Vietnamese Buddhist Peace Delegation to the Paris peace talks. This organization was not officially recognized, but Thich Nhat Hanh and Cao Ngoc Phoung were a whirlwind of activity, publicizing the sufferings of ordinary Vietnamese while the talks dragged on.[19] After the peace accords were signed in 1973, Thich Nhat Hanh and his small band of followers withdrew to a suburb of Paris and later to southern France and what was to become Plum Village. Apart from efforts to rescue Vietnamese "boat people" seeking escape from the new regime governing the country, efforts that were thwarted by numerous nations refusing to accept these refugees, the group focused on building community and cultivating its path of "being peace":

> Love tries hard to express itself
> What can we do?
> Our hands are available. . . .
> The answer will certainly come
> if we know how to remain faithful and calm
> in the midst of turbulence.[20]

In 1982 Thich Nhat Hanh concluded a five-year period of seclusion and began to offer retreats in many countries. Through these retreats and the many books that he published, he and his followers, such as Sister Chan Khong, found a new way to express their love. After forty years of spreading the message of being peace, Thich Nhat Hanh died on January 22, 2022, in Hue, Vietnam, near his ancestral home.

The Poet's Prophetic Wisdom

Thich Nhat Hanh's collected poems are offered in *Call Me by My True Names*, which he divided into two sections: "The Historical Dimension" and "The Ultimate Dimension." From Thich Nhat Hanh's Mahāyāna standpoint, these two dimensions are one. The tones of the two sections are strikingly different. The "Historical Dimension" includes poems written in the crucible of war from the early sixties through the late seventies and extending to the tragedy of the "boat people" seeking asylum after the fall of Saigon in 1975. Some of these poems were chanted by activists demonstrating in the "Don't Shoot Your Brother" peace campaign of 1965. Both sides of the conflict denounced these antiwar poems.[21] Each of these poems is an act of resistance.

"Don't listen to me," says the bodhisattva in the guise of a prophet in "Mudra." "Please don't."[22] Nevertheless, we can't help but listen. Transforming anger into urgency, these poems rivet our attention. Grief suffuses these antiwar poems. We are compelled to witness the senseless wasting of life, forced to walk a devastated landscape with the poet. My conviction is that these poems bear a striking similarity to the anguished cries of the Hebrew prophets. To be clear, Thich Nhat Hanh never explicitly borrowed a prophetic voice as Rita Gross did. I have been stressing all along that prophecy as a spiritual practice is not restricted to any single tradition but, consciously or unconsciously, can be accessed from multiple standpoints.[23]

For a Buddhist monk there is no divine call, no burning bush, but something akin to that happened for Thich Nhat Hanh when in June 1963 a young monk, Thich Quang Duc, immolated himself protesting the oppression of Buddhists by the Diem regime. Jeremiah spoke of the compulsion to speak out as having a "fire in the bones" that must be let out (Jer 20:9). In Thich Nhat Hanh's case the fire was all too literal. "The fire that burns him/ burns in my body," the poet cries,

> And the world around me
> burns with the same fire
> that burns my brother.
>
> He burns.

The very heavens reverberate with the cries of the young monk. The poet, speaking out of unquenchable pain, promises lasting fidelity. He will take up the task of teaching the youth and denouncing the war.[24]

Many in the West were confounded by Thich Quang Duc's self-immolation and those that followed. They saw it as suicide, a senseless taking of a life. "Wasn't it also a violation of the Buddhist precept against the taking of a life?" they asked. Thich Nhat Hanh countered that this extreme act expressed "the unconditional willingness to suffer for the awakening of others." "Every action for peace," Thich Nhat Hanh concluded, "requires someone to exhibit the courage to challenge the violence and inspire love."[25]

In chapter 1 we discussed how prophetic words and symbolic actions were a form of "moral chemotherapy" for an extreme situation. While Thich Quang Duc's action sincerely expressed the compassion of a bodhisattva, it just as surely challenged all of us who lived through this painful and disastrous era to shed the suffocating skin of complacency.[26]

Prophetic denunciation appears most dramatically in two poems: "Condemnation" and "Resolution." In the first poem, the poet, standing "in the presence of the undisturbed stars," denounces the perfidy of a village leveled by bombs killing all its inhabitants simply because a Viet Cong squad had passed through it. He calls upon those who hear his voice to join in his condemnation of this war. "Be my witness," he exclaims. "I cannot accept this war./ I never could,/ I never will."

> I am like the bird who dies for the sake of its mate . . .
> crying out
> "Beware! Turn around and face your real enemies—
> ambition, violence, hatred and greed."

If we kill our fellow human beings, the poet laments, "with whom then shall we live?"[27] In "Resolution," the denunciation is even more pointed. Without naming names the poet challenges us in a litany that uses the second-person plural: "You fight us. . . . You curse us. . . . You condemn us. . . . And you murder us. . . . And all because "we fight hatred/ while you feed on hatred and violence."[28]

This shift to a dualistic framework is only momentary. Much more often the poet addresses his plea to his "brother." In "Our Green Garden," he bares his breast to his brother: "I know it is *you* who will shoot me tonight/ piercing our mother's heart with a wound that can never heal." The murder of brother by brother lets loose an ecological catastrophe: "Terrible winds . . . blow from the ends of the Earth, hurling down our houses and blasting our fertile fields." As in the case of Jeremiah, chaos among human beings finds a correlate in nature.[29] Only in this case the ecological devastation is all too literal. In the midst of a wildfire world, the poet begs, "Don't sacrifice our green garden/ to the ragged flames."[30] Seeing into this interlocking connection, the poet must act. "How could we not struggle/ when even the prairie flowers/ and mountain grass/ moaned from the pain of injustice?"[31]

A central part of the struggle of the third way was the role of the young men and women from the SYSS who worked to help refugees from the violence to rebuild their homes. A grenade attack on one such group that could have come from either side left a dozen dead or wounded "and ripped apart the sky." Their grieving leader expresses his outrage with cutting irony in "Those That Have Not Exploded":

> What was their crime?—
> to hear the voice of compassion
> to come and live in a hamlet
> to help the villagers
> teach the children
> work in the rice paddies?[32]

The poet's grief cuts most deeply over the death by immolation of Nhat Chi Mai on May 16, 1967, one of the first group of six to join the Tiep Hien Order. In "Flames of Prayer," the poet takes on the persona of Nhat Chi Mai living her last day: "Waking up early, oh how I want to live forever!" She is transfixed by the beauty of the world that she is about to leave. Each precious leaf, each group of school children, "chirping like birds," each aunt, uncle, brother, and sister is embraced and held dearly. Her own grief and the poet's as well are transformed into compassion.[33] In a play written by Thich Nhat Hanh to remember six of the SYSS youth murdered one night, *The Path of Return Continues the Journey*, the alchemy of eliciting compassion from grief is developed still further. Here it is Nhat Chi Mai who picks up six murdered SYSS youth from the riverbank where they were executed and ferries them on their continuing journey. As they travel, they discuss the interweaving of life and death. They take on the role of protectors of human life. It is the living who are shrouded in the fog of war, who create labels such as "enemy or "adversary" and then shoot the person on whom they have pinned the label.[34]

Nhat Chi Mai appears once more in a Thich Nhat Hanh short story, "The Ancient Tree," written to commemorate her sacrifice. Here the forest home and the ancient mother of all trees are threatened by wildfire. Birds and animals flee, but many do not make it. One giant bird struggles in vain to put out the flames with water dripping from her body. Finally, in desperation, the bird "let forth a piercing cry. The cry was tragic and passionate and was suddenly transformed into the rushing sound of a waterfall. All at once the bird felt the fullness of its existence. . . . Without anxiety the bird plunged into the forest fire like a majestic waterfall."[35] The story, it seems to me, is a seamless fusion of Avalokiteshvara's listening to the cries of the world with the prophetic voice (the tragic and passionate cry), together producing the action of a bodhisattva whose compassion embraces even conflagration.³⁶

War's Cancer Metastasizes

"Those That Have Not Exploded" expresses Thich Nhat Hanh's outrage at the grenade attack on the young members of SYSS whom he had taught and whose actions he had nurtured. But the poet pulls us more deeply into this heart of darkness. There are more grenades that have not exploded:

> They remain
> still
> in the heart of man—
> unknown the time of their detonation.³⁷

War does not end with the cessation of hostilities. Violence reshapes the psyche of all who are touched by the conflagration of war. In a later poem, "Defuse Me," the poet makes it clear that he alone cannot defuse the bomb inside himself: "I need you to defuse me."³⁸ You, when it is your turn, will need me to defuse the bomb inside you.

War's disease spreads in other ways. In "The Sun of the Future," the poet assumes the persona of an African American soldier sitting in a wet trench waiting for "Victor Charlie." "Why do I have to hate you, Victor Charlie?" he asks. "When did we sow the first seed of hatred and anger?" As the soldier agonizes, his wife and children in Chicago remain ensnared in poverty. The money for the "War on Poverty" has been siphoned into war's swamp. "This is not what we meant to do!" the soldier sighs as he waits for Victor Charlie.³⁹

War's corrosive power damages all who come in touch with it, but none more than those who look elsewhere to find the enemy; deluded, they remain unaware that the enemy waits within. "The Lonely Watchtower" takes us into the depths of war' depravity, the effects of which are all too visible:

> High
> on top
> of the spiked heel

of the joy-woman's shoe,
you build your watchtower.

Devastation surrounds the tower. Burnt-out paddies and withered gardens. Stripped barren, the landscape is a literal wasteland, a land defiled by waste:

At noon:
You throw down
your empty sardine cans
your empty beer cans
your empty Coke bottles
your cigarette butts.

You point your guns at the body of our motherland, but at night "our souls come back and dance." It will not be the enemy's mortars that topple that tower. Rather the tears of millions, flowing together, will flush away "the joy-woman's lipstick" and "your power." This flood

will wash away
your garbage
your waste
your junk.[40]

Not even Jeremiah can match this poem's explosion of metaphors of war's cancer: the joy-woman's stiletto heels, the empty beer cans, the cleansing tide of tears. It is hard to imagine a more trenchant or prophetic biopsy of war as metastatic cancer. Unless we undergo the suffering of moral chemotherapy, we will die, alone, in our watchtower as a tide of tears washes it away.

It would be wrong to intimate that Thich Nhat Hanh, forced to live in exile after 1967, lost his prophetic edge. The *Fourteen Mindfulness Trainings of the Order of Interbeing* maintained the practice of dismantling ideologies that sanction killing, calling Buddhists to speak out against injustice without stoking partisan rancor.[41] Thirty years and more after the end of hostilities in his homeland, Thich Nhat Hanh still called upon people to wake up, to hear the bell of mindfulness sounded by melting glaciers, roaring wildfires, and howling hurricanes: "We need a . . . collective wakening," he said. "We have created a system we cannot control."[42] "The poisoning of our ecosystem, the exploding of bombs, the violence in our neighborhoods and in society, the pressures of time, noise and pollution—all of these have been created by the course of our economic growth and they are all sources of mental illness."[43] Decades later, the toxic culture metaphorically depicted in "The Lonely Watchtower" had spread across the globe.

The Poet-Prophet in Exile

The Hebrew prophets dealt with the catastrophic loss of Israel and later of Judah and of Jerusalem, the Holy City. With the destruction of the temple in Jerusalem came a sense of a shattering of cosmic meaning. For some of the prophets this meant wrestling with the trauma of a forced exile from their homeland. A mid-seventies conversation in Paris between Thich Nhat Hanh and Daniel Berrigan, a Jesuit priest and radical peace activist, sheds light on the poems gathered under the "Ultimate Dimension." They are crafted in the midst of exile. Thich Nhat Hanh tells Berrigan of a recurrent dream:

> From time to time, I see in my dream a green hill—a hill of green grass where I spent time playing as a child. . . . Every time I leave, I leave things on that hill. I have grown trees here and there. . . . From time to time I have returned to that hill, and in the space between two dreams, the hill had grown. The hill is not a static image, it is growing like myself; and every time I come to the hill, I see that's the place where I should be. And each poem that I have written is in the form of a plant, a leaf, a flower. . . .
> From time to time it has happened that something has stood in my way and I haven't been able to reach the hill . . . and each time like that I woke up with a feeling of sadness. Even in dreams you are not allowed to come back.[44]

While the war raged on and close friends or the young SYSS students were in danger, imprisoned, or killed, the pain of isolation was nearly unbearable.[45] Throwing himself into the work of the Buddhist peace delegation was one way of coping with exile. A stronger antidote to the loneliness of exile was finding and building a community, a sangha, as he had done as a young monk building the hermitage at Phuong Boi. "Community building," he would later say, "is our true practice."[46]

Prophets appear to be dogmatically certain in their utterances, and Thich Nhat Hanh's condemnation of the war, too, was unequivocal. Their moral stance, however, arises out of a dark night of the soul that must be endured. Jeremiah, at the end of his rope, even curses the day of his birth (Jer 20:14–18). The poignancy of Thich Nhat Hanh's conversation with Daniel Berrigan is striking. He speaks of being a "fish out of water," more ominously as being a stateless person pushed from place to place by the few who hold the reins of power: "Even in dreams you are not allowed to come back."[47]

Most if not all of the poems in "The Ultimate Dimension" are either in the present tense or in the present perfect tense. This squares with the Buddhist sense of the fullness of the present moment and of how we sleepwalk through time, wandering in the past while anxiously awaiting the future. In this light the conversation between Daniel Berrigan and Thich Nhat Hanh takes on added significance. Berrigan introduces the topic of memory but suggests that we think of memory as a creative force that re-members what has been broken. It puts the broken world back together. Thich Nhat Hanh, for his part, sees such re-membering as the beginning of awakening: one recovers from forgetfulness, from one's dispersion.[48]

Buddhists are often suspicious of common affirmations of hope. Such hope appears to be a turning away from the present moment, orienting the self toward a not-yet future. Our life becomes a series of hurdles that must be surmounted, each of which gives rise to the next. Thich Nhat Hanh shows us how the process works: "Usually we say, 'Wait until I finish school . . . then I will be really alive.' But then when we obtain it, we say, 'I have to wait until I have a job in order to be fully alive.' After the job, we need a car, and after the car, a house. . . . We always postpone being alive to the future."[49] Thich Nhat Hanh is particularly concerned that peace not be interpreted as a future goal. "Peace Is Every Step," as the title of one book puts it. Digging into the present moment taps the wellspring of energy to move forward. Hope postpones being peace, lures us away from touching the "Ultimate Dimension."[50]

The war poems sound a different note. There, trauma is accompanied by longing and grief by hope:

In darkness Earth, my homeland,
yearns for the miraculous event
when . . . Maitreya comes to my land. . . .

> Let my homeland, let Earth pray
> for Vietnam—
> her deaths and fires,
> grief and blood—
> that Vietnam will rise from her suffering
> and become the soft, new cradle
> for the Buddha-to-come.[51]

Hope born of agony is hope against hope. The stars witness that another world is possible. That Maitreya, the Buddha-to-come, might come to a land wasted, a place where "Mara's hand bears down in violence and hatred," is itself an expression of radical hope. At least in these war poems, hope as the fruit of trauma, grief, and longing transformed into compassion offers a contrast to hope as wishful thinking that escapes the present moment. I suggest that Thich Nhat Hanh overcomes this discordant interpretation of hope by offering Saint Francis as an alternative model: "When St. Francis asked the almond tree to tell him about God, in just a few seconds the tree was covered with beautiful flowers. St. Francis was standing on the side of the ultimate dimension. It was winter. There were no leaves, flowers, or fruits, but he saw the flowers. . . . When we touch one thing with deep awareness, we touch everything. Touching the present moment, we realize that the present is made of the past and is creating the future."[52] In the present moment to re-member and to see what confounds common sense is a form of radical hope: "he saw the flowers."

Conclusion

In the crucible of war, Thich Nhat Hanh and his followers developed new forms of insight and practice that in time sprouted as a new branch, a new form of Engaged Buddhism. While most of his postwar prolific writings breathe "being peace," the war poems strike a different chord. They bear a family resemblance to prophetic modes of witness, diagnosis, denunciation, and compassion. They challenge all those caught in war's death grip to wake up. We see this in specific poems:

- Trauma and pain compel the poet to act, to protest and resist. Thich Nhat Hanh saw his war poems as forms of nonviolent action.[53]

- The poet/prophet denounces the war in Vietnam and even those who perpetuate it. Human beings are not our enemies.

- The poet grieves. In "The Path of Return Continues the Journey" the poet identifies with the murdered School of Youth for Social Service students. Their deaths are not final; they give birth to compassion for the living.

- War short-circuits efforts to build a just society. "The Sun of the Future" expresses compassion for an African American soldier victimized by the war while his family suffers from poverty in Chicago.

- War is a cancer that metastasizes. In "The Lonely Watchtower" we see war's moral corruption at its worst. It demands a moral chemotherapy that in this poem takes the form of a flood tide of tears.

- War buries bombs deep inside of us that can explode decades later. The poet shatters our complacent amnesia, encourages us to "look deeply," and calls us to defuse each other's bombs.

- "Liberate us from your liberation," the poet-prophet demands. In so doing he performs a necessary critique of the ways in which the prophetic stream turns deadly.

- The poet, like some of the Hebrew prophets, is condemned to exile and must forge a new form of Engaged Buddhism in an alien land.

- Unlike the prophets, the poet does not draw on a subversive memory and does not—except for one poem that expresses longing for Maitreya, "The Buddha-to-Come"—proclaim an alternative future.

We must be careful not to separate these poems and the dark night of the soul that they reflect from those of the Ultimate Dimension. They inter-are. Just as he was being called back to Vietnam from teaching at Columbia University in 1963, Thich Nhat Hanh wrote "Butterflies over the Golden Mustard Fields." He remembers those who have died. The wind is their breathing. "It was only yesterday that you told me/'If one day you find everything destroyed/ then look for me in the depths of your heart.'" The poet asks what he can do to help and the wind replies: "Smile. Life is a miracle. /Be a flower.'" Commenting on the poem, Thich Nhat Hanh says, "If we stop being joyful and stop singing, we are caught in a kind of prison." In the midst of collective dukkha, the poet, "a bubbling spring," breaks free.[54] This way of being, he insists, is available in each present moment:

> The good news is that you are alive,
> and the linden tree is still there,
> standing firm in the harsh Winter.[55]

Buddhist Reflections in a Prophetic Key #3
Sea Pirates, Nazis, and the Need for Moral Judgment

Of all the poems that Thich Nhat Hanh wrote during or immediately after the war in Vietnam, his signature poem, "Please Call Me by My True Names," has generated the most heated discussion. Critics have focused on the central stanza that reflects Thich Nhat Hanh's agonizing reflection on the plight of the "boat people," refugees from the victorious North Vietnamese regime:

> I am the twelve-year-old girl.
> refugee on a small boat
> who throws herself into the ocean
> after being raped by a sea pirate.
> And I am the sea pirate,
> my heart not yet capable
> of seeing and loving.[1]

I, like many others, gagged reading the sentence "I am the sea pirate." The poem throws the moral life up for grabs. I must recognize my complicity in creating the world that has shaped the sea pirate. Yet, in his own commentary on the poem in *Being Peace,* Thich Nhat Hanh seems to go further by stripping away the pirate's responsibility for his actions. If we grew up under the social conditions that the pirate did, he suggests, likely we would end up as pirates.[2] One problem here is that such an interpretation undercuts moral integrity and agency. Not all who grew up under those social conditions became pirates. They and we make moral choices. Later Thich Nhat Hanh points out that we do not blame a tree when it fails to thrive. We look for the underlying causes. "Blaming . . . never lead[s] to any positive effect."[3] Prophets, on the other hand, point to the entire population of Judah, but especially its powerful elite, for failing to live up to their covenantal obligation to do justice. Are we face to face with intractable differences in moral stances?

Sallie King's commentary in *Being Benevolence,* her study of Engaged Buddhist ethics, is very helpful here. The poem, she argues, releases many from "the prison of judgmental thinking." It "counters the tendency to complacent self-righteousness, distancing oneself from the 'evil doers,' while judging them like God from above."[4] We are challenged to enlarge the scope of our compassion to include sea pirates, as painful as the process may be.

Read in this light the poem vaccinates the reader who takes it to heart from the very disease endemic to a prophetic moral stance, specifically, a propensity to self-righteousness, setting oneself on a moral mountaintop above the evil doers and assuming a firm grasp of the divine will to the point of calling for a violent divine retribution. If we kill the pirate, Thich Nhat Hanh counters, we kill some part of ourselves.[5] Such an uncovering of the virus endemic to the prophetic calling is itself a form of moral chemotherapy. In my mind the poem does not suspend moral judgment and accountability but only raises them to a higher register.[6] We inevitably make moral judgments, but not "like God from above."

As if this challenge to our moral stance were not enough, Sallie King raises the ante. King spent a term teaching Engaged Buddhism to German students at the University of Hamburg. When she taught Thich Nhat Hanh's signature poem, she was met with strong resistance. The students insisted that some events, movements, institutions, and even individuals' actions are morally evil and should be judged as such. They had been raised in a nation that—after two decades of emphasizing itself as the victim—made it a matter of collective principle to face its moral culpability for the suffering perpetrated by the Third Reich and to call out any signs of a recurrence of Nazism. Germany has made the prophetic voice a part of its public discourse.[7] King points to the long delay in Japanese Buddhists coming to terms with their complicity in Japanese imperialism, the lack of a prophetic discourse around Cambodia's "killing fields," and the failure of Buddhist communities—with some exceptions—to denounce the virulent Buddhist nationalism in Sri Lanka and Myanmar.[8] Cultivating nonjudgment in such circumstances is ethically deficient.

Surely Thich Nhat Hanh's antiwar poems condemning the violence of all sides of the Vietnam war and America's disastrous involvement in it remain a Buddhist witness to and condemnation of moral evil and the suffering it produced. Thich Nhat Hanh, we can be sure, would add that strong moral condemnation must be tempered with compassion and the recognition that we who judge evildoers are never as free of the taint of complicity as we like to think. The metastatic cancer diagnosed in "The Lonely Watchtower" ravaged the collective body of all who were caught in the maelstrom of the Vietnam war. I suggest we juxtapose that poem with "Please Call Me by My True Names." The ensuing dialectic might be one way of addressing the moral concerns of King's German students.

Chapter Four

Joanna Macy and the Work That Reconnects

> How can I be fully present to my world—present enough to rejoice and be useful—when we as a species are destroying it. . . . This query was clearly my life koan.
>
> —Joanna Macy, *A Wild Love for the World*[1]

> There comes a time when all life on Earth is in danger. Barbarian powers have arisen. Although they waste their wealth in preparations to annihilate each other, they have much in common: weapons of unfathomable devastation and technologies that lay waste to the world. It is now[,] when the future of all beings hangs by the frailest of threads, that the kingdom of Shambhala emerges. . . . You cannot go there, for it is not a place. It exists in the minds of the Shambhala warriors. . . . Now comes the time when great courage is required of the Shambhala warrior. . . . For they must go into the very heart of the barbarian power and dismantle the weapons. The Shambhala warriors know that they can do this because the weapons are . . . mind made. . . . So they can be unmade by the human mind. [The Shambhala warriors] train in the use of two weapons. . . . The weapons are compassion and insight.
>
> —Joanna Macy, *Widening Circles*[2]

Joanna Macy has told the Shambhala prophecy to her wide circles of friends, fellow Buddhists, and people in many countries trying to come to terms with the looming devastation of a nuclear holocaust or the climate change that blights our lives. In 1965, Macy was in India along with her family while her husband, Fran, was assistant director of the Peace Corps for India. At the urging of a volunteer, she traveled north from New Delhi to Dharamshala, and from there onward, up twisting mountain roads to a settlement of Tibetan refugees. There she met a young Tibetan monk, Choegyal Rinpoche, who was to set her on the path of the Buddha and who became her lifelong friend.[3] After numerous postings abroad, Joanna found herself back in India renewing her friendship with Choegyal. It was he who told her the Shambhala prophecy and it is his version that she has passed on.

If Rita Gross was the first Engaged Buddhist to explicitly borrow a prophetic voice, Joanna Macy is the first of our Engaged Buddhists to convey a prophecy and clearly, in her case, she is *proclaiming* it. Macy's treatment of the Shambhala prophecy bears several family resemblances to the ancient Israelite examples of the genre. There is, first, the Shambhala warriors themselves training with the weapons of compassion and insight. The Hebrew prophets are the warriors battling their rulers, who lack insight and compassion, who have descended into barbarism in their treatment of the marginalized. These prophets stand up to God no less, emboldened by their compassion for a suffering people. Neither the Shambhala prophecy nor those of the Hebrew prophets predict the future. They read the signs of the times. They show keen insight into what is threatening in the present moment. Always that moment is one of crisis, a time when everything is at stake. Both call their hearers to act. Likewise in both cases "the line between good and evil runs through every human heart."[4] Finally, both versions of the genre hold fast to hope that another world—one of justice and peace—may be born.

Eventually Joanna Macy began to tell the Shambhala story in every workshop that she led. It set what she called the "work that reconnects" in a larger context. We are volunteers in an army of Shambhala warriors who wield the weapons of compassion and wisdom. "These two weapons represent two essential aspects of the Work That Reconnects. One is the recognition and experience of our pain for the world. The other is the recognition and experience of our radical, empowering interconnectedness with all life."[5]

Joanna Macy has contributed to prophetic wisdom in four areas. First, she calls us to face the trauma, the collective dukkha, of our age. Second, through her workshops, she introduces mindful practices designed to break us out of the shell of psychic numbness into which we have crawled. Macy overturns Buddhists' widespread negative valuation of emotions such as anger and despair. Third, her definition of active hope as "something we *do* rather than *have*" transforms a prevailing Buddhist suspicion of hope as wishful thinking, as an escape from the present moment. She sees hope as a wellspring of action.[6] Finally, using her early studies of systems theory, she explores the affinities between Buddhist understandings of interdependence and "deep ecology." In the process she calls us to participate in "the Great Turning."

Widening Circles

Joanna Macy was born on May 2, 1929. She had a difficult childhood dodging the anger of her tyrannical father. For a time, she found refuge in the Presbyterian church and studied in college to be a Christian missionary. She found her studies in church history and Christian dogma stultifying and she abandoned her earlier aspirations. For a short period after college, she worked for the CIA. Initially it was a heady experience: "I liked belonging to a small elite that knew more than other people," she said. That arrogance quickly dissolved when she, one of the inner circle, viewed a classified film of the early tests of a hydrogen bomb. "I felt stupid, and sick and unprepared," she lamented, while her colleagues chatted undisturbed. "There it was again, the same chilling foreboding that had come over me . . . with the news of Hiroshima, the same sense of an irrevocable shift of fate, like a shudder in the ground beneath my feet."[7]

Her trip to the Tibetan refugee community in 1965 led to many subsequent trips, to a meditation practice, and to formal commitment to follow a Buddhist path.[8] This practice gave birth to numerous transformative experiences. One example is worth mentioning as demonstrating a distinctive characteristic of Macy's practice. On one of her trips to the Tibetan community in an Indian train crammed with passengers she felt her body expand to the point where it included all the others: "Everything out there—each gesticulating, chewing, sleeping form; each crying baby and coughing heap of rags . . . was as intimately my body as I." What bears mentioning in our examination of Macy's prophetic overtones is, first, the very visceral and emotional sense of what Thich Nhat Hanh calls "interbeing" in her experience and, second, her reaction to this event: "My mind when it could think repeated one thing: 'released into action.' Now we can be 'released into action.' "[9]

Systems Thinking and Buddhist Interbeing

Eventually Macy's path led her to doctoral studies at Syracuse University. The key intellectual breakthrough for her came when she realized that the Buddhist teaching of dependent coarising (*pratītya samutpāda*) and contemporary systems theory illuminate one another. Dependent coarising encapsulates the Buddhist understanding of causality, the mutual conditioning of all phenomena that reveals their lack of any isolated or enduring substance. Its intent is soteriological. Realizing our internal relations with all that is, we become free to work for the liberation of all.[10] That work, in turn, becomes our joy.

For its part, systems theory offered an irreplaceable lens for examining the natural world as interwoven ecologies: "A system is less a thing than a pattern. It is a pattern of events, its existence and character deriving less from the nature of its components than from their organization. As such, it consists of a dynamic flow of interactions. . . . The organized whole found in nature, then, is not only a system but an *open* system. It maintains and organizes itself by exchanging matter and energy and information with its environment. These flow through the system and are transformed by it. These exchanges and transformations are the system's life and continuity for no component of the system is permanent."[11] Open systems, then, are self-organizing and self-regulating. Macy specifies three further defining qualities of such systems. First, every level of reality, from atoms to bodies, from societies to galaxies, is a whole and cannot be reduced to the workings of its parts. Second, systems are dynamic. They do not simply maintain their equilibrium but instead strive for greater complexity. Finally, each whole is composed of subsystems and is, in turn, a subsystem nested in a greater whole.[12]

Christopher Queen labels the underlying principles of systems theories as "adaptation, emergence, integration and nestedness." They offer "a new paradigm for analysis," but Queen suggests that Macy goes further. She adopts "a rhetoric of urgency and empowerment," asking her audiences to "re-member our collective body" and to "recover the capacity of open living systems for exploratory self-organization."[13] One further quality of open systems would become of central significance as Macy moved beyond her graduate studies: new organizing principles arise only when the old system has undergone a "positive disintegration." While we feel a loss of bearings, staying open to the experience and its feedback leads to breakthrough and thriving.[14] This process has recurred frequently in our evolutionary history.

Macy suggests that the juxtaposition of systems theory to the Buddhist understanding of dependent coarising can uncover the mutual causality inherent in, among other things, our moral life. Systems theory challenges the frameworks that we implicitly draw upon to interpret Buddhist teachings. It uncovers misinterpretations of Buddhist teachings that arise when we consciously or unconsciously operate out of a frame of linear causality.[15]

Despair and Empowerment

Decades before "climate change" became a menacing reality and a painful part of our consciousness, Macy attended a conference on planetary survival in 1977 at the Boston Coliseum. The conference talks offered a nonstop barrage of bad news. Riding back to a dinner date on the Boston T, Macy plunged into a dark night of the soul. "At that moment something gave way inside me," she remembers. "I found myself looking at the faces across the aisle through tears that I was powerless to stop or hide. It felt like the collapse of some inner scaffolding that for years had been holding the kind of information I had harvested all day, holding it up and out of the way, on a shelf in my mind. As that scaffolding crumbled, years of stored knowledge about what we were doing to our planet—to ourselves—cascaded into my heart and body, bringing a realization I could no longer keep at bay: yes—we can succeed now in destroying our world."[16] "I had no idea how to live with [this awareness]," she realized.[17] One way to deal with this traumatic awareness of the probable mass extinction of many species would have been to rebuild the scaffolding. Robert Jay Lifton, a psychiatrist, had earlier studied survivors of the Hiroshima bombing. He coined the term "psychic numbing" to describe the psychological mechanisms by which these survivors blocked out the horrors that they had experienced.[18] Later when the nuclear arms race shifted into high gear, he applied this concept to understand how people living under the specter of nuclear annihilation could go about their business as usual. What Hiroshima represented, Lifton argued, was the possibility of extinguishing all life on earth. "Destroying most or all of human life is, to say the least, an extreme transgression. But to destroy nature itself in the process is a still further transgression around which we experience a quality of dread, hidden guilt and nothingness—these emotions frequently amorphous and beyond our grasp but on the order of an ultimate deadly sin."[19] To avoid the pain of this awareness a socially orchestrated, collective numbing (I was one of the children crouching in the school hallway, hands over our heads, as if this might save us from a nuclear blast) became part and parcel of the national security state. This collective sensibility rested not on indifference but on blocked emotions and a disconnected imagination. Our ability to imagine a meaningful future was undercut: "In its extreme varieties, numbing itself becomes a symbolic death. One freezes in the manner of certain animals facing danger, becomes as if dead in order to prevent actual physical or psychic death."[20]

What kept Macy from succumbing to psychic numbness throughout a protracted period of grieving was her Vipassana Buddhist practice and the intellectual framework provided by systems theory's understanding of positive disintegration. What Macy saw as remaining open and aware of her grief and despair, her Buddhist friends called clinging. Her pain for the possible extinguishing of life on this planet they saw as futile. "All you can change is yourself," they said.[21] Psychic numbing masqueraded as Buddhist wisdom. Despite these "friendly" admonitions, Macy's radical honesty kept her open.

One year after her experience on the Boston T, and still struggling with the existential dread that it raised, Macy, chairing a seminar at Notre Dame University on the topic of a possible extinguishing of any future, acknowledged her emotions and invited others to do the same. The result of just a brief sharing radically opened the seminar: "It unleashed energy and mutual caring." At the conclusion of the seminar a small group searched for an explanation of what had just happened. They compared the upsurge of feeling to grief work. Unblocking and acknowledging one's grief or, in this case, despair was a first step beyond paralysis: "We knew that it had something to do with a readiness to face the dark and take that darkness into us, that it had to do, in other words, with a willingness to acknowledge and experience pain, and that this pain for the world, like pain for the loss of a loved one, is a measure of caring. We also knew that the joint journey into the dark had changed us, bonding us in a special way."[22] Of key importance was this group's intuitive understanding that they—and we—were not likely to be able to take the journey alone. From these touchstone events Macy and numerous colleagues evolved what were first called "Despair and Empowerment" workshops and later "the Work That Reconnects."[23] The early workshops were clearly grounded in the theory that Macy had developed linking systems theory with a Buddhist understanding of interdependent coarising. As open systems, we, both as individuals and as a species, undergo periodic, painful reorganization, but our interconnectedness is also a source of energy. The addition of Lifton's diagnosis of collective psychic numbing proved to be transformative. So also, Macy insisted, were her years of experience teaching meditation techniques to those involved in struggles for peace and justice.[24]

Macy's deliberate efforts to elicit strong emotions that many Buddhists would see as negative symptoms of dukkha—including despair and dread—is one of her most salient innovations. We learn to accept these emotions as realistic responses to global threats to the survival of our species and many others. The emergence of these emotions is a sure sign of a crack in the armor plate of denial and psychic numbness. They are the shadow side of deep reservoirs of caring.

In chapter 1 we saw that biblical scholars have applied trauma studies to illuminate the work of the Hebrew prophets to enable their people to come to terms with the overthrow of the monarchy, the destruction of the temple, and the exile of the power elite in Babylon. Above all, the royal ideology that offered a divine guarantee that Judah would remain unscathed for all time lay in ruins. The prophets of exile modeled the grief that had to be felt if collective numbness was to be shattered and the people were to open up to a radical reorientation of their faith in a liberating God.

Despair and Personal Power in the Nuclear Age, published in 1983, during a period of an escalating nuclear arms race, is a record of Macy's early experiments in dealing with trauma and the tangle of emotions that lay buried under a layer of numbness. It was clearly designed to be a handbook for those who might take up this work of coming back to life. There are descriptions of numerous exercises, sample agendas, and lists of organizations to connect people with. There is a solid understanding of how to evoke emotions, how to honor them, and, above all, how to facilitate a workshop without playing therapist or offering bogus optimism.[25] Macy and her colleagues were inventing a new pedagogy that combined Buddhist practices with exercises that involved bodies, emotions, and minds. Antinuclear activist Kathleen Sullivan for example, confided in Joanna Macy at one of these workshops the fury that fueled her activism. "Yes, feel your anger and rage," Macy replied. "And breathe that through as you fuel your motivation." "What a relief," Sullivan reflected on this transforming awareness. "I had finally found a home for the matrix of emotions I felt as a young woman growing up in a world under threat."[26]

One example of an exercise used in these workshops provides a clear indication of how Macy has transformed Buddhist spiritual practices. "Breathing through" begins with a straightforward attention to one's in and out breaths. Then the participants are counseled to visualize their breath "as a stream or ribbon of air," moving through the nostrils, the windpipe, and the lungs, and from there to the heart and then out into the universe. Next the group is asked to open themselves to concrete images of suffering, "your fellow beings in pain and need, in fear and isolation, in prisons, hospitals, tenements, refugee camps," and to breathe in these images, riding on the stream of air into and then out of the heart, not trying to solve anything, not holding on to the pain, but allowing one's good heart to do its work. "Let all sorrows ripen in me," Macy said, quoting Shantideva. Trust your heart. "Remember that the heart that breaks open can hold the whole universe."[27]

Through her reinvention of Buddhist practice in the form of the "Work That Reconnects," Joanna Macy has taught us, first, to recognize the emotional blockage that short-circuits the connection between worldviews and behavior, and then to see apathy not as a moral flaw but as a form of psychic numbing that offers a costly and disempowering protection from our fears, despair, and sense of isolation. The Work That Reconnects encourages us to acknowledge our pain for the world as the token of our great care. This pain can be a sign of a systemic realignment of our sense of self. Finally, we learn how to tap into "negative emotions" as a source of positive commitment. In Buddhist terms we embrace our collective dukkha not by transcending or quenching our emotional responses but by transforming them, releasing the energy in our underlying care for the earth and its sentient beings. Our pain reveals our connectedness, our interbeing. Our connectedness is a vast root system that nourishes us. This, Macy concludes, is what *deep ecology* captures. We are not individual but ecological selves.[28]

Deep Ecology and Deep Time

Macy found a way to integrate her systems theory, and her Buddhist understanding of interdependence, while directing her work in a normative direction through the concept of deep ecology. Originally developed by Arne Naess, a Norwegian philosopher, deep ecology affirms the interrelatedness and radical equality of all life. The biosphere that sustains us is a self-regulating system within which all life is nested. Our well-being is dependent upon the well-being of others and of the biosphere itself.[29] Nonhuman life as well as human life carries intrinsic value that must be recognized and respected as essential to the whole. Other life forms must not be reduced to a purely utilitarian means to human ends. All beings exist as events within a field of internal relations.[30] Reckless pursuit of self-centered benefit by a dominant species threatens the balance of this system. The consequences are now painfully evident: climate change, extreme weather events, wildfires, and the relentless unfolding of the sixth great extinction.[31] Deep ecology does more than illuminate the present crisis. Decentering human life, it overthrows frameworks that have shaped Western traditions for several millennia.

One exercise developed by Macy in the mid-1980s with John Seed in Australia but adopted by many others is the "Council of All Beings." It serves as a metonym for our interconnected world. This ritual reminds us that "respect for the web of life is our birthright, it evokes both sorrow for its loss and a yearning for its return. In systems terms, this exercise allows 'self-referencing'—that is, seeing ourselves and our actions from the perspective of the larger context." Before meeting John Seed, Joanna says that deep ecology was just a useful concept. With the invention of the council exercise, it became tangible, encompassing.[32]

The heart of the Council of All Beings exercise is when the participants allow themselves to be chosen by a life form and speak on its behalf in the council. These beings first express their power, the unique and beautiful manifestation of life that they are, then they detail the hardships that human greed and ignorance have imposed upon them. Finally, they offer gifts to awakening humans to be used in repairing the web of life. The council serves to decenter human beings. Taking her turn sitting in the center of the circle and compelled to just listen to the other beings, Macy felt a strong desire to protest her innocence. The exercise revealed how much she clung to an anthropocentric view.[33]

Accompanying this council is a litany, "The Bestiary," a lamentation for dying species. "How do we honor the passing of life?" Macy asks, when so many species are nearing extinction.

> Reed Warbler
>   Swallowtail Butterfly
>   Bighorn Sheep
>   Indian Python
>   Howler Monkeys
>   Sperm Whale
>   Blue Whale

> Dive me deep, brother whale. . . . Deep in our mother ocean where I once swam, gilled and finned. The salt from those early seas still runs in my tears. . . . Give me a song, a song for sadness too vast for my heart, for a rage too wild for my throat.[34]

Through such exercises we begin to "break free from the species arrogance" that threatens life on this planet. As this process unfolds, our "wild love" for the world widens.[35] Overcoming species arrogance, addressing the sixth great extinction and climate change, may well be the toughest challenge that humans have faced. Macy's ecological self faces the challenge joyfully and hopefully.

More than any Engaged Buddhist that I am aware of, Joanna Macy has developed a prophetic Buddhist understanding of hope. As we saw, Macy defines "active hope" as "something we *do* rather than *have*" (italics in original). Recall Rebecca Solnit's powerful metaphor of hope as an ax for breaking out of our anthropocentric prison. Hope is a practice that recurs again and again. We see reality clearly, we identify what we hope for, and we take a step to move things in that direction.[36]

In her advocacy for active hope Macy seems to depart from mainstream Buddhist understandings. Buddhists are often suspicious of common affirmations of hope. Such hope appears to be a turning away from the present moment, orienting the self toward a not-yet future. In chapter 3 we examined Thich Nhat Hanh's critique of common understandings of hope as postponing being alive to a future that is always beyond our reach. Rita Gross argues that hope expresses both an aversion to the present and attachment to a desired future. "Hope and fear," she argues, "are merely two sides of the same coin. . . . We hope that things will go a certain way and we're afraid that they won't." Instead, she sees Buddhism as affirming "settling and soaring": "Settle into the edge of nowness, soar off that edge. Settle and soar endlessly."[37]

Despite his suspicions about conventional understandings of hope, Thich Nhat Hanh saw the present as multidimensional.[38] The past is gathered and incorporated in the ever-changing present that is the womb of the future. Subversive memory and active hope are dimensions of the present. Radical hope transcends rational expectations. It transforms conventional hopes for some particular change, event, or thing.

Eventually the Work That Reconnects developed a spiraling process as its spine. The spiral begins with gratitude, with what the text celebrating Joanna's life and work calls "a wild love for the world." The spiral curves forward to "honor our pain for the world," breaking the cultural taboo that admonishes "pull yourself together; where is your Buddhist equanimity?" From honoring our pain, the spiral moves to "seeing with new eyes," drawing from ancient wisdom as well as from exercises in deep ecology and deep time. Finally, "going forth" embraces active hope in taking a few steps forward. Following this recurrent spiral, we begin to realize that the whole world is acting with us and through us.[39]

Macy's approach to an alternative understanding of hope relies upon a concept of "deep time." Ecologists work out of a sense of deep time, thinking in terms of millions, even billions of years. Our culture functions within narrow temporal frameworks. Our economy rewards those who think in terms of short-term gains—the quarterly financial report. Long-term consequences are offloaded to a nebulous future. Such narrow frameworks undercut the meaning of our lives.[40] In the West, during the Middle Ages, craft persons worked with an expansive understanding of time as they built magnificent cathedrals fully aware that it would take generations to complete them.

"The Work That Reconnects" revives a sense of deep time connected to a scientific understanding of deep ecology. Macy credits her Tibetan friends for acting out of an understanding of deep time. During periods of moderation in Chinese rule, the Tibetans, like the medieval craft worker, simply placed stone upon stone to rebuild temples and monasteries destroyed in the Chinese Cultural Revolution. When crackdowns occurred, they waited patiently, knowing that the work would not be completed in their lifetime. Active hope does not hanker after success; it persists.[41]

The image and possibility of a nuclear holocaust or apocalyptic scenarios of climate change threaten any sense of temporal continuity, to say nothing about deep time. "We are thus among the first," Robert Jay Lifton says, "to live with a recurrent sense of biological severance."[42] So, as Macy conceived of it, the work that reconnects must enable us to reinhabit time. Thich Nhat Hanh argues that when we meditate, we bring all of the suffering in the world with us. Meditation is an act of re-membering.[43] Similarly, the reality of interdependence entails bringing a sense of deep time to our meditative practice. Our ancestors sit with us. The Work That Reconnects asks us to remember the gifts that they have bestowed on us and the responsibilities that they bequeathed to us. Yet we do not sit with our ancestors alone. Bridging the chasm—the possibility of our own species extinction at our own hands—one exercise in the Work That Reconnects asks participants to compose a letter written by their future descendants. We sit face to face with the faceless ones, those yet to be born. They certainly will hold us accountable. "What did you do with the poison fire, the Plutonium waste that will poison our world for 240,000 years?" they will surely ask. And then Macy envisions them asking, "What did you do during the Great Turning?"[44]

The Great Turning

The Great Turning represents Macy's prophetic challenge to the present generation.[45] As with the prophets, we are confronted with a crisis that is total in its impact. Jeremiah, wearing an iron yoke, bears witness to imminent disaster. Amos, with his plumb line, sees his present society—built upon injustice—as a wall that is not set true; the shock waves that will cause it to collapse can already be felt. Macy shines a laser beam on the actual structures that constitute our collective life. One way of engaging this crisis—Business as Usual—is a recipe for disaster. A runaway economic system predicated on ravaging the earth and turning it into commodities that are rapidly consumed and then discarded is suicidal. While those imprisoned by Business as Usual live in denial and succumb to psychic numbness, the end of this system can be felt in the shock waves that convulse the present. Because of its heedlessness and hubris, the prevailing system, call it what you will—runaway capitalism, death-dealing nationalism, rampant racism—defaults to the Great Unraveling with horrendous implications for life on earth.[46] As with the prophets, the present crisis offers a stark choice: either the Great Turning or the Great Unraveling.

The phrase "The Great Turning" should also be read as a riff on the Buddha's "turning of the wheel."[47] In this critical age a new dharma is emerging with roots solidly in the Buddhist long history of creating new "vehicles" as it moved into new cultures with new challenges. The Great Turning represents a shift to create a self-sustaining political, economic, and spiritual system that cares for all living beings. It is by no means guaranteed. If we are to survive the Great Unraveling, it will be by a combination of three kinds of actions. First, "holding actions": boycotting corporations that trash the biosphere, passing laws that remove fossil fuel subsidies, holding vigils at places of ecological destruction, and engaging in acts of civil disobedience, as in the case of the Standing Rock pipeline protests. Holding actions buy us time, and time now is in short supply. Second, structural change entails creating alternative institutions in the shell of the old system. It includes a multitude of creative transformations already well underway: community-supported agriculture and urban gardens, land trusts, cooperative industries, and even such basic innovations as creating bike lanes for commuting to work. The third kind of action involves shifting consciousness by employing systems theory to illuminate our interconnectedness, fostering an ecological awareness and drawing on the resources and practices of Engaged Buddhism, ecofeminism, creation spirituality, liberation theology, and other forms of spirituality that call into question the ongoing commodification of all aspects of our life.[48] The prophetic ethos is manifest in all three of these actions. In each we glimpse the dharma of the ecological self.

Conclusion

We can now take stock of what we have learned about prophetic wisdom from Joanna Macy's incorporation of systems theory, deep ecology, and deep time into her Buddhist theory and practice:

- Both the Shambhala prophecy that guides Macy's engagement with the world and the Hebrew prophets read the signs of the times as a critical period in which we are called to make a choice. Both offer an active hope grounded in compassion and insight.

- Systems theory provides a useful tool for revising traditional understandings of the Buddhist concept of dependent coarising. It guides analyses of systemic oppression and alienation and enables the development of the concept of interbeing in ways that link it to the theory and practice of deep ecology and deep time.

- The concept of psychic numbness developed by Robert J. Lifton offers a diagnosis of our paralysis in confronting the threats to life on this planet of a nuclear holocaust and climate change. Macy's exercises uncover the buried trauma that has arisen with these twin threats. In exercises such as the Council of All Beings we tap into reservoirs of caring.

- Reinterpreting the role of emotions in pursuing the Buddhist path, Macy offers an alternative to traditional Buddhist approaches to dealing with "negative emotions" such as grief, anger, and despair. Rather than seeing them as forms of ill will and clinging, she enables us to see how they express our underlying solidarity with all living beings.

- The Work That Reconnects draws upon "deep time." Mindful practice links us to the ongoing process of evolution. We express our gratitude to our ancestors for their insights and compassion. We also connect with the faceless descendants who rely upon our acts in the present.

- The concept of "active hope" addresses the Buddhist critique of commonplace hope. Macy's vision of the Great Turning offers an analogue to the prophets' active hope. The world is not all Egypt. It is also a riff on the Buddha's "turning of the wheel." Holding actions, the creation of alternative institutions, and shifts in consciousness are the skillful means for bringing about liberation and another possible world.

Despite Macy's early Christian aspirations and education, I do not see her drawing upon the Hebrew prophets in any explicit fashion. My argument is that a prophetic mode of being religious and ethical is an aquifer that Macy has tapped into while remolding Buddhist concepts, and drawing upon the insights of systems theory and deep ecology. More explicitly, she draws upon the prophecy of the Shambhala warriors who fight—with the weapons of compassion and insight—against the "Great Unraveling" and for a future that already exists in our hearts and minds.[49] This myth is Macy's recruiting story. Those who enlist may draw upon ancient ancestors and a newly imagined Buddhism. In the end, Macy appeals to those who come after:

> You live inside us, beings of the future
> In the spiral ribbons of our cells, you are there
> In our rage for the burning forests, the poisoned fields
>   the oil-drowned seals
> you are here
>   stir us awake.
> Fill us with gladness for the work that must be done.[50]

Buddhist Reflections in a Prophetic Key #4
Bearing Witness to the Suffering of Our Time

One way of deepening the transformative power of "the work that reconnects" would be to develop a hybrid practice that combines Macy's exercises with the mindfulness practice of the Zen Peacemaker Order founded by Bernie Glassman Roshi and Jishu Holmes. The order is grounded in three tenets: "not-knowing," or letting go of fixed ideas; bearing witness to joy and suffering; and taking action to heal ourselves and the world. The second tenet led Glassman to develop innovative forms of mindfulness practice. Glassman brought people from diverse religious and secular traditions to places of great suffering. He led retreats on the streets of New York for groups who came to live with and as the homeless. He also conducted ecumenical retreats at Auschwitz-Birkenau. Here participants sat in silent meditation while leaders chanted the names of the dead. Glassman speaks movingly about how Auschwitz strips participants bare as it did its prisoners. "We sat in our circle for four days," he reflects on one such retreat, and sitting created "a special place for us, a space of bearing witness." In the stories that participants told one another in the evenings, silence, anxiety, anger, and, above all, pain gave way to love for one another.[1]

In the sheer immensity of its evil, the Holocaust brings on psychic numbness. Glassman's bearing witness calls us to sit with that immensity and dissolve the numbness. No quick resolution, no placing this evil in a safe compartment labeled "the past." "Never again," we may say. Yet it has happened again and again—in, for example, Myanmar, an ostensibly Buddhist country, which has conducted an "ethnic cleansing" of its Rohingya Muslim minority.

Something akin to the witness evoked by the Zen Peacemaker Order's retreats took place in 1992 when Joanna Macy, as part of her activism about the dangers of nuclear waste, took her "Despair and Empowerment" workshop to towns in Belarus, Ukraine, and Russia that were exposed to lethal radiation by the Chernobyl meltdown in 1986. Novozybkov, a Russian town of fifty thousand, was directly in the path of the radioactive cloud released by the meltdown. Russian authorities, fearing that the cloud would reach Moscow, with its millions of residents, seeded the cloud, and radioactive rain poured down on Novozybkov. No evacuation. No warning. No follow-up with special care for those affected. The rain embodied the carelessness of unaccountable authority. The people of Novozybkov were disposable; their subsequent birth defects and cancers were treated as unconnected with the catastrophe at Chernobyl. "Our workshops, we soon realized, were not so much to help people recover from a catastrophe as live with an ongoing one," Macy concluded.[2]

Simply put, the workshop tore away the shroud of silence that surrounded the event. "Why have you done this to us?" one woman put it. "What good does it do? I would be willing to feel the sorrow—all the sorrow in the world—if only it would save my two daughters from cancer."[3] To her credit, Macy recognized that any discourse at that moment on the value of confronting despair would be obscene. The next day, however, the same woman talked about how her heart had been broken open. "It feels right," she shared. Another participant said that for the first time he felt clean, "uncontaminated." Macy, for her part, promised that the people of Novozybkov would not be forgotten. She would take their story to other groups exposed to the "poison fire." "I wanted these men and women of Novozybkov to know," Macy insists, "that they are not alone in their suffering, but part of a vast web of brothers and sisters who are determined to use their painful experiences to help restore the health of our world." Their lives and suffering would not be reburied in silence.[4]

We can imagine a group of Novozybkov students like the ones that Sallie King encountered in Germany attending Macy's workshop. While healing would be a paramount goal, these students might insist that the "authorities" be held accountable for their actions in seeding the radioactive clouds without warning or evacuating the residents of Novozybkov. Who decided to seed the clouds? Why were no emergency actions taken to rescue the villagers? Was decision making and moral responsibility lost in a bureaucratic maze? Above all, what restorative steps were taken to aid the people affected by the fallout? What steps should have been taken?

Radioactive waste that remains lethal for hundreds of thousands of years is an example of "slow violence" that does its damage over so many generations that the original cause becomes obscured if not forgotten.[5] Climate change is another example of slow violence. The half-life of carbon dioxide in the atmosphere is one hundred years. The emissions from the first car I ever owned more than fifty years ago are still there, still contributing to the greenhouse effect. Slow violence is notoriously hard to recognize. Similarly, numerous advocates speak of how difficult it is to get people to imagine their actions contributing to a sixth great extinction. But we could imagine a mindfulness retreat at the edges of the Alberta tar sands, a retreat that would include not only Macy's exercises but also action in solidarity with the Beaver Lake Cree Nation, who are fighting to defend their ancestral lands from toxic waste.[6] Imagine a Buddhist peace and justice group or even a sangha holding a mindfulness retreat once a quarter at sites of fracking, at oil refineries, and at the corporate headquarters of fossil fuel giants. They too are places that create suffering. Prophetic wisdom calls us to sit with the immensity of the evil of our times and then, like Macy, be released into action.

Chapter Five

B. R. Ambedkar

The Annihilation of Caste and the Liberation of the Dalits

Why do you remain in that religion that does not treat you as human beings? Why do you remain in that religion that does not allow you to educate? Why do you remain in that religion that prohibits you from entering a temple . . . ? A religion which does not recognize a man as a human being, is not a religion but a disease. . . . A religion that compels the illiterates to be illiterate, and the poor to be poor, is not a religion but a punishment.

To become human, convert yourselves.
To get organized, convert yourselves.
To secure equality, convert yourselves.
To get liberty, convert yourselves.

—B. R. Ambedkar, "What Way Emancipation?"[1]

The world owes much to rebels who would dare to argue in the face of the pontiff that he is not infallible.

—B. R. Ambedkar, *Annihilation of Caste*[2]

The man who leveled this indictment and exhortation was Dr. Bhimrao Ambedkar, who was speaking at a convention of Dalits in May 1936 before an audience of thirty-five thousand.[3] This conference was a follow-up to a previous one in October 1935 in which Dr. Ambedkar vowed that although he was a Hindu by accident of birth, he would not die a Hindu. Because he was the most recognized leader of Indian Dalits, his vow was a bombshell. No less than Gandhi himself—the one that Ambedkar sarcastically refers to as "the pontiff"—tried to downplay the impact of Dr. Ambedkar's oracle, declaring that religion was not like a cloak that you could change as you pleased. He called upon Dr. Ambedkar to "assuage his wrath."[4]

It took more than twenty years for Ambedkar to make good on his promise, and he did so by converting to Buddhism before a massive gathering of between three hundred and five hundred thousand Dalits whom he then led through their own rite of conversion. The form of Buddhism to which he and they converted was a distinctly modern variety and one decidedly geared toward social transformation. For some Buddhist scholars, Dr. Ambedkar's modernist interpretation and pragmatic reformulation cut the heart out of the Buddha's teachings. For more sympathetic critics, he offered a Navayāna, a new "vehicle" akin in its revolutionary implications to the three Buddhist vehicles before it.[5]

Apart from the meticulous analyses of Christopher Queen, most scholars of Engaged Buddhism have neglected Ambedkar's writings, and especially the multipronged forms of action that he initiated. So who was this man who by all accounts was a fiery and galvanic speaker, a fearless polemicist who did not shy away from excoriating the most holy of Hindu scriptures? Who was this fierce opponent of Gandhi's romantic espousal of a reformed caste system as the necessary basis of Indian social order, the man who challenged the Mahatma for his failure to end the caste system once and for all?

A Life Sentence without Parole

B. R. Ambedkar was born on April 14, 1891, to a family of Mahars, one of many Dalit ethnic groups. This makes him the oldest of our elders, one generation ahead of Thich Nhat Hanh and Joanna Macy and two generations before Rita Gross. Ambedkar's father served in the British army and instilled in his children a love for learning. As a young child, Ambedkar experienced directly what he later called the "veritable chamber of horrors" that was the caste system.[6] Because of British legislation he was able to attend a public school, but he had to sit on a burlap sack so as not to pollute the desk and he was forbidden to drink water from the same tap as the other students. Across India Dalits were subject to daily humiliations and the pervasive threat of physical violence. Dalits who dared to better their family's wealth, Dalit women carrying water in metal pots, men wearing shoes to a wedding, women wearing clothing with fancy embroidery, and Dalits serving ghee to guests at a feast were subjected to mob violence. In some places contact with a Dalit's shadow was considered polluting and access to Hindu temples was forbidden to Dalits, as was learning the sacred language of Sanskrit.[7]

The whole of Indian society was crammed into a purity/pollution framework that, in turn, was linked to fixed ancestral occupations that fated some to be priests and others street scavengers. "Each region of India," novelist and political activist Arundhati Roy recognizes, "has lovingly perfected its own unique version of caste-based cruelty based on an unwritten code that is much worse than Jim Crow laws."[8] For the Mahars that version, at one point, required wearing a spittoon around one's neck to catch any spit that might pollute the road. Mahars were responsible for removing dead cattle from public roads and for taking care of the cremation grounds, among other duties.[9] Ambedkar's metaphor for the caste system was a multistoried tower with no doors and no staircases. For a Dalit, this meant life in prison without parole.[10]

Given this prison tower, Ambedkar's escape was nothing short of miraculous. He was the only Dalit in his high school. The Maharaja for his region was a reform-minded Hindu and he financed Ambedkar's college education. Later he funded Ambedkar's graduate work. Ambedkar completed graduate studies in 1916 for his PhD at Columbia University, studying under the American philosopher and educator John Dewey. He then proceeded, after a hiatus in India, to complete a second doctorate in economics at the London School of Economics, and still later he completed studies leading to his admission to the bar. Returning home in 1923 after years abroad was an education of a brutal sort. Working as a secretary to the Maharaja, he would have files literally thrown at him by clerks to avoid inadvertently touching him. They rolled up the carpet when he entered the office so that he would not pollute it. Worse still was his inability to find lodging. In desperation he rented rooms under a false name as a Parsi. When his subterfuge was discovered, a mob armed with clubs drove him out. He fled to Bombay (now Mumbai), where he took up a position as a college teacher.[11] Convinced that education was the key to liberation, Ambedkar created a system of hostels as places of refuge for Dalit students that later became colleges organized by the People's Education Society that he founded.[12]

From the mid-1920s through the mid-1930s, Ambedkar also pursued a different track to achieve basic rights for Dalits. Dalits created several *satyagraha* (truth force) movements that employed Gandhian methods but focused on specific forms of caste oppression, not British colonialism. These movements sought permission to walk on restricted public roads, to be allowed to enter Hindu temples for worship, and to gain access to public water sources. One of the marches that Ambedkar led was to a lake where animals could safely drink but Dalits could not. "We are not going to Chavadar Lake merely to drink its water," he declared. "We are going to the lake to assert that we too are human beings like others."[13]

The Dalits who gathered around Ambedkar to engage in nonviolent direct action for such basic rights fully expected Gandhi to join this *satyagraha* movement. In this they were sorely disappointed. Gandhi briefly joined one such action and argued—ineffectively—with Hindu priests that they should allow Dalits to enter their temples. He failed to counter the argument of the priests that the Dalits' impure condition was a karmic consequence of their previous lives.[14] Gandhi subsequently remonstrated with the protesters that they should fight for their rights "by sweet persuasion and not by *satyagraha* which becomes *duragraha* (demonic force) when it is intended to give a rude shock to the deep-rooted prejudices of the people."[15]

Ambedkar found Gandhi's rejection of his own method for pursuing freedom unconscionable. He responded sarcastically that Gandhi was unwilling to "hurt the feelings" of caste Hindus. He contrasted the timidity of reform-minded Hindus with the American abolitionists. Are you willing to fight a civil war with your caste fellows to abolish the evil of caste? he asked.[16] For Ambedkar what was needed was precisely the "rude shock" that Gandhi deplored. But it would have to go beyond tough words. Direct action was necessary because, as Dr. Martin Luther King would later put it, those in power rarely give up their power unless forced to do so. "The Caste Hindu," Ambedkar argued, must be "made to think and . . . forced to feel that he must alter his ways. For that you must create a crisis by direct action against his customary code of conduct."[17] Like the Hebrew prophets, Ambedkar did not believe that the crisis would be created with sweet words.[18] Strong feelings had to be elicited to sustain a social revolution.

Ambedkar's most dramatic act of symbolic resistance to the ideology of caste came in 1927, when he publicly burned the *Manusmriti*, the ancient work of Indic jurisprudence. The power of this act of resistance lay in its total repudiation of the legal underpinnings of the caste system. While these actions were underway, Ambedkar, the lawyer, also sought vindication of Dalits' rights through the courts, but this led to lengthy litigations.[19]

For the most part these efforts to gain full inclusion in public life for Dalits and for Dalits to be able to exercise the most basic rights failed. The failure of *satyagraha* made Ambedkar skeptical that the Hindu majority would ever recognize the equal status of Dalits as full citizens. He became concerned about a possible tyranny of the majority in a future "democratic" India. So, representing the Dalits, at two Round Table Conferences with the British in London in 1930 and 1931—a position that Gandhi challenged claiming that he represented the Dalits—Ambedkar negotiated a "separate electorate" for Dalits as had been granted to Muslims and Sikhs. In such a system Dalits would vote for Dalits running for election to reserved seats and then would vote for a larger slate in the general election. Without such a system, Ambedkar feared that the Hindu majority would elect only those Dalits whose views did not challenge the caste system. Gandhi abhorred this proposition because of his romanticized vision of a unified India. He felt that separate electorates for Dalits would amount to a "vivisection" of the Hindu community.[20] Also, as a shrewd politician, he did not want to see the Hindu majority watered down by a possible alliance of Dalits with Muslims and Sikhs.

When the British included Ambedkar's proposal in the official outcome of the second Round Table Conference, Gandhi was outraged. He vowed to fast to the death unless this provision was removed from the pact. When Gandhi began his fast, the British, quickly shifting responsibility, countered that they would not remove the provision unless Ambedkar signed on to the revision. This placed immense public pressure on Ambedkar. Ambedkar feared that if the Mahatma died, it would let loose a torrent of violence against Dalits across all of India. Cornered, Ambedkar signed the repeal but only after extracting a commitment to nearly twice as many reserved seats for Dalits as promised in the British pact. Nevertheless, Ambedkar remained convinced that Gandhi had violated his own *satyagraha* principles and committed what he called a "foul and filthy act."[21]

In some ways this breach between two powerful leaders was inevitable. The two men differed not only on the focus of *satyagraha* but, most especially, in their core visions of a truly free Indian society. Arundhati Roy argues that the battle between these two giants was ultimately a tragic conflict between two utopian visions. Gandhi saw India's salvation in the swaraj (self-rule) of its thousands of villages. He saw the main currents of the Western model of development (urbanization, industrialization, centralized government) as utterly hostile to Indian civilization. He held a highly romanticized view of village life, one at severe odds with Ambedkar's view of it as a "chamber of horrors." For his part, Ambedkar saw liberty, equality, and fraternity, the principles of the French Revolution (and those, he later argued, of Buddhism), as the magna carta for a just society. His "city of justice," as Roy puts it, was grounded in a Deweyan sense of free association in many spheres of life, enabling all persons to exercise their powers. Both were right, Roy claims, and both were terribly wrong. Gandhi saw "the seed of cataclysm that was implemented in the project of Western modernity." That project carried out Marx's prediction that under capitalism's glare "all that is solid melts into air." Tough-minded Ambedkar, however, held no truck with romanticized village rule. Cities represented the possibility of liberty, the opportunity to actualize one's powers and one's gifts in the context of equality. His understanding of liberty and equality blended individualism with the solidarity born in a social revolution and grounded in Buddhist *maitri*, loving-kindness toward all living beings.[22]

It would be a mistake to see this confrontation between the two giants of twentieth-century India as the tragic climax of their relationship. Ambedkar by no means dragged himself off the public stage to lick his wounds. He doggedly pursued Dalits' liberation with new strategies whenever one approach proved inadequate. Gandhi was the unavoidable giant. Any program of social amelioration had to pass muster with him. Gandhi for his part acknowledged that Ambedkar was his most uncompromising challenger. So Ambedkar and Gandhi would meet and wrestle, again and again.

It would also be a mistake to think that Gandhi was indifferent to the oppression of Dalits. From the moment he returned to India he included the abolition of untouchability as a key element in his social program.[23] However, Gandhi's approach to the issue of untouchability differed radically from that of Ambedkar. Gandhi believed that untouchability could be stripped out of the caste system while leaving that system's determination of occupations in place. Untouchability was a "sin" that called for repentance on the part of caste Hindus, and his appeals were to that group. He called for a process of self-purification on the part of caste Hindus. Ambedkar bridled at the paternalism expressed in Gandhi's analysis. Gandhi's approach, Ambedkar was convinced, turned Dalits into the passive recipients of caste Hindus' noble penitence. For him liberation was a matter of Dalits gaining self-respect. As moral agents, Dalits must declare their radical equality—a principle that is incompatible with any caste system—and conversion would enact that equality.[24]

The Prophet as Subversive

In chapter 1 we discussed what Walter Brueggemann called the royal consciousness, the belief in God's invincible protection and blessing for the central institutions of ancient Judah. The royal consciousness assured Judah of its continuity as the focus of God's favor for all time. Ambedkar's diagnosis of Hindu society as one of "graded inequality" rendered sacrosanct by its most sacred scriptures bears a strong analogy to the prophets' attack on the royal consciousness. The Hindu caste system, too, is a seamless fusion of the religious, political, and social imagination, canonized in the codes of purity/pollution.[25] A system in which every form of inequality is predestined cannot be trimmed of one or two dead branches, argued Ambedkar. It must be rooted out—annihilated.

The first of the two major works of Ambedkar that we need to examine in more detail is *Annihilation of Caste*. The caste system is irredeemable. It must be rooted out—and for Ambedkar the roots of the system are found in the Vedas, Hinduism's most sacred texts.[26] The opportunity to make this case to erstwhile social reformers came with an invitation to preside and speak at a national conference to be held in May 1936. It was sponsored by Jat-Pat Todak Mandal, an organization of caste Hindus committed to the abolition of the caste system. Ambedkar was skeptical about reformist Hindus and agreed to speak only after concerted persuasion. At the conference sponsor's request, Ambedkar submitted an advance copy of his speech. The organization, under a great deal of recrimination for inviting Ambedkar, bridled at his attack on the Vedas. They saw it as unnecessary and highly inflammatory and asked Ambedkar to revise his speech. He saw the offending passages as the linchpin of his argument and refused to alter his text. After some back and forth, the speech and the conference were cancelled, and Ambedkar published *Annihilation of Caste* on his own.[27]

Repeatedly Ambedkar insists that caste is a mental construct rooted in the human imagination. To uproot caste, one must transform the human imagination. To eradicate caste, Hindus would need to leave the world imagined in their holiest of scriptures. The insidiousness of the caste system of "graded inequality" is that there is always a group below one's own. Even outcastes have grades of untouchability. The system blurs the bright line between oppressor and oppressed. All groups except the very top and the very bottom function as fierce boundary protectors against those below it in the caste hierarchy while also experiencing similar restrictions from those above it. So all but the lowest of the low have a stake in clinging to the "reality" imagined in sacred texts and cemented in the social structure. Each group jealously guards its privileges and power over the ones below it. Because each group vigilantly and viciously polices its borders, the caste system is self-enforcing. It is, Arundhati Roy insists, "the ultimate means of control."[28] Such a system, Ambedkar concluded, creates "an ascending scale of hatred and a descending scale of contempt and might be a source of perpetual conflict." Such a system is inimical to the working of democracy, which depends upon cooperation and solidarity.[29] Nevertheless, all do not suffer equally. At their worst, reprisals directed towards those who transgressed their restrictions as outcastes included a "social boycott" in which no one would buy from or sell to the perpetrator, denying employment and literally starving the person to death.

If caste is a form of mental slavery, what are the criteria by which we can discern whether we or others are truly free? Ambedkar replied in "What Way Emancipation?" that only those are free who are awake and who are not imprisoned by traditional teachings and customs but test them critically. Only those are free who are conscious of their "rights, responsibilities and duties." And are prepared to defend them. Finally, those are free who are not enslaved to circumstances defined by others but who carve out their own purpose. "In the light of the above observations," Ambedkar asked, "are you free?"[30] As in the case of the Israelites wandering in the wilderness in the Exodus story, there needed to be a protracted process of decolonizing one's mind to rid oneself of a slavish mentality.

The enforcement of caste boundaries by one caste upon those below it was, Ambedkar maintained, "a matter of system . . . a matter of principle." The recognition of systemic or structural violence sets Ambedkar apart from those who, like Gandhi, thought you could purge the caste system of its oppressive elements and retain it as structuring the social order. Ambedkar challenged the Gandhian movement's focus on a struggle for *political* independence while holding in place the Indian *social* structure. Social tyranny, Ambedkar countered, was worse than political tyranny. "History bears out the proposition," he argued, citing Luther as the precursor of political emancipation in Europe, "that political revolutions have always been preceded by social and religious revolutions."[31]

In some interesting respects *Annihilation of Caste* bears a family resemblance to Dr. Martin Luther King Jr.'s "Letter from a Birmingham Jail."[32] Both are directed to a group of self-styled religious moderates. Both detail how Jim Crow and the caste system penetrate the everyday lives of the oppressed group even in absurd regulations of minutia. Both expose the ways in which the system frustrates human aspirations at every turn, locking whole classes of people into subordinate roles. Both recognize how the system is kept in place by the daily threat of physical violence. No tinkering around the edges will suffice. Caste and Jim Crow must be annihilated, and their religious justifications must be overturned. King spelled out for the so-called moderate clergy what it would entail to live up to their sacred calling. For his part, Ambedkar challenged reform-minded Hindus: "Hindus hold to the sacredness of the social order. Caste has a divine basis. You must therefore destroy the sacredness and the divinity with which caste has become invested." "Will you show that courage?" he demanded.[33] Both Ambedkar and King were, as it were, Moses inviting the Egyptians and not simply the Jews to undertake an Exodus, a moral journey.

Ambedkar was a disciplined politician who fought for the rights of Dalits both within the Congress Party and in opposition to it. As the first minister of law in the newly independent India, he chaired the committee that drafted the Indian Constitution, a process that took several years (1947–50). Yet he was under no illusion about the efficacy of rights written into law. "If the fundamental rights are opposed by the community," he concluded from painful experience, "no Law, no Parliament, no Judiciary can guarantee them."[34] And in India, social tyranny persisted. When a bill to guarantee basic gender equality was shelved for fear of alienating orthodox Hindus, Ambedkar resigned his post.

On the cusp of his resignation, Ambedkar leveled one more prophetic judgment on the newborn democracy. He declared that India was on the verge of entering "a life of contradictions. In politics we will have equality and in social and economic life we will have inequality." How long the nation could live with this contradiction he could not foretell.[35] Here Ambedkar was judging India based on the capacious understanding of democracy that he had inherited from John Dewey: "A democracy is more than a form of Government. It is primarily a mode of associated living. The roots of Democracy are to be searched in the social relationship, in the terms of associated life between the people who form a society." Three principles, Ambedkar continued, undergird a democratic form of social life:

> Some equate Democracy with Equality and Liberty. Equality and liberty are no doubt the deepest concern of democracy. But the more important question is what sustains equality and liberty. Some would say it is the law of the state that sustains equality

and liberty. This is not a true answer. What sustains equality and liberty is fellow-feeling. What the French Revolutionists called fraternity. The word fraternity is not an adequate expression. The proper expression is what the Buddha called Maitree [*sic*]. Without Fraternity liberty would destroy equality and equality would destroy liberty. Fraternity is therefore the root of democracy. The main . . . question is—wherein lie the roots of fraternity without which Democracy is not possible? Beyond dispute, it has its origins in Religion. . . . One must go to the Religion of the people and ask—does it teach fraternity or does it not?[36]

After decades of political engagement, Ambedkar focused his final years on catalyzing a religious revolution as the key to an emancipated India.

Buddhism Reconceived

In his October 1956 speech during the mass conversion of (mostly) Dalits, Ambedkar responded to those who argued that he sought to impose Western values on Indian civilization: "This path has not been borrowed from anywhere. This path is from here, it is purely Indian." Furthermore, he said, "we have not got stuck with a corpse around our neck," no dead past, no weight of oppression. In Buddhism there is a provision for change with the change of time.[37]

The path that Ambedkar himself had taken to this climatic ceremony was, indeed, a long one. More than twenty years had elapsed since he had proclaimed that while he was Hindu by accident of birth, he would not die a Hindu. His search had entailed an extensive examination of multiple traditions. Ambedkar's criteria for sifting through these multiple religious traditions included the following: it must be compatible with modern science; it must foster liberty, equality, and fraternity; it must support a moral life; and it must not sanctify poverty.[38] Along the way he would make ample use of the liberty declared by the Buddha to follow one's own lights, and of the generosity of Buddhism in incorporating multiple versions of the Dhamma.

So it goes without saying that Ambedkar drew on the "Kalama Sutta" in the *Aṅguttara Nikāya*, which describes the Buddha's encounter with the Kalamas, who had been thrown into doubt by rival prophets who claimed divine authority for their teachings. Rather than add to the doctrinal free-for-all, the Buddha forces them through a process of interrogation to rely upon their own reason. Does the teaching promote craving, hatred, delusion, or violence? Is it likely to lead to the violation of the five precepts? Above all, does it foster suffering? The criteria here are pragmatic. Does the teaching foster a righteous life? The Buddha models ideology critique to encourage the Kalamas to liberate themselves from the competing claims to orthodoxy.[39]

While insisting that only Buddhism meets the criteria for a truly modern religion, Ambedkar saw one handicap to the dissemination of this revisionist interpretation: Buddhism lacks a presentation that is akin to the Christian's Bible and is both compact and comprehensive. *The Buddha and His Dhamma* was intended to provide this missing element. The prologue to *The Buddha and His Dhamma* opens with a long quote from James Hastings's *Encyclopedia of Religion and Ethics*. Certain key periods, Hasting argues, force us to reconsider inherited beliefs. This is one such moment. Across the globe there are movements to reform religious traditions.[40] Immediately Ambedkar situates his interpretation of the Buddha's life and teachings within a worldwide transformation process. He sees himself, the Dalits, and all of India as having entered this critical juncture, a time when political revolution, that is, the movement for national independence, must be accompanied by a social revolution. The latter requires a profound reshaping of the mind if genuine liberation from engrained habits, customs, and traditions is to occur.[41] Christopher Queen sees this epigram from Hastings as signifying Ambedkar's commitment to a modernist agenda as expressed in the Western Enlightenment and the French Revolution.[42] Queen pushes further when he outlines a kinship between Ambedkar's this-worldly Buddhism and the Christian Social Gospel, which was in its American heyday while Ambedkar was at Columbia University, and with the later emergence of liberation theology. A common thread in all three is a professed commitment to the deconstruction and reconstruction of religious traditions to uncover their prophetic dimension.[43]

Ambedkar is quite direct in laying out the places where he sees the traditional presentation of the Dhamma leading to dead ends. He takes issue with key presentations of the Buddha's teachings that wear the mask of orthodoxy yet raise barriers to modern seekers. First, Ambedkar sees as "absurd" the standard account of Gautama's leave-taking precipitated by an encounter with old age, sickness, and death. That someone twenty-nine years old would not have been exposed to these signs of human finitude and impermanence challenges our credulity. Ambedkar offers an alternative narrative in which Gautama as a member of a protoparliament offers a lonely prophetic resistance to escalating war fever over a water rights dispute with a neighboring country. Forced into exile, Gautama resolves to get at the root of human conflict in all its manifestations. This account of Gautama's leave-taking immediately forces us to think in a new way about (collective) dukkha. The cause of Gautama's leave-taking is not an existential/psychological crisis but fear-generating group thinking and ideological fixation igniting war fever.[44]

Second, Ambedkar argues that the Four Noble Truths, as they stand, throw a pall of pessimism over the entire Dhamma. Ambedkar does not abandon these teachings tout court, rather they are reconceived. The traditional interpretation attributes the causes of human suffering to mental states (the three poisons: craving, aversion, and ignorance). This places responsibility on the individual alone and for a Dalit that would only add to their crushing psychological burden. On the contrary, Ambedkar's own deepest experiences of dukkha were rooted in a massively oppressive social system, a system that hounded him and threatened him with violence daily. Ambedkar shifts the discussion of dukkha from the existential plane of finitude to the plane of socially structured human life.

Third, Ambedkar redefines Nibbana in his rendition of the Third Noble Truth. Too many, he claims, have made a nonsense of it: "They hold that Nibbana means extinction of all human passions, which is equivalent to death." The Buddha's famous Fire Sermon does not say life is on fire but that passions are on fire with the three flames of craving, aversion, and ignorance. Nibbana means sufficient control of one's passions so that one does not short-circuit engagement in a righteous life. The ultimate goal of Buddhism is to live that life by observing the Five Precepts (The Path of Purity), following the Eightfold Path (The Path of Righteousness), and realizing the Ten Perfections (The Path of Virtue). As Christopher Queen points out, this reverses the traditional order in which following the Eightfold Path leads to Nibbana. What this means is that the Dhamma is inherently social in its intent: "Dhamma is righteousness which means right relations between man and man in all spheres of life."[45]

Several other changes should be underlined. The traditional interpretation of karma that sees one's condition in one's current life as predetermined by previous lives is unconscionable because it cuts the nerve of action and, in our terms, blames the victims of oppression for their own unalterable condition. This is a position that Ambedkar shares with virtually all Engaged Buddhists.[46]

Analyses of Buddhist modernism most commonly stress meditation—especially by lay people—as the preeminent form of spiritual practice within modernist Buddhist communities.⁴⁷ Not so Ambedkar. In *The Buddha and His Dhamma* meditation plays an instrumental role in developing the "spirit of universal love." Action, not contemplation, is central. This decentering is presented in a dramatic way in Ambedkar's treatment of the Buddha's post-enlightenment decision to begin to spread the Dhamma. "He realized," Ambedkar begins, "that what is necessary is not to escape from the world. What is necessary is to change the world and make it better. . . . It was his duty to return to the world and serve it *and not sit silent as the personification of inactive impassivity*" (italics added), Nothing less than a rejection of the universal iconography of the sitting Buddha is presented here. The Buddha rises and strides forth. Similarly, Ambedkar argues that the monastic sangha exists not for the perfection of individuals but to serve fellow human beings.⁴⁸ Christopher Queen nicely sums up the implications of these revisions: "In each of these examples, the ethical—we might say 'prophetic,' recalling the Hebrew prophets' passionate insistence upon 'justice' and 'righteousness'—dimension is lifted up at the expense of what might be called the spiritual or sapiential dimension."⁴⁹

Buddhism versus Marxism

Toward the end of his life and in the aftermath of a communist takeover in China, Ambedkar saw the fate of Asia as hinging upon a struggle between two world-transforming ideologies—that is, Buddhism and Marxism. In speeches shortly before his death and in the early drafts of what was to be a book, Ambedkar laid out his comparison between Buddhism and Marxism.⁵⁰ After listing ten major theses of Marxism, Ambedkar argues that history has disproven, or critics have demolished, key tenets of Marx's claim to have created a "scientific socialism." What remains are four affirmations: (1) the purpose of philosophy is to reconstruct the world; (2) class conflict is pervasive; (3) private ownership of property is the source of that conflict; and (4) for the general good private property must be abolished. Buddhism, Ambedkar maintains, agrees with Marxism on each of these points but made them central to the mission of the sangha more than two thousand years before Marx.⁵¹

Echoing Marx's "Theses on Feuerbach" on the purpose of philosophy, Ambedkar says, "The purpose of Religion is to explain the origin of the world. The purpose of Dhamma is to reconstruct the world."⁵² Ambedkar argues regarding Marxism's second point that, while the Buddha does not use the term "exploitation," he does see the pervasiveness of dukkha. While some see dukkha as referring only to the endless rounds of birth-death-rebirth, Ambedkar does not agree. In plenty of places the Buddha uses the term "dukkha" to refer to poverty. Misery is a product of unending class conflict. Dukkha should be interpreted as exploitation. Only socialism can bring about a cessation of exploitation: "To emancipate those depressed and poor people is the principal task of the Buddhist religion." Finally, like communism, the monastic sangha prohibited private ownership of all but the most necessary of personal items, robes, and a begging bowl.[53]

Given these similar analyses of social suffering and ultimate goals, the difference between Buddhism and Marxism comes down to the means chosen to reach these ends. Marxism commits itself to a violent usurpation of political power and to the installation of a dictatorship whose dissolution is indefinitely postponed. Marx's theory of a fixed teleology short-circuits the freedom of association and action that generates history as the temporal expression of humanity's self-creation. Buddhism seeks a bloodless revolution; the Buddha's method was to change minds. Ambedkar, following Dewey, distinguishes between force as violence and force as energy. Only Maitri allows force as energy to unfold in fruitful ways. "Let the ambit of your Maitri be as boundless as the world," Ambedkar insisted, for only through boundless virtuous action will a true social revolution be brought about.[54]

Conversion as Emancipation

On October 14, 1956, Ambedkar fulfilled his promise to convert. He did so before a gathering of three hundred thousand to five hundred thousand mostly Mahar Dalits. According to legend, this was the date on which the emperor Ashoka converted to Buddhism. Ashoka, renowned for his this-worldly application of Buddhist teachings in service to his people, was a model for Ambedkar and for each of the converts.[55] The oldest monk in India, Bhikku Chandramani, offered the three refuges to Ambedkar and his wife.

Having modeled the process of conversion for his followers, Ambedkar immediately broke with the traditional deference to the monastics by inviting the gathered white-clad mass to rise and voluntarily take the three refuges. He led these followers in reciting twenty-two vows. Recognizing how deeply rooted Hinduism was in the minds of Dalits themselves, Ambedkar began with eight vows to renounce specific Hindu beliefs and rituals. The very structure of the vows performs a decisive break with one's past. Vows nine and ten are the hinges of the set. Having renounced a system of graded inequality, they vowed "I believe in the equality of mankind" followed by an injunction to act: "I shall endeavor to establish equality." For the remaining vows "I shall" replaces "I shall not." Those who take refuge vow to follow the Eightfold Path and take on the Ten Perfections while upholding the Five Precepts. Vow number twenty-one puts the whole process in simple terms: "I believe I am entering the new life," while the final vow pledges to put into action the Buddha's teachings.

The following day Ambedkar spoke to the newly converted. He traced his own journey, praised the Buddha for his openness to change, and applauded Buddhism as a radical indigenous tradition. Then he stated the task before them: "We must resolve to follow Buddhist religion in the finest way. It should not happen that the Mahar people brought the Buddhism to disgrace, so we must have a firm determination. If we accept this, then we will thrive ourselves, our nation and not only that but the whole world also. Because the Buddhist religion only will be the saviour of the world."[56] Less than two months later, Dr. B. R. Ambedkar was dead.

Conclusion

Ambedkar's revision of the Buddha's Dhamma is not a form of "secular Buddhism." The kingdom of righteousness is a refocusing of the traditional concept of Nibbana. Striving for that kingdom is a sacred engagement on the level of human interconnectedness. Like other "convert" Buddhist modernists, Ambedkar boldly recasts traditional teachings and practices, but not to the same ends. Christopher Queen's argument that Ambedkar shifts the focus of Buddhist practice from the sapiential/spiritual to the prophetic/ethical captures the religious valence of his multiple forms of action.

Ambedkar's tapping into the prophetic dimension challenges both the theory and practice of Engaged Buddhism in several ways.

- First, Ambedkar, as Aishwary Kumar puts it, was "a master of agonistic rhetoric." He saw rhetoric as a form of *satyagraha* necessary to bring underlying forces and conflicts to the surface.[57] His forceful advocacy of the rights of Dalits, his call for the annihilation of caste, and, most especially, his willingness to challenge Gandhi directly bear this out. Learning from Ambedkar requires that Engaged Buddhists reconsider what constitutes "right speech."

- Second, just as the prophets challenged the "royal consciousness," Ambedkar directs his penetrating critique at the religious/social/political imagination that colonizes the mind of every Hindu. The Israelites needed to wander in the desert to free themselves of their slave mentality, so all Hindus, not just Dalits, need to free themselves from a mentality that imagines social reality as "graded inequality." Ambedkar's own long search for an alternative to Hindu teachings modeled a process of decolonization not only for Indians but for all Engaged Buddhists who seek to emancipate themselves from ideologies that cement injustice in place.

- Third, just as Rita Gross recovered an indigenous Buddhist feminism, Ambedkar finds an indigenous resistance to caste in early Buddhism. His annihilation of caste is not an alien imposition. The rejection of Brahmanism as the ideological framework for the caste system is manifest in the earliest texts that describe the formation of the Buddhist sangha. The sangha included members from all castes and outcastes. It gathered Brahmins and barbers, servants and street sweepers, criminals and lepers, and it included women.[58]

- Fourth, of our four elders, Ambedkar was the most engaged in politics and in devising ways to pursue justice. Like the prophets' compassion for a people undergoing the trauma of exile, Ambedkar's multiple forms of action and advocacy emerge from the collective trauma, the monstrosity of injustice, the daily "chamber of horrors" that was village life for a Dalit.

- Fifth, Ambedkar offers a utopian vision of Indian society that rivals Gandhi's romanticized vision of self-sufficient village republics and Marxism's vision of a classless society founded on violence. While Ambedkar's vision can be accused of uncritically accepting a Western modernist model, his fusion of radical equality and *maitri* and his appropriation of Dewey's understanding of democracy as associated living offer a distinctive vision of another possible world. Arundhati Roy calls this vision the "city of justice."

- Finally, in contrast to the Hebrew prophets, who grieve for their people's destruction and reluctantly carry out a divine command, Ambedkar relished the battle that he fought on numerous fronts—in the courts fighting for the rights of Dalits, in the streets as a *satyagraha* warrior, in the newly independent government as the principal drafter of the Indian constitution, and in the sangha as the Buddhist who brought about one of the largest mass conversions in human history. "The battle to me," he insisted, "is a matter full of joy. The battle is in its fullest sense spiritual. . . . For ours is not a battle for wealth or power. It is a battle for freedom. It is a battle for the reclamation of the human personality. . . . My final words of advice to you [are] educate, agitate and organize. Have faith in yourselves and never lose hope."[59]

Buddhist Reflections in a Prophetic Key #5
Gautama's Leave-Taking

Many modern Buddhist teachers and practitioners have reacted with consternation to the standard version of Gautama's leave-taking. Sneaking off in the middle of the night and leaving a sleeping wife and newborn baby hardly comport with the image of the Buddha as an exemplar of compassion or even one who practices basic respect. So some Buddhists feel a great sense of relief when they find in one of the ancient Buddhist schools a story in which Yasodhara, Gautama's wife, who has been a partner to the Buddha in many previous lives, consents to his leave-taking. No midnight escape. The two make love and conceive a child. Yasodhara then endures the discipline of a six-year pregnancy, matching Gautama's six-year process to give birth to his enlightened self. "Yashodhara, the one who stayed home, dug into her own spiritual life right where she was."[1] Here the prophetic element is realized in wrestling a woman from the shadow of silence to share, step by step, in Gautama's journey. Ordinary life, a child as a fetter, women as dangerously alluring, and enlightenment through renunciation of home are challenged as cloudy perspectives "of the all-male founding fathers of Buddhism."[2]

Ambedkar takes a different tack in challenging the standard version. He sees the story of the future Buddha's leave-taking that is precipitated by an initial encounter with sickness, old age, and death as "absurd." Any twenty-nine-year-old would have encountered all three on numerous occasions. What is not reasonable on the face of it, Ambedkar insists, should be set aside.[3] Ambedkar instead offers a countervailing myth, extrapolated from canonical sources.

In Ambedkar's version, Gautama is a representative in a Sakya assembly, a protoparliament under the rulership of the king of Kosala. A conflict with the neighboring state of Koliya over water rights has broken out and a resolution to go to war with Koliya has been presented to the assembly. Gautama speaks against the resolution and proposes negotiation with Koliya. "Dharma, as I understand it," the already wise Gautama argues, "consists in recognizing that enmity does not disappear by enmity. It can be conquered by love only." But Gautama's proposal is rejected. A large majority votes to go to war and calls for all able-bodied males to take up arms. Gautama refuses to do so and he is confronted with an ultimatum: join, have your family's lands confiscated, be hanged, or go into exile. Gautama proposes that he be allowed to go into exile as a wandering mendicant, and the assembly agrees to this proposal.[4]

The story does not end there. Gautama discusses his decision with his parents and then with Yasodhara. "Your decision is the right decision," she responds. "You have my consent and support." Gautama then takes his leave in full daylight with the blessing of his grieving parents.[5]

Then Ambedkar's revision takes a new twist. Public opinion turns in favor of Gautama's peaceful approach to the conflict, and the assembly begins negotiations with the Koliyas. This puts Gautama in a dilemma: Does this reversal absolve him of his vow? he asks. "The problem of war is essentially a problem of conflict. It is only part of a larger problem. This conflict is going on not only between kings and nations, but between nobles and Brahmins, between householders, between mother and son, between son and mother, between father and son, between sister and brother, between companion and companion. The conflict between nations is occasional. But the conflict between classes is constant and perpetual. It is this which is the root of all sorrow and suffering in the world. I have to find a solution to the problem of social conflict."[6] It is worth pausing here to let the full import of this passage sink in. Ambedkar has taken a key moment in the hagiography of the Buddha and boldly recast it. In the new story parents and wife still grieve but they consent to Gautama's radical action. Bonds are reinforced even as Gautama leaves Kapilavastu. His action leads to a peaceful resolution of conflict between two countries on the brink of war.

The power of the standard recounting of Gautama's leave-taking lies in the existential universality manifest in old age, sickness, and death. In Ambedkar's version we also have a species of universality—the presence of conflict at all levels of human society. Gautama's search is not for a private enlightenment but a collective transformation. Gautama has not left society, rather he has brought society and its collective dukkha with him as he undergoes his search.

Postscript: As I write, war rages in Ukraine, including massive attacks on civilian populations, widespread displacement, and war crimes. Historian Piotr Kosicki, reflecting on the rupture of more than seven decades of relative peace in Europe, sums up his commentary by saying, "Thinkers since Plato and Augustine have understood peace as but a fleeting dream, a pause between inevitable returns to a state of war, *because conflict is intrinsic to the human condition.* In the study of international relations this worldview is called realism" (italics added).[7] Viewed from this perspective, Ambedkar's version of Gautama's leave-taking becomes a prophetic contrast not only to the war fever in his country but also to Augustine and his many disciples, a bold declaration that conflict can be ended.

Part Two

Liberation in the American Context

Chapter Six

The American Jeremiad

Creating the City upon a Hill

Thus stands the cause between God and us. Wee are entered into Covenant with him for this worke.... For this end..., wee must Consider that wee shall be as a Citty upon a Hill, the eies of all people are upon us; soe that if wee shall deale falsely with our god in this worke we have undertaken and cause him to withdrawe his present help from us, wee shall shame the faces of many of gods worthy servants, and cause theire prayers to be turned into Curses upon us till we be consumed out of the good land whither wee are goeing. And to shut upp this discourse with that exhortacion of Moses... in his last farewell to Israell, Deut. 30 Beloved there is now sett before us life, and good, deathe and evil in that wee are Commaunded this day to Love the Lord our God and to love one another, to walke in his ways and to keepe his Commaundements... that the Lord our God may bless us in the land whither we goe to possesse it.... Therefore, let us choose life.

—John Winthrop, "A Modell of Christian Charity"[1]

The deep hope ... is that Black prophetic fire never dies ... and that a new wave of young brothers and sisters of all colors see and feel that it is a beautiful thing to be on fire for justice.

—Cornel West, *Black Prophetic Fire*[2]

The generation of the elders is passing. New Buddhist voices have arisen, challenging Buddhist communities in new ways. As we heed those voices, it remains critical not to cast the wisdom of the generation of elders to the winds. Part 1 of this volume took stock of the legacy of four elders, investigating those traits of their thinking and action that bear a family resemblance to the vision and actions of the Hebrew prophets. Liberation theology teaches that religious thought is contextual. It arises out of a real situation of human suffering from injustice, reflects on it, and offers a framework for engagement. Gustavo Gutiérrez calls this process of creating a framework for action "critical reflection on praxis."[3] This is clearly evident in our four elders: Rita Gross's rootedness in the feminist movement, Thich Nhat Hanh's struggle for peace in Vietnam, Joanna Macy's workshops on the dangers of nuclear brinksmanship and climate change, and B. R. Ambedkar's struggle to liberate the Dalits.

When we shift to the American context, as we do here in part 2, we find a particular discourse and a framework adopted by movements for change both on the left and on the right. Scholars have labeled it "the American Jeremiad." Given their minority status, Engaged Buddhists seeking social justice will need to collaborate with like-minded movements for social change if they wish to be effective. This will entail adapting this discourse by learning from its most ethically nuanced and challenging exemplars.

Most Americans are familiar with the image of their nation as a City upon a Hill. It is a rhetorical staple of presidents who extol America as a beacon for all humankind. In his 1630 sermon "A Modell of Christian Charity," John Winthrop, the first governor of the Massachusetts Bay colony, intended the metaphor to be a cautionary image—as foreboding as it was challenging. The City might become a slum shrouded in a dark cloud if the Puritan settlers failed to live up to the terms of their covenant with God and with one another. Given their important "commission," failure would surely wreak severe consequences. Choose life, Winthrop said, calling to mind the Exodus narrative and echoing—more precisely, reenacting—Moses's final admonition to the Israelites, as they approached their promised land.

We begin with Winthrop because our focus is on social liberation in the American context. It took Buddhism traveling over the silk road to China over six centuries or more to adapt to Chinese culture. In the process of adapting, a whole new galaxy appeared in the heavens. New schools, new scriptures. What Buddhists call a turning of the wheel was completed. In *Radical Dharma*, Reverend angel Kyodo williams argues that Buddhism at its best has adopted key aspects of the culture in whose soil it has planted its roots.[4] She and her colleagues argue that in the American context Buddhism should adopt a "radical dharma." Buddhism's initial connection with America's self-help industries, with their cult of the individual, runs the risk of fostering an "entitled solipsism." With it comes a disengagement from confronting and overcoming "injustice, inequity, pain, injury, disease, violence."[5] Instead, I suggest that Buddhism in the American context should *selectively* appropriate the tradition of the American Jeremiad, with its connection to movements for social justice, a tradition that spans close to four hundred years.

A scant thirty-two years after Winthrop's admonition, Michael Wigglesworth in a visionary poem spelled out in great detail "God's Controversy with New England":

> Beware, O sinful Land, beware;
> And do not think it strange
> That sorer judgments are at hand,
> Unless thou quickly change. . . .
> Or thou art undon:
> Wrath cannot cease, if sin remain,
> Where judgment is begun.
>
> Ah dear New England! dearest land to me
> Which unto God hast hitherto been dear,
> And mayst be still more dear than formerlie
> If to his voice thou will incline thine ear.[6]

A New Discourse for a People on a Mission

Within less than a generation the elements of the American Jeremiad had established themselves as perhaps the first literary genre of the European settlers. Allusions to the Exodus narrative provide the basic frame. Myth and history are fused within this frame that the Puritans sought to reenact.[7] Violations of communal norms place the entire community under divine judgment. A crisis of impending consequences includes the possibility of a catastrophic derailing of the divine mission. Consequently, its vision of a brighter future is conditioned upon the people acting immediately to rectify the situation. Forged in the world-transforming mission of expatriate English Puritans, the American Jeremiad was a new genre. By contrast, Sacvan Bercovitch, professor of American history, maintains, "The European Jeremiad developed within a static hierarchical order, the lessons that it taught about historical recurrence and the vanity of human wishes, amounted to a massive ritual reinforcement of tradition. . . . The American Puritan jeremiad was a ritual of a culture on an errand. . . . Crisis was the social norm it sought to inculcate. The very concept of errand, after all, implied a state of unfulfillment. The future, though divinely assured, was never quite there. . . . Denouncing or affirming, [the Puritans' vision] fed on the distance between promise and fact."[8] The power of the jeremiad depended upon shared moral norms. Despite the impending divine wrath—which was always impending—return to those norms would avert disaster and New England would be "still more dear than formerlie." Lamentations and indictments were intended as goads to close the gap between fact and ideal.[9] By the nineteenth century this discourse was well on the way to embracing the nation and articulating its manifest destiny. "Escaped from the house of bondage," Herman Melville wrote in his early novel, *White Jacket,* "Israel of old did not follow after the Egyptians; to her were given new things under the sun. And we Americans are the peculiar, chosen people—the Israel of our time; we bear the ark of the liberties of the world."[10]

It is hard to read Melville's evocation of the Exodus narrative today without cringing. Bearing the ark of liberty, America has repeatedly stumbled, if not fallen. Yet the presence of the jeremiad in our own time is unquestionable. Cornel West labels "Black prophetic fire" as one stream of the jeremiad tradition that has not run dry. Multiple prophetic critiques of oppression tap into that aquifer even though they may do so unwittingly. Like Moses, West calls for "a new wave of young brothers and sisters of all colors" to rekindle prophetic fire.

Sacvan Bercovitch saw the American Jeremiad as a ritual of consensus morphing into a doctrine of America's manifest destiny contingent upon confronting a series of crises that threatened to swamp the enterprise. Cathleen Kaveny, however, argues that as early as the American Revolution the focus of the jeremiad shifted from shared norms to a vision of norms that *should* become the core of the nation's ideology, that is, a focus not on recurrent violations of the covenant but on the terms of the covenant itself and on contested applications of those terms. So the abolition movement labeled slavery as a "national sin" whose continuance threatened to destroy the cancerous republic.[11] The jeremiad changed "from a mechanism enforcing social consensus to a vehicle propelling social change."[12] The Social Gospel movement straddling the nineteenth and the twentieth centuries is a prime example of the use of the jeremiad to redefine the meaning of the vocation of a "Christian" nation. In *Christianity and the Social Crisis* (1907), Walter

Rauschenbusch, the foremost spokesperson for the Social Gospel, defined the crisis in terms that still resonate:

> The continents are strewn with the ruins of dead nations and civilizations. . . . Nations do not die by wealth but by injustice. . . . Progress slackens when a single class appropriates the social results of the common labor, fortifies its evil rights by unfair laws . . . and consumes in luxury what it has taken in covetousness . . . In the last resort the only hope is in the moral forces which can be summoned to the rescue. If there are statesmen, prophets, and apostles who set truth and justice above selfish advancement, if their call finds a response in the great body of the people, if a new tide of religious faith and enthusiasm creates new standards of duty and a new capacity for self sacrifice, . . . then the entrenchments of vested wrong will melt away, the stifled energy of the people will leap forward, . . . and a regenerate nation will look with the eyes of youth across the fields of the future.[13]

Dueling Jeremiads

We need only recall the impact of social Darwinism as the ideological justification of the robber barons' laissez faire capitalism to recognize that Rauschenbusch's redefinition of the national compact was strenuously contested. Here we see what Cathleen Kaveny calls "dueling" Jeremiahs. As in the case of the prophet Jeremiah, the key issue during times of moral crisis becomes who is the true prophet, that is, the one whose analysis reveals the roots of the crisis and whose vision offers a path beyond the crisis. Given the jeremiad's role as a form of "moral chemotherapy," the danger becomes that every crisis is viewed as a mortal threat to the soul of the nation and the conflicting jeremiads harden into rigid ideological positions. The result can be what Kaveny calls a "moral balkanization."[14]

A first step in in evaluating dueling jeremiads is the presence or absence of a consciously self-critical dimension expressed as the willingness to criticize one's own foundational narratives in the name of those narratives themselves. So Daniel Berrigan, a Jesuit priest and decades-long peace activist who drew heavily on the Hebrew prophets, minced no words when he confronted the Exodus narrative and "its serpents' tangle of means and ends." He challenged the pharaonic god who orders the deaths of the Egyptian firstborns. From Berrigan's standpoint any jeremiad grounded in the liberating message of Exodus must say "no" to any deity—any ideology—that renders "children expendable, invisible, inaudible."[15]

Assuming that the American Jeremiad is so rooted in America's religious and political life that it cannot simply be dismissed, Cathleen Kaveny pushes further. She offers Abraham Lincoln's second inaugural address and Martin Luther King Jr.'s sermons as the gold standards for evaluating competing jeremiads.[16] The issue that the jeremiad addresses must be both systemic and entrenched. Jeremiads are not meant to be all-purpose moral rants. Fundamental values of the social compact must be at stake, and reform efforts must be, at least for the present, stymied.[17] King's analysis of a nation on the verge of spiritual death, suffering from the poisons of militarism, racism, and economic exploitation, exemplifies this criterion.[18] The jeremiad brings to light the sufferings of those who have been rendered invisible or treated as "collateral damage." It draws upon a subversive memory but also places the issue within a "horizon of hope."[19]

A jeremiad that does not succumb to dualistic thinking foreswears what is called in the case of the Hebrew prophets the "oracles against the nations," that is, denunciations that project the "other" as an irredeemable enemy.[20] So, Lincoln's second inaugural address can be read as a repudiation of the demonization of the other by both sides in the Civil War.[21] Neither side can truthfully claim that it fully adheres to God's will. God's purposes exceed human understanding. Such a jeremiad remains not only in solidarity with the oppressed but recognizes as well one's shared complicity with the injustice that is condemned. Leavened with this strong dose of intellectual and moral humility, Lincoln can end by urging the nation to press on "with firmness in the right as God gives us to see the right."[22] Tragic suffering accompanies any struggle against oppression. So, finally, the jeremiad's call to confront injustice should eventuate in compassion. We must act, Lincoln urges, "with malice towards none, with charity for all."

Lincoln sets the bar high—perhaps unattainably so. "The American public square," Kaveny recognizes, "is not a seminar room." "The conversations it hosts," she goes on to say, "are often cacophonous. . . . In examining issues of grave moral and political import, [participants] offer comments that are fueled not only by reason but also by passionate moral and religious commitment. In short, discourse in the American public square includes prophetic condemnation of great moral and social evils as well as nuanced consideration of competing values and policy goals."[23]

The African American Jeremiad

The African American Jeremiad is a distinct strand within the tradition of the American Jeremiad. It is not possible to grasp fully the import of the latter without examining the multiple contributions of the former. Cornel West sees the prophetic voice cultivated, expressed, and transformed in an unparalleled way by African Americans. They created a genre that combined the best of what Euro-American modernity offered—a developed critique of illegitimate authority and arbitrary power—with New World African modernity:

> New World African modernity consists of degraded and exploited Africans in American circumstances using European languages and instruments to make sense of tragic predicaments—predicaments disproportionately shaped by white-supremacist bombardments on black beauty, intelligence, moral character and creativity. New World African modernity attempts to institutionalize critiques of white-supremacist authority and racist uses of power, to bestow dignity, grandeur and tragedy upon the denigrated lives of ordinary black people. . . . Prophetic criticism rests on the best of New World African modernity by making explicit the personal and political aspects of existential democracy implicit in the visions, analyses and strategies of American African victims of Euro-American modernity.[24]

Several points in Cornel West's argument are worth underscoring. First, prophetic criticism embodied in the jeremiad is a modern creation by those English Puritans whom Michael Walzer called the first "world transforming activists." Second, in the voices of African Americans the jeremiad was even more a modern product, a hybrid form created in the teeth of white supremacy. Third, what West calls "Black prophetic fire" is as close as we get to a vibrant, persistent tradition of the jeremiad in the American context.

It goes without saying that the Exodus narrative was the pervasive frame through which African Americans imagined themselves and their world. Within this frame, Black people saw themselves as "a chosen people *within* a chosen people." America, however, was Egypt as well as the promised land. Slavery, in the African American Jeremiad and in the abolitionist movement, constituted the Chosen Nation's original sin, a curse upon its soul. Retribution awaited America if it did not collectively repent and abolish its sinful state.[25]

Exodus, in short, formed a counternarrative to the dogmas of white supremacy. In the face of a virulent ideology, Exodus declared that this oppressive Egypt was doomed to collapse. "Oh Mary don't you weep, don't you moan," the enslaved sang in the midst of a war for emancipation, "Pharaoh's army got drowned."

The Exodus frame of the African American Jeremiad did not function to reinforce the status quo. In its most salient manifestations, it grounded hope in a movement toward freedom. So, one hundred years after the end of the Civil War, John Lewis, the stalwart and bloodied freedom rider, leader of the Student Nonviolent Coordinating Committee, and a veteran of numerous arrests, saw the confrontation at the Pettus Bridge outside of Selma, Alabama, in March 1965 as the struggle to cross the Red Sea. "We were God's children wading in the water," he declared. "Our struggle was the modern day struggle of the children of Israel and we were on our way out of Egypt land to a better land, to a Promised Land. . . . We would sing 'Go down Moses, go down in Egypt land, and tell old pharaoh to let my people go, go down in Alabama, down in Selma, tell Sheriff Clark, tell George Wallace to let my people go.'"[26] The civil rights struggles were not *like* the Exodus narrative. They were the Exodus journey unfolding in the present, expressed in sermon and song, and bodily enacted in marches and demonstrations. Putting one's body on the line became a transcendent experience of the story both for the empowered agents and for all of those caught up in the drama.[27]

Working within this framework, African Americans crafted a distinctive literary genre—the African American Jeremiad. Willie Harrell argues that the African American Jeremiad differed in purpose from its Puritan counterpart. It served three distinctive purposes: as "the foundation for Black empowerment," as a call for Black solidarity, and, as an abolitionist tract put it, "to effect a mighty revolution."[28] Examples of the genre stretch from David Walker's 1829 pamphlet "Appeal to the Coloured Citizens of the World" to Jesmyn Ward's *The Fire This Time*.[29] My treatment of this long tradition necessarily will be very selective.

David Walker was born in 1785 in the South to a free mother and an enslaved father. He migrated to the North, where he became an early abolitionist. In what was arguably the first full-blown African American Jeremiad, he advocated for African Americans to free themselves using any available means, including slave rebellions. God, he argued, will not allow the oppressors to rest comfortably forever: "Slavery is ten thousand times more injurious to the country than all of the other evils put together, and which will be the final overthrow of its government. . . . I tell you Americans! that unless you speedily alter your course you and your Country are gone! For God Almighty will tear up the very face of the earth."[30] A looming crisis, unequivocal denunciation, a call to act before it was too late—each of these elements of the jeremiad was forcefully articulated. Moreover, Walker altered slaves' understanding of time by insisting that slavery would end "this side of eternity."[31] Finally, Walker's "Appeal" directly confronted early America's foremost intellectual, Thomas Jefferson, whose influential *Notes on the State of Virginia* claimed both that Black Americans were morally, physically, and intellectually inferior and that the enslavers treated their slaves humanely. The slaveholding plutocrats, Walker argued, had created a repressive state that was *less* morally evolved than Egypt was toward its Hebrew slaves.[32]

Frederick Douglass: On Fire for Freedom

Walker's "Appeal" was magnified in the fiery rhetoric of Frederick Douglass. Douglass was a colossus of the nineteenth century, a fierce abolitionist in the run up to the Civil War and a persistent advocate for Reconstruction in its aftermath. As a young child, born into slavery, Douglass was sent to live in Baltimore with relatives of the enslaver. There, for about two years, Sophia Auld taught him to read until her husband forbade it, telling her it was unlawful to teach a slave to read in the state of Maryland. But it was too late; young Frederick had crossed over into a new world. He collected pages of the Bible in the gutters of Baltimore. The metaphors, vision, and cadences of the King James Bible became engrained in his very being. Above all, Douglass absorbed the rhetoric and message of the Hebrew prophets. "Their great and terrible stories," argues David Blight, "provided Douglass the deepest well of metaphors and meanings for his increasingly ferocious critique of his own country. . . . Douglass not only used the Hebrew prophets, he joined them."[33]

Douglass's three autobiographies and numerous biographers tell the story of the rebellious slave, his dangerous flight to the North, and his finding a voice through preaching at the AME Zion church in New Bedford, Massachusetts. In August 1841 he addressed an antislavery society convention where William Lloyd Garrison was in the audience. Profoundly moved by Douglass's speech, Garrison recruited Douglass as a lecturer in the American Antislavery Society. Nathaniel Rogers, a New England abolitionist and editor, described the young Douglass as a "volcanic outbreak," "outraged humanity . . . at last bursting its imprisonment."[34] Douglass took to the American Jeremiad as his native tongue.

We can get some sense of Douglass's rhetorical power by examining his most famous speech and one that exemplifies the African American Jeremiad. "The Meaning of July Fourth for the Negro" was delivered at a July 5, 1852, gathering in Rochester, New York.[35] Douglass begins his speech with declarations of humility. It is, he says, indeed, an awesome distance between his birth as a slave and the platform on which he stands. He immediately sounds a hopeful note: the reform-minded can take courage from the fact that America as a nation is still young. Her pathways are not yet carved in fixed grooves. America claims a golden memory in the saga of its founders. It is tempting to bask in the reflected glory of their accomplishments, but in their day they were branded "agitators and rebels, dangerous men" (190). The Declaration of Independence offered "saving principles" (191). Cling to them "at whatever cost," Douglass insists, for the founders lived, did their work, and died. Now you must do yours. With that challenge, Douglass shifts from the remembrance of the founding era to the heart of the jeremiad. "My business . . . is with the present," he declares. "The accepted time with God and his cause is the ever-living now" (193).

We can imagine Douglass pausing for a moment and then intoning, "Fellow citizens, pardon me, allow me to ask, why am I called upon to speak here today? What have I, or those I represent, to do with your national independence?" (194). "The rich inheritance," he continued," of justice, liberty, prosperity and independence, bequeathed by your fathers, is shared by *you*, not by me. . . . This Fourth of July is *yours* not *mine*. *You* may rejoice. *I* must mourn" (194). "Standing with God and the crushed and bleeding slave on this occasion, I will, in the name of humanity, which is outraged, in the name of liberty, which is fettered, in the name of the Constitution and the Bible, which are disregarded and trampled upon, dare to call in question and to denounce, with all the emphasis I can command, everything that serves to perpetuate slavery—the great sin and shame of America!" (195).

To those who object to Douglass's jeremiad on rhetorical grounds and believe that he would do better to provide rational grounds for his abolitionist cause, he responds, "Must I undertake to prove that the slave is a man?" Must we debate that a system based on violence and bloodshed is morally wrong? All persons know that slavery is morally wrong—*for themselves* (196). "O! had I the ability and could reach the nation's ear, I would to-day pour out a fiery stream of biting ridicule, blasting reproach, withering sarcasm and stern rebuke. *For it is not light that is needed but fire*" (196; italics added). To the slave the Fourth of July is "a day that reveals to him, more than all other days in the year, the gross injustice and cruelty to which he is the constant victim" (196). Is there any other nation as barbarous and hypocritical as America? Douglass delivers on his own challenge focusing blow by blow on the domestic slave trade and the Fugitive Slave Act that made the entire nation complicit in this crime against humanity (196–98).

Having leveled this indictment, Douglass shifts his focus to the Christian churches that have utterly failed—with a few exceptions—in their prophetic mission. Quoting Isaiah, he says, "Your hands are full of blood. . . . Cease to do evil. . . . Seek justice" (Isa 1:15–17). Do you think, he asks, that slavery would last even one hour if the churches would together denounce it? "The existence of slavery brands . . . your Christianity as a lie" (201).

Unlike Garrison, Douglass sees the Constitution as not entirely corrupted. Encouraged by the "saving principles" of the Republic, he ends with the assurance that slavery is doomed (205) and quotes the abolitionist anthem:

> God speed the year of jubilee. . . .
> When from their galling chains set free,
> Th' oppress'd shall vilely bend the knee,
> And wear the yoke of tyranny
> Like brutes no more. . . .
> When none on earth
> Shall exercise a lordly power,
> Nor in a tyrant's presence cower;
> But all to manhood's stature tower,
> By equal birth. . . .
> Until that year, day, hour, arrive,
> With head and heart, and hand I'll strive,
> To break the rod, and rend the gyve, . . .
> So witness heaven! (205)[36]

Douglass's Fourth of July speech is about as uncompromising a version of the African American Jeremiad as one can imagine. The voice of the prophet thunders. His aim is to rouse the conscience of the nation, to awaken a people who have been comatose for 233 years. He will not stoop to debate those who deny both facts and moral certainty. It is time for fire.

All of the elements of a jeremiad are expressed with unparalleled rhetorical power: the sacred memory of the founding; the "saving principles" as the terms of the social compact; indictment and denunciation of the nation for its failure to abide by its own norms; a time of mortal crisis; the failure of the religious communities to uphold their prophetic mission; and a glimmer of hope in a dark time if only the people in the religious communities, and the nation, will act.

If Douglass calls upon the ancient law of jubilee to provide a glimmer of hope, in a later speech, "The Significance of Emancipation in the West Indies," he offers a deeply ironic counter "City upon a Hill" to the one promised by Winthrop and extolled by American presidents. The eyes of humanity look not on any American city but upon a British colony. Douglass celebrates the emancipation of all slaves in the British West Indies on August 1, 1834: "The day and deed are both greatly distinguished. They are as a city set upon a hill, all civilized men at least, have looked with wonder and admiration upon the great deed of justice and humanity. . . . The event we celebrate is the finding and restoration to the broken ranks of human brotherhood eight hundred thousand lost members of the human family. It is the resurrection of a mighty multitude from the grave of moral, mental, social and spiritual death where ages of slavery and oppression, and lust and pride, had bound them."[37] This event, Douglass goes on to say, is an authentic form of progress that transcends the marvelous inventions and burst of prosperity that mark the nineteenth century. Nations are preserved not by "the gilded splendors of wealth" but by the grandeur of virtue. The emancipation of slaves in the West Indies testifies to the triumph of freedom and justice over "devilish brutality."[38] Compared to this achievement, even the most prosperous American city is a foul and fetid slum.

Ida B. Wells's Anti-Lynching Campaign

Certainly, Frederick Douglass was unmatched in the rhetorical power with which he challenged the nation's "original sin." But we also esteem many of the prophets for their lonely persistence in times when the community refused to listen. In an era when Booker T. Washington's acquiescence to Jim Crow prevailed, one fearless woman stood up and stood out. Ida B. Wells "is not only unique," Cornel West insists, "but she is the exemplary figure full of prophetic fire in the face of American terrorism . . . when lynching occurred every two and a half days for over fifty years in America."[39] Born a slave during the Civil War, Wells was propelled into action by the March 1892 lynching in Memphis, Tennessee, of three African American men—one of whom Wells knew—whose only "crime" was to own and run a grocery store in competition with white-owned stores and to defend it against an attack from a white mob. This event "opened my eyes," Wells recollected, "to what lynching really was. An excuse to get rid of Negroes who were acquiring wealth and property and thus keep the race terrified. . . . I then began an investigation of every lynching I read about."[40] A pioneer investigative journalist, Wells shattered the white supremacist myth of lynching as a justifiable defense of white womanhood from rapacious Black men. She did it by marshalling statistics, for example, in less than one-fifth of the cases were the men even accused of rape, let alone guilty of it. She exposed trumped-up charges, or in some cases no charges at all.[41] What she exposed was mob violence as calculated terrorism designed to enforce the subjugation of African Americans to the Jim Crow caste system.

In the late nineteenth and early twentieth century, Wells may have been hampered in the kinds of rhetoric considered as respectable when voiced by a woman, but it did not keep her from speaking out in over two decades of leadership. Her fearless rage must be read between the lines:

> Why is mob murder permitted by a Christian nation? What is the cause of this awful slaughter? This question is answered almost daily—always the same shameless falsehood that "Negroes are lynched to protect womanhood." . . . All know that it is untrue. The cowardly lyncher revels in murder, then seeks to shield himself from public execration by claiming devotion to woman. But truth is mighty and the lynching record discloses the hypocrisy of the lyncher as well as his crime. . . . The only certain remedy is an appeal to law. Lawbreakers must be made to know that human life is sacred. . . . Lynching . . . is . . . a blight upon our nation, mocking our laws and disgracing our Christianity. . . . Let us undertake the work of making the "law of the land" effective and supreme upon every foot of American soil.[42]

Conclusion

Beginning with the New England Puritan settlers, the jeremiad became a staple of American moral discourse. This use of the prophetic voice was generally accepted as appropriate where fundamental ideals, the norms of communal life, were being abrogated. As we have seen, it subsequently entered the bloodstream of American religious and political life, energizing numerous movements for social change. While the fiery rhetoric of Douglass and others resembled the Hebrew prophets in many respects, we should be clear that these prophets are *modern* reincarnations. They see injustice as systemic. So the abolitionists referred to America as the "slaveholding republic," indicating thereby how slavery had insinuated itself into every aspect of society, corrupting the whole fabric and making a mockery of democratic ideas. The American Jeremiad became a discourse for a people on a mission. The City upon a Hill needed to be built or, more precisely, rebuilt.

What might it mean to open our Buddhist practice to transformation by this prophetic fire? How might Buddhists incorporate the jeremiad into their own discourse? I understand that some Buddhists might object, saying, "Don't we have enough contenders in the public square, right and left, righteously denouncing everyone and everything? What we need is more civility and loving speech, which is precisely what Buddhists have to offer." Certainly, loving speech is often the most appropriate form of discourse, especially for resolving conflicts over important values. But not always. The teaching of "skillful means" suggests that different circumstances require *phronesis,* practical wisdom tailoring rhetorical forms to fit the situation.

Engaged Buddhists, seeking to address injustice within American society, need to come to terms with a form of discourse that will be widely used by other religious and secular advocates for social reform. We cannot simply close our ears to the jeremiads that pepper the movements whose goals we share. Can Engaged Buddhists offer a model of the jeremiad that is not divisive?

I suggest, first, that we revisit Kaveny's gold standard of the jeremiad, Lincoln's tragic theology as expressed in his second inaugural address, but now to draw out what Buddhists can borrow from Lincoln's prophetic voice. In developing their own transformed model, Engaged Buddhists can learn a great deal about the utility of the jeremiad as a genre not from the loudest voices dominating social media but from its most nuanced and carefully formulated examples.

- *The Almighty has His purposes.* Lincoln recognizes the limits to our knowledge, but more importantly to our moral discernment.
- *The prayers of neither side have been answered fully.* In a conflict neither side can claim an exclusive monopoly of truth. Fiery rhetoric must be tempered by humility.

- *With malice toward none.* In a society with a history of racism that has invaded our laws, behaviors, and institutions, no one can claim to be cancer free. Embedded injustice must be confronted. Yet no person is incapable of self-transformation. No one can be written off as irredeemable.

- *With firmness in the right.* Delusions are endless, but that is no excuse for inaction. The lotus has no choice but to grow in a sea of mud. We do have what Douglass called "saving principles" and, for example, Thich Nhat Hanh's mindfulness trainings to guide us.

- *Bind up the nation's wounds.* Restorative justice, not retributive justice, is called for, and restorative justice must be carried forward with compassion.[43]

Second, as we have seen, Kaveny herself argues that the prophetic voice is appropriate as a form of *moral chemotherapy* to address a situation in which the very norms of a democratic communal life have been undermined and in which *our capacity for moral discernment and for moral agency have been compromised.* Buddhists are not immune to such an eclipse of moral awareness. The psychic numbness that Macy addressed bleeds over into moral numbness when we cocoon ourselves in a self-involved practice. How do we know when our practice breeds not equanimity but moral complacency? When social sickness has metastasized from within, prophetic discourse is more than an appropriate "skillful means"; it is required.[44]

- *Moral chemotherapy.* It is appropriate when core values are at stake, or when collective forms of the three poisons (greed, ill will, and delusion) have metastasized.[45] Fiery rhetoric is called for in these cases and when a complacent society has rendered a group invisible and voiceless.

- *Prophecy without contempt.* Contempt is despising the other as a vile (sub)human being, placing the other beneath oneself as utterly worthless.[46] Dualistic thinking flirts with contempt. A Buddhist jeremiad—both in tone and substance—will recognize that all beings have a Buddha Nature and that those who have identified with entrenched injustice are able to change.

- *Used sparingly to address systemic ills.* Chemotherapy is not a skillful means for the common cold. Rita Gross's careful analysis of the Buddhist tradition grounded her critique of patriarchal Buddhism as a systemic impairment of Buddhism's deepest intentionality.

Now, more than ever, we need to take stock of our legacy of prophetic fire. In the twentieth century one person, Dr. Martin Luther King Jr., stood above all others in reinventing and carrying forward the jeremiad tradition. His legacy, despite all the accolades, remains largely untapped.

Chapter Seven

Dr. Martin Luther King Jr.
America's Jeremiah

> All over the world like a fever, freedom is spreading in the widest liberation movement in history. The great masses of people are determined to end the exploitation of their races and lands. . . . In Washington Irving's familiar story of Rip Van Winkle . . . the most striking thing . . . is not that Rip slept twenty years but that he slept through a revolution that would alter the course of human history. One of the great liabilities of history is that all too many people fail to remain awake through great periods of social change. . . . But today our very survival depends on our ability to stay awake, . . . to remain vigilant and to face the challenge of change.
>
> —Martin Luther King Jr., "The World House"[1]

> The whole future of America will depend upon the impact and influence of Dr. King.
>
> —Rabbi Abraham Heschel[2]

More than fifty years after Dr. Martin Luther King Jr.'s murder, the nation still thrashes with the nightmare of racism, and Rabbi Heschel's prophetic words ring ominously true. Dr. King's jeremiad remains largely unknown, hidden, as Willis Jenkins puts it, in a "hagiographic haze."[3] We have canonized Dr. King; his life has been treated as a completed narrative, not one cut short by murder. That narrative has been redacted; whole sections blacked out. What did we fail to see while he lived, and what has been hidden in the haze of his canonization? What were the teachings and praxis of the man that Cornel West calls "the radical King?"

Engaged Buddhists who immerse themselves in the thought of the radical King will find that he, too, is one of our elders. Dr. King offers new meaning—a new turning of the wheel—to the Buddhist experience of waking up. Through his cautionary tale of Rip Van Winkle, and his commitment to treating the present crisis without flinching, Dr. King calls us to realize our sociospiritual quest. Nonviolent action is one form of practice for those who form the intention (*bodhicitta*) to wake up all beings.

On July 21, 1955, not yet one year into his pulpit and five months before the start of the Montgomery bus boycott, Dr. King delivered a sermon to the Dexter Avenue congregation called "Death on the Seashore." As he was to do repeatedly in the next thirteen years, Dr. King placed the southern Black community within an Exodus framework as the encompassing narrative of the triumph of good over evil.[4] He began by reciting a litany of evils both personal and political. For too long we have seen, he said, "imperialistic nations crushing other nations by the iron feet of oppression."[5] Next he called the congregation's attention, as he would do much later in "the World House," to a revolution, the uprising of people of color across the globe throwing off the shackles of colonial oppression. Liberation movements are a tsunami sweeping away dehumanizing structures. He then connected these movements to the epochal Supreme Court decision in *Brown v. Board of Education*. "Many years ago," Dr. King argued, "we were thrown into the Egypt of segregation. . . . For years it looked like we would never get out of this Egypt. . . . But one day, through a world shaking decision by the Supreme Court of America . . . the Red Sea was opened and freedom and justice marched to the other side." As for the latter-day Egyptians, they will be swept aside by the tide of history.[6] Dr. King ended this sermon with a call to a personal decision: "My friends, get out of Egypt!" While there was an active NAACP chapter in Montgomery, there was not yet any mass movement that he could exhort them to join. But what he did do, Gary Selby argues, was to give his congregation a new way of looking at their circumstances. He sought to convince those for whom the prospects of social change seemed bleak that the journey to freedom had already begun and that they were called to participate in a dramatic global transformation that was already underway, one that was supported by a liberating God.[7] It was a wake-up call.

Key elements of the African American Jeremiad were announced in this early sermon: the Exodus narrative as a framing or interpretive device;

America as Egypt, not (yet) the Promised Land for African Americans; a global perspective; a sense of kairos, living on the verge of an epochal change. But this sermon lacks a sense that this moment is also a moment of crisis, when concrete action is called for as opposed to a vague appeal to get out of Egypt, and it does not yet identify specific targets of imperial oppression. Before the year's end, all that would change. A one-day boycott would galvanize the Black community and spark a protracted struggle to desegregate buses, and these missing elements would fall into place. Later, as the movement spread throughout the South, the Exodus narrative ceased to be simply a framing device. Just as the Hebrew prophets transformed Exodus from a past event into an ongoing liberating journey, the Black community and its allies reenacted the Exodus narrative in their bodies under the lash of Pharaoh's sheriffs, defeating the white supremacist armies.[8]

The Prophet's Calling

Dr. King heeded the call to be the spokesperson for the Montgomery bus boycott but he did not choose to become a twentieth-century prophet. In fact, as we saw in chapter 1, in his classic "kitchen experience," a troubled and sleepless King prayerfully confessed his inability to carry the burden of leadership of the boycott in the midst of death threats to himself and his family only to receive an assurance of God's abiding presence.[9] Through a gradual process of interaction with the Montgomery boycotters, he became invested with a prophetic persona, that is, no longer simply borrowed a prophetic voice but now reenacted the prophetic archetype.[10] The prophetic persona, in other words, was not a private possession but a relational process.[11] Keeping this dialogical understanding of the prophet's role in mind, I suggest that we can see Dr. King's jeremiad in full bloom in three key texts: a letter, a sermon, and a visionary parable of global freedom and peace.

Birmingham Jail

The first of our three major texts is the classic argument for nonviolent direct action, "A Letter from Birmingham City Jail."[12] The letter was drafted while King was in jail April 12–20, 1963. Birmingham was a city in which apartheid ruled in almost all areas of public life—even the songs in jukeboxes were split into Black and white songs. Dr. King was in jail because the campaign to desegregate these public facilities in Birmingham was faltering.[13] Sheriff Bull Connor had launched fierce attacks on the marchers, bringing the brutality of the system to the surface. But the movement was having a hard time gathering people ready to go to jail. To make matters worse, an Alabama state court had declared an injunction against further marches.

Dr. King knew that something dramatic had to happen if the movement was not to be defeated. On Good Friday, King set out to commit civil disobedience in Birmingham but with fewer than fifty followers. He was quickly arrested. In jail King was placed in solitary confinement. Cut off, he became very anxious, undergoing his own Passion.[14] Then he read a letter, published in a local newspaper, from leading clergy, including an Episcopal, a Catholic, and a Methodist bishop and a Reformed rabbi, charging King with fomenting violence, recklessly endangering gradual progress for African Americans, and breaking the law in violating an Alabama state court's injunction against marching while asking white Southerners to obey the Supreme Court's decision in *Brown v. Board of Education*. Finally, they charged that Dr. King was an outsider disturbing an otherwise peaceful city.[15]

King's letter itself is complex in form—a letter that, first, rebuts the charge that he is an outsider fomenting discord; second, lays out a case for nonviolence as a method for pursuing justice; third, presents a theological treatise on justice that provides a norm for judging just versus unjust laws; and, finally, levels a harsh prophetic denunciation of both Southern white "moderates" and the Southern white churches.[16]

Above all, this is a letter, a genre that assumes the possibility of a dialogue, as opposed to, say, a manifesto. In his salutation, "My dear Fellow Clergymen," King establishes a basic equality. He is not petitioning a higher court. Later referring to "my Christian and Jewish brothers," he implies a common respect for one another that is necessary for any genuine dialogue. Even his most caustic remarks are encased within this dialogical framework. He assumes a common commitment to fundamental religious values (289, 295). Writing in jail, Dr. King immediately associates himself with the Apostle Paul, also in jail and writing a letter, a man who accepted no boundaries to the spread of the Gospel. Just as the eighth-century BCE prophets were compelled to carry God's word far beyond their villages, "I am in Birmingham," King insists, "because injustice is here. . . . I too am compelled to carry the gospel of freedom beyond my particular hometown" (290).

The long discussion of nonviolence as a practice with a disciplined set of steps counters the charge that King, as an "outside agitator," is a disrupter of the peace. The careful method leading to nonviolent direct action is anything but reckless.[17] Dr. King lists four steps that must be taken in any nonviolent campaign (290–91): First, study the situation. Is there an injustice that demands remediation? Second, negotiation. Can we come to an agreement without disrupting society? Third, spiritual preparation. Are the resisters ready to remain nonviolent even when provoked? And fourth, direct action. This is undertaken only when negotiations have failed to produce an agreed-upon change and it should lead to renewed negotiations. In Buddhist terms, nonviolent action is a practice. To the clergy's plea for a negotiated settlement, Dr. King, in effect, says, "I couldn't agree more." That is precisely the aim of nonviolent direct action, namely, to create a crisis that will force all parties to sit down and negotiate. It is the merchants of Birmingham who have failed to honor the terms of previous negotiations (290–92). To those who counsel patience (including President John F. Kennedy and the major media), King replies that from the African American perspective "wait" has almost always meant "never."[18] Time does not automatically bring progress. "History is the long and tragic story," as he will state repeatedly throughout his struggle, "of the fact that privileged groups seldom give up their privileges voluntarily." Freedom must be demanded by the oppressed (292).

Nonviolent direct action intends to create a crisis, but it is not the cause of violence. Like a boil—King's own visceral metaphor—violence is impacted. It must be brought to the surface if healing is to occur (291, 295). Nonviolence represents a middle path between the passivity of those who have acquiesced in their oppression and the hatred of those who espouse a retaliatory violence.

In response to the charge that he is a lawbreaker, King offers a synthesis of Thomas Aquinas, Martin Buber, and personalist philosophy to present his theory of justice. A just law is one that reflects natural or divine law. More specifically, a law that uplifts the human personality is just, and one that degrades it is unjust. Just laws establish I-Thou relationships, not I-It relationships in which the person is treated as a thing, a means to others' ends (293).[19]

King offers a litany of the violence, both overt and covert, perpetrated against African Americans, ranging from the terrorism of lynch mobs to police who curse, kick, and kill African Americans with impunity to life under the cloud of daily humiliations, to the psychological damage to his six-year-old daughter, Yolanda, when he had to tell her that "Funtown is closed to colored children" (292–93). Faced with this pervasive, multilayered violence, King embraces the label of "extremist." Jesus was an extremist for love and Amos an extremist for justice. "The nation and the world," he concludes, "are in dire need of creative extremists" (296–98). Casting his lot with Amos and Jesus, King shifts from appeals to the clergies' moral conscience to prophetic denunciation.[20]

The American Jeremiad is a genre of moral discourse appropriate for extreme situations. Having sided with those extremists for justice and love, Dr. King directs his controlled ire against the white "moderates" and against the Southern white churches. Dr. King has been sorely disappointed by both overlapping groups. The white "moderates" have shown themselves to care more for law and order than social justice. "Maybe I expected too much," he laments. "I guess I should have realized that few members of a race that has oppressed another race can understand the deep groans and passionate yearnings of those that have been oppressed and still fewer have seen that injustice must be rooted out by strong, persistent and determined action" (295–96, 298).

Dr. King, however, saves his harshest criticism for the Southern white churches. He has traveled all over the South looking at the beautiful churches but wondering, "What kind of people worship there?" Cutting to the quick, he asks: "Who is their God?" Behind the stained-glass windows of the beautiful churches were the clergy who preached "peace, peace" when there was no peace (cf. Jer 8:11), clergy whose sentimental religion shied away from the realities of power. By contrast, King offers a "subversive memory." The earliest Christians "were too God-intoxicated" to give way to fear. No, they courageously attacked ancient evils. Today, he charges, "the judgment of God is on the churches as never before" (298–301). The church risks becoming an irrelevant social club if it continues to support a negative peace with order rather than a positive peace with justice (295). The jury may be out on the fate of the Southern white churches, but King closes his letter confident that freedom will be reached in Birmingham and throughout the nation because "the goal of America is freedom" (301).[21]

A Time to Break Silence

A sermon that more closely conforms to the genre of the jeremiad is Dr. King's "A Time to Break Silence" that was delivered at Riverside Church in New York City on April 4, 1967, one year to the day before he was murdered.[22] A lot had happened since he had written his Birmingham letter in some degree of desperation. The Birmingham campaign had been successful, only to be followed quickly by a church bombing that killed four young girls and horrified a nation. Landmark civil rights legislation was passed in 1964 and 1965. In their wake King broadened the focus of the movement to deal with social and economic injustice but ran into an avalanche of hate when marching for a fair housing ordinance in Chicago in the summer of 1966. Now the shadow of the war in Vietnam threatened to derail all efforts at social reform. By the beginning of 1967, the escalating war in Vietnam was already draining funds from President Lyndon Johnson's "War on Poverty." It disproportionately was wasting the lives of young Black men drafted into the military. At Riverside Church, Dr. King publicly declared his opposition to the war in Vietnam. In so doing, he broke with his closest advisors and liberal supporters. The civil rights establishment accused King of betraying the cause of the African American people. The last thing the civil rights establishment wanted, argues Jonathan Rieder, "was to get into a smackdown with President Lyndon Baines Johnson."[23] The clearest indication that King was perilously out on his own came from the Southern Christian Leadership Conference (SCLC) board, which refused to endorse King's opposition to the war.[24] Nevertheless, speaking to Andrew Young, Dr. King said, "I feel so deep in my heart that we are so wrong . . . and the time has come for a real prophecy and I am willing to go that road."[25]

Dr. King's understanding of the cost of speaking out is reflected in the sermon's opening remarks: "The calling to speak is often a vocation of agony but we must speak" (231). Twenty-five hundred years ago Jeremiah had testified to a similar vocation: God's word was "like a burning fire shut up in my bones." "I am weary," Jeremiah lamented, "with holding it in and I cannot" (Jer 20:9). Compelled to speak, King lists seven reasons why the war was a moral disaster. First, like a "demonic destructive suction tube," it has siphoned off skills and funds that would have been directed to the war against poverty. Second, it has cruelly deceived poor Black and white men, sending them to their deaths in greater numbers than the more well off. Third, it has subverted appeals to African Americans to seek social change through nonviolence when they see their country relying on violence. America, he charges, "is the greatest purveyor of violence in the world today" (232–33). Fourth, by frustrating the hopes of peoples for freedom, it has violated its own ideals and injects the poison of cynicism into America's veins. Fifth, sixth, and seventh, his Nobel Peace Prize, his ministry in service to the one who said "love your enemies," and his calling as a son of the heavenly

Father all commit him to go beyond narrow nationalist commitments. Those who counsel silence, King insists, "have not really known me" (232–34).

Having laid out these charges, King takes his listeners through a process of envisioning the war in Vietnam from the point of view of its victims. That section ends with a five-point peace plan (234–39). This, if followed by a glimmer of hope, might seem an appropriate end to his jeremiad. But King then proceeds to level, if possible, a more serious indictment: "I wish to go on now to say something even more disturbing. The war in Vietnam is but a symptom of a far deeper malady within the American spirit." If we fail to cure it, he argues, accurately predicting the disastrous course of the next half century, we will be organizing peace rallies for an endless series of Vietnams. "I am convinced," he insists, that if we are to get on the right side of history, we as a nation must undergo a radical revolution of values" (240). Such a revolution must confront the three poisons of "racism, materialism and militarism" if America is to avoid "spiritual death" (241). A Buddhist will immediately see a connection between King's three isms and collective forms of Buddhism's three poisons—greed (materialism), ill will (militarism), and delusion (racism).[26] "History," he concludes, "is cluttered with the wreckage of nations and individuals that pursued this self-defeating path of hate. . . . We are confronted with the fierce urgency of now. . . . The 'tide in the affairs of men' does not remain at the flood, it ebbs. . . . Over the bleached bones and jumbled residue of numerous civilizations are written the pathetic words: 'Too late.' . . . We still have a choice today: nonviolent coexistence or violent co-annihilation" (242–43). As with Jeremiah, Dr. King's prophetic words were met with charges of treason by his detractors and consternation by his supporters. The *Washington Post* provided a comparatively restrained denunciation. King, it editorialized, "has done grave injury to those who are his natural allies . . . and an even graver injury to himself. . . . He has diminished his usefulness to his cause, to his country and to his people. And that is a great tragedy."[27] When even his closest advisors chided him, Dr. King replied, "I really feel that someone of influence has to say that the United States is wrong, and everybody is afraid to say it."[28]

The World House

Following the Riverside speech and at a SCLC retreat in May, Dr. King set the context for a new phase of the organization's work: "We have moved," he said, "from the era of civil rights to the era of human rights. . . . [W]e have been in a reform movement. . . . But after Selma and the voting rights bill we moved into a new era, which must be an era of revolution."[29] The third jeremiad that we will examine is the final chapter of *Where Do We Go from Here: Chaos or Community?*[30] Dr. King's new vision for a revolutionary era, his new dream, is organized around the metaphor of "the World House." Human beings have reached the stage of development where they must live together or die together on one earth. A scientific and technological revolution has compressed the globe. A second revolution, the rise of masses of the disinherited throwing off their chains, is spreading contagiously. It is, in fact, "the widest liberation movement in history." It is as if the globe's billions of disenfranchised are chanting the civil rights anthem: "Ain't gonna let nobody turn us around" (196–98).

Then Dr. King offers us a parable—the story of Rip Van Winkle, the man who slept through a revolution. We are, all too many of us, like Rip, dead asleep as the revolution marches on. Today, however, our very survival depends upon staying awake. King offers Buddhists a new turning of the wheel, a new interpretation of what it means to wake up. Remaining calm on our cushions while the world house burns down is a false liberation. King elaborates on the three systemic forces that might already be setting the house aflame: Racism is the "hound of hell which dogs the track of our civilization." One of its Hydra heads is neocolonialism. The white, Western world lives in abundance wrested from exploited labor while across the globe awareness dawns that those who do not have a share in the abundance are, largely, people of color. Racism in tandem with economic exploitation could well burn the house down, unless, of course, militarism triggers a nuclear conflagration that sweeps all away (204–11). Confronted with this litany of the palpable injuries to the body politic perpetrated by these systemic poisons, those who have awakened declare, "This is not just!" (218–19). In the face of these dire threats, King calls for a third revolution, a revolution of values (216). It begins with the most basic of principles. "From time immemorial," King argues, "men have lived by the principle that 'self-preservation is the first law of life.' But this is a false assumption. I would say that other-preservation is the first law of life precisely because we cannot preserve self without being concerned about preserving other selves. . . . The self cannot be a self without other selves. . . . All men are interdependent. . . . Whether we realize it or not, each of us lives eternally 'in the red.' We are everlasting debtors to known and unknown men and women" (209–11).[31]

Having in effect redefined the Buddhist concept of interdependent coarising to focus on a revolution of values, Dr. King offers a moral challenge to we who would live in the "World House." The first two revolutions have compressed the globe and charged it with the electricity of liberation, but only the third revolution can make the house livable. Only awake agents can recognize that racism, poverty, endless war, and preparations for war are the arsonist's tools that could burn the house down. For Dr. King, however, the issue is not just waking up but staying awake to carry out the third revolution. Here, I suggest that we recall Robert Jay Lifton's and Joanna Macy's treatments of "psychic numbness," particularly as it affects all of us who are still living under the cloud of a nuclear holocaust. Psychic numbness shuts down our emotional reactions to that threat, as we succumb to the illusion of security promoted by a militarized state. We go about our everyday lives, buying groceries, meeting work deadlines, dealing with a depressed teenager, dealing with our own depression, all seemingly very compelling demands, which, of course, they are. Confronted by the mind-numbing realities of endless wars, by climate change with its runaway wildfires and floods, by capitalism's pillaging of the planet, and by the contagion of white supremacy, we shut down. We add layers and layers of armor imprisoning our hearts. Given multiple disasters, one tripping on the heels of the last, psychic numbing can be lethal. We need Jeremiahs more than ever.

Conclusion

I have focused on Dr. Martin Luther King Jr. as the quintessential embodiment of the prophetic ethos that compelled Amos, Isaiah, Jeremiah, and their kin in all ages. He was America's twentieth-century Jeremiah. In theory and practice he propelled the jeremiad to a new level of meaning and relevance. Cornel West is surely right when he argues that there is a "radical King" who can be discovered behind the "hagiographic haze" of our collective narrative of Saint Martin. A master of the synthetic imagination, King fused the jeremiad tradition with elements drawn from the American civil religion, and from the Protestant Social Gospel mixed with the Christian Realism of Reinhold Niebuhr. All the while, he remained solidly rooted in the spiritual life of the Southern Black church. He harnessed these multiple sources to nonviolent practice. This synthesis points a way forward for the American jeremiad, saving it from degenerating into an alienating harangue, a blanket condemnation that smothers any possibility of hope. Dr. King epitomizes what West calls an "organic intellectual," namely, a person who embodies in action what he argues for intellectually and one whose core ideas have been incubated in community.[32]

Engaged Buddhists rooted in American culture can see Dr. King as our elder and as one who with many others put his shoulder to a new turning of the wheel. Having examined three examples of Dr. King's jeremiad, we can point out more explicitly how his thinking and practice overlap with and expand that of Engaged Buddhists.

- The world is not fixed. Two revolutions are transforming the globe, and a third revolution of values is called for if the world house is not to burn to the ground. In this historical moment, the law of impermanence faces us with a choice: chaos or community?

- Dr. King's understanding of interdependence includes the imperative to address the collective forms of three poisons: materialism/economic exploitation/poverty (greed), militarism (ill will), and racism (delusion) that pollute, warp, and, at worst, eat away at the network of mutuality that binds us all together.

- Systemic injustice: Good will and a general commitment are not enough. King's discourse maintains a prophetic edge. Ignorance and evil must be denounced and confronted in practice. The impacted "boil" of structural violence must be brought to the surface. Each poison demands a specific strategy, a specific antidote.

- Transformation of the self and the work for social change must not be bifurcated. Nonviolence, as Dr. King practiced it, is a disciplined form of action that requires careful spiritual preparation and a deep personal commitment. Its specific stages bear family resemblances to aspects of the Buddhist Eightfold Path: investigation (right view), spiritual preparation (right intention), cultivating discipline (right effort), and willingness to put one's life on the line (right action). Taken as a unified practice, nonviolent resistance becomes a form of right concentration.

- King's jeremiad is directed most sharply against religious communities and their leaders. They merely echo popular opinion instead of shaping it through a prophetic message. In Buddhist terms they (and we) mistake complacency for equanimity, "law and order" for peace, and well-meaning intentions for effective love. With notable exceptions (e.g., Rita Gross's forceful critique of patriarchal Buddhism), Engaged Buddhists have not similarly challenged Buddhist sanghas.[33] If we agree with Dr. King that the collective poisons do indeed pervade American society, how might sanghas shape their teachings and practices to offer an antidote?

- Closely related to Dr. King's judgment upon the religious communities is his claim that America is sick unto death. The parable of Rip van Winkle adds a new layer of meaning to waking up. We all are in danger of sleeping through a revolution. This raises the question: Has America been in a moral coma for the past fifty plus years? If so, what do Buddhists have to offer to reawaken us from our collective coma?

- As with the classical prophets, Dr. King's understanding of time diverges sharply from the American myth of progress. He focuses upon "the fierce urgency of now." That "now" is shaped by the subversive memory of Exodus, and it gives shape to an alternative future, the future of King's "World House" dream. How does Dr. King's understanding of time lead us to a reconsideration of Buddhism's emphasis on "the present moment?" What do Buddhist have to draw upon as a subversive memory and an alternative future?

In a piece published only after his murder, King restates his concern that America is courting spiritual death and that she risks ending in ruins as did so many empires of the past. African Americans will no longer be confined in a wretched present. They and their white allies will batter down the prison walls. "Today's dissenters," he states unequivocally in his final words, "tell the complacent majority that the time has come when further evasion of social responsibility in a turbulent world will court disaster and death. America has not changed because so many think it need not change, but this is the illusion of the damned. . . . America must change."[34] More than fifty years later, America still turns a deaf ear to its most compelling Jeremiah, even as it elevates him to sanctity. In this light, Rabbi Heschel's prophetic claim that America's future depends on what it creates from King's legacy sounds foreboding. Only by collectively heeding the prophetic voice might we, Americans, prove that it is not too late. Faced with such a challenge, we might well tremble at King's own haunting words at Riverside Church: "You have not really known me."

Buddhist Reflections in a Prophetic Key #6
Reinventing Buddhism in a Hostile Society

In the case of the Japanese, their oriental habits of life and their . . . inability to assimilate biologically, and what is more important, our inability to distinguish the subverters and saboteurs from the rest of the mass, made necessary their class evacuation.

—Lt. Col. William A. Boekel to Col. Karl Bendetsen, Western Defense Command[1]

A viper is nonetheless a viper wherever the egg is hatched.

—*Los Angeles Times* editorial, February 1942[2]

Following the days of Pearl Harbor, doubt, fear and suspicion have arisen, hindering the progress of our religion. . . . Many are reluctant to say with pride that they are Buddhists. In spite of all this I still choose Buddhism. . . . It is the newest of religions, brought over by our fathers and mothers from their homeland. . . . We [second generation], too, can follow this path. . . . By our actions and deeds, the American public will come to know Buddhism is nothing to fear and suspect but a religion that will be an asset to a greater and a finer America.

—Misao Yumibe[3]

Dr. Martin Luther King Jr. challenges us to confront the three poisons: militarism, racism, and exploitation/poverty. Racism, a collective delusion, has warped the American experience since 1619. Slavery is the paramount institution created by racism but only one of its products. Think of racism as a rhizome that sends up its shoots in many times and places but all of which are connected to a common subterranean root. In this light the imprisonment of American citizens of Japanese ancestry and Japanese legal residents in concentration camps during World War II may appear to be of lesser rank, but, surely, unjustly imposed suffering should never be ranked. For those confined, the experience was devastating.[4] While the Germans herded Jews into concentration camps, so did America with its citizens of Japanese ancestry. While Germans forced Jewish citizens to wear a yellow star, so Japanese American citizens living under martial law in Hawaii were forced to wear a black badge. They were restricted from holding certain jobs just as Jews in the Netherlands under German occupation and elsewhere were excluded from whole classes of employment.[5] So, the wheel of evil turned in a new direction; the old visage donned a new mask.

We can see the first shoots of racism directed against Asian immigrants in the Chinese Exclusion Act of 1882 and its follow-up in the Oriental Exclusion Act of 1924. These laws together denied to Asian immigrants the possibility of becoming naturalized citizens. I, however, cannot get past the fact that had my parents been Japanese Americans and not Irish Americans, I would have been born in one of those concentration camps. While the Chicago chapter of the Buddhist Peace Fellowship has participated in and helped organize an annual vigil at the site of the Manhattan Project to remember the crime against humanity in the atomic bombing of Hiroshima and Nagasaki, Buddhist sanghas—with notable exceptions—have not faced up to the trauma inflicted on fellow Buddhists in early 1942. How can we rid our sanghas of this serpent when its presence is hidden in amnesia?

In *American Sutra: A Story of Faith and Freedom in the Second World War,* Duncan Ryuken Williams blows away the smog of ignorance. He documents the resilience of the Japanese American community, their determination to publicly proclaim their loyalty to America while resisting being stripped of their religious and cultural identity, as can be seen in the proud declaration of Misao Yumibe. In the process, Williams maintains, they forged "an American Sutra," a lotus born in a literal sea of mud, or, depending on their camp's location, in an ocean of sand.[6]

Japanese American Buddhists were doubly suspect as both a racial "other" and as "heathens" within a "Christian civilization." The government explicitly targeted the leaders of the Japanese American community in Hawaii. Well before Pearl Harbor it had created a list of leaders who were to be arrested on national security grounds in case of war. Within hours of the bombing at Pearl Harbor hundreds of first-generation priests in Hawaii were arrested by the FBI as well as a few leaders on the West Coast. With many priests held in segregated locations, it was up to Buddhist lay persons, wives of priests, and some second-generation priests to keep Buddhism alive in the camps. They did so by introducing some elements of American Protestantism: Sunday services, singing hymns, and conducting "Dharma schools" while retaining key elements of their Japanese traditions. In so doing they resisted the clear intention of Dillon Myer, the director of the War Relocation Authority, to foster assimilation to "Christian European American norms" as the solution to "the Japanese problem."[7]

What is striking is the virulent racism that spawned the ideology that Japanese American citizens were of a different species, unknowable and, therefore, not to be trusted. Combined with public hysteria over early Japanese conquests in the Pacific, this racism created a volatile mixture that fostered such attitudes as expressed in the *Los Angeles Times* "vipers" editorial. Racist attacks persisted after the war, when Japanese Americans returned to their homes to find refusals of service, vandalism, looted household goods, and blatant death threats.[8]

American Sutra tells the story of Japanese Americans' resistance to assimilation to the "Christian civilization," confident that they could be both committed Buddhists and loyal Americans. This is also a story of reinventing Buddhism, offering in a situation of extreme duress a new turning of the dharma wheel. In so doing they proclaimed a vision of America as a multiethnic, multiracial, and multireligious society. But my question is this: How do we, Buddhists in the American context, come to terms with the fact that the earliest groups to plant Buddhist communities on these shores were subjected to racism expressed in attitudes, laws, and unjust incarceration? I do not see in the Beat Generation or in the convert sanghas that formed in the following decades any pointed, sustained—prophetic—efforts to come to terms with the shameful legacy of racism as it manifested in tearing citizens and legal residents from their homes and placing them in concentration camps. A prophetic American Buddhism will ferret out the tangled history of racism, its trail of dukkha, as it extends its tentacles into the present. Given that new generations of Asian immigrants in the post-1965 period have faced racist attacks, as did those who "looked Asian" during the Covid pandemic, what does solidarity with our coreligionists demand of all American Buddhists if we are to awaken from our historical amnesia?

Part Three

From Prophecy to Praxis:
Strategic Action and Social Liberation

Chapter Eight

Nonviolent Action

The Dynamics of Love, Power, and Justice

What most people call power, Buddhists call cravings.

—Thich Nhat Hanh, *The Art of Power*[1]

When collective power, whether in the form of imperialism or class domination, exploits weakness, it can never be dislodged unless power is raised against it. . . . Social injustice cannot be resolved by moral and rational suasion alone. . . . Conflict is inevitable, and in conflict power must be challenged by power.

—Reinhold Niebuhr, *Moral Man Immoral Society*[2]

Social activists often have difficulty understanding and accepting the importance of political power. For many, power is a negative term. Power is corruption. Power is what we are fighting. . . . For many, power is the very antithesis of morality. . . . Yet power is fundamentally important to political change. Social activism is all about power.

—David Cortright, *Gandhi and Beyond*[3]

Part 3 argues that social transformation requires strategic action. Neither compassion nor jeremiads is enough to guide action. Strategic thinking is necessary. In the last two years of his life, Dr. Martin Luther King Jr. was confronted by a younger generation of Black leaders who had been bloodied organizing Black communities in the South. They repudiated King's grounding of nonviolence in love and espoused a gospel of Black Power. King listened deeply to his challengers and responded by calling for a dialectic of love, power, and justice. Chapter 8 wrestles with this dialectic as a koan for social activists. Chapter 9 argues that Engaged Buddhists must couple a prophetic imagination with a historical diagnosis, and a critical social theory to uncover the delusions propagated by the prevailing ideologies. Finally, chapter 10 illustrates how a diverse group of Engaged Buddhists, committed to deep listening, might analyze America's endemic pathology of racism, sketch a vision of an alternative future, and weigh a number of strategies for action as an antidote to this disease, and then move to act.

Nonviolent action is central to Engaged Buddhism and an indispensable method for pursuing complete liberation. It is also an exercise of power. An aversion to the exercise of power, David Cortright and Reinhold Niebuhr imply, is a handicap for any Engaged Buddhist. However, many Engaged Buddhists share Thich Nhat Hanh's reservations about the exercise of power. Thich Nhat Hanh's and Cortright's social activists recognize how the will to power powerfully generates ill will and delusion. The Hebrew prophets too spurned the power politics of their day. They saw how the possession of power easily blinds one to its impact on others. But not all Engaged Buddhists agree. We have seen how Dr. Ambedkar employed numerous skillful means to empower Dalits. He stated forthrightly, "What I want is power—political power for my people—for if we have power, he continued, we have social status."[4] Power in all its permutations, I suggest, is a koan that Engaged Buddhists must wrestle with.[5]

Power Redefined

Hannah Arendt, the renowned political theorist of totalitarianism and revolution, may help us in our wrestling with this koan. In *On Violence,* Arendt developed an understanding of power that directly opposes the common view that violence is the ultimate form of power, and that to rule is to dominate other human beings by means of physical and structural violence. The idea that all power derives from the barrel of a gun and that the threat of violence alone can produce an obedient citizenry was grounded on a fundamental misunderstanding of power.[6] "Power and violence," Arendt insisted, "are opposites. . . . Violence appears when power is in jeopardy but left to its own course it ends in power's disappearance."[7]

Sound strange? We first need to understand that Arendt holds that the ability to act, to bring forth something new, is what distinguishes human beings from other animals, and it is what makes us political animals: "It enables [a person] to get together with his peers; to act in concert, and to reach out for goals and enterprises that would never enter into his mind, let alone the desires of his heart, had he not been given this gift—to embark on something new."[8] The key here is the phrase "to act in concert." Power arises out of a meeting of minds on a course of action. Power endures until enough actors no longer see its form and exercise as legitimate and withdraw their support.[9] In those circumstances, those who are "in power" may be tempted to substitute violence for their eroding power.

Clearly Arendt does not equate power with domination and its command-obedience framework. To further complicate matters, Arendt maintains that the phrase "nonviolent power" is redundant.[10] Another way to put it is that what Thich Nhat Hanh sees as power rooted in craving is not actually power at all but a form of violence, a will to power that expresses ill will toward all but the self. Coercion on the part of those "in power" eats away at the authority invested in the regime, becoming its own worst enemy.

Among the proponents of nonviolence, Gene Sharp has developed the most complete analysis of and argument for nonviolent action as an expression of power. He, like Arendt, subscribes to a social interaction view of power that "sees rulers or other command systems, despite appearances, to be dependent on the population's good will . . . and support. . . . Power always depends . . . upon a replenishment of its sources by the cooperation of numerous institutions and people—cooperation that does not have to continue."[11] More specifically, any regime depends on a pervasive sense of legitimacy. Those in power are invested with authority. "No matter how great their means of physical coercion," Sharp continues, "all rulers require an acceptance of their . . . right to rule and command. *The key to habitual obedience is to reach the mind*" (italics added).[12] It is this acquiescence that must be overcome. Nonviolent action—whether or not it breaks any law—begins with an act of disobedience. The authority of the ruler or of a law or custom is called into question. So, the first step in a nonviolent campaign is not to convert the opponent but to change the mind of the oppressed, to transform passive resignation into felt agency.[13] Sharp and Arendt offer complementary arguments. Sharp sees the importance of an initial break, a mental liberation that Buddhists can affirm. Arendt sees action-in-concert as most important in bringing forth something new.

If Engaged Buddhists are to integrate a prophetic voice, it would be helpful to see where the Hebrew prophets stood on the exercise of power. They undoubtedly exercised the power of direct confrontation of unjust authority. At God's instruction, Jeremiah dictates a scroll to his amanuensis, Baruch, who reads it both in the temple and before officers of the royal court. The king, presented with the scroll, cuts it to pieces and burns it, at which point Jeremiah dictates a new scroll with an added denunciation of the king's recalcitrance (Jer 36). Neither Jeremiah nor any of the prophets are the kind of persons who seek a meeting of the minds. But that is hardly fair to them. The prophets' God was not arbitrarily willful. The prophets' judgment was that the covenant—the social contract—had been abrogated by the elites and their beneficiaries and that their power had become illegitimate in God's eyes. The callousness toward the vulnerable (the widow, the orphan, and the stranger in their midst) of those craving power was a form of violence. The power of the king of Judah or, for that matter, of the Babylonian empire is ephemeral.

James Jasper, who studies contemporary "moral protests," sees power anchored in what he calls "legitimating frames." The Hebrew prophets call those frames into question and outline an "injustice frame." They claim that those wielding power have abandoned shared social principles, that is, the covenant.[14] They tear off the mask of divinely sanctioned authority; they strip away the illusion of eternity from the established institutions; they uncover the hidden cancer threatening the nation. "This people—/to what /compare them?" writes peace activist Daniel Berrigan, translating Isaiah 30:12–13, "a firm-seeming wall/ a mortal crack runs through./ It sways, it heaves and buckles/ and falls asunder!"[15]

The injustice frame includes an alternative reading of history. The trajectory of the idealized past has veered away from the established institutions of the present. The prophets do not subscribe to history as the self-glorification of the empire du jour. Nor do they sanction the political maneuvers of the vassal states, including Judah. They denounce the charade that is called realpolitik. Jeremiah, walking the streets of Jerusalem wearing an iron yoke, declares what will come of that gambit.

Love and Power

Prophets are not pastors, nor are they reformists working within established institutions. In *The Prophet and the Bodhisattva*, I argued that prophetic action under the conditions of modernity aligns with social movements, movements that consciously confront injustice.[16] Similarly, what Rabbi Ward-Lev argued about the Hebrew prophets' transforming the Exodus event into an ongoing moral journey fits with how social movements function in modern societies. "Social movements," James Jasper argues, "are . . . an important source of innovation and creativity in modern society."

> Much like artists, [protestors] are at the cutting edge of society's understanding of itself as it changes. Moral protesters are often sensitive to moral dilemmas the rest of us ignore; they sometimes generate new ways of understanding the complexities of the human condition. . . . Even when we disagree with their positions, they frequently force us . . . to decide if our intuitions are consonant with our basic values. They extend our moral languages. . . . In the face of social change, protesters are like the proverbial canaries in the mines, except that they sing out rather than quietly expire.[17]

The foremost proponent of nonviolent movements as a form of power after Gandhi was Martin Luther King Jr. Engaged Buddhists committed to social change can learn a great deal from a careful examination of Dr. King's theory of nonviolent action. As we saw in the previous chapter, nonviolent action expresses a commitment to dialogue at its heart. Nonviolence, as a complex form of concerted and strategic action, pushes forward to breach the walls of exclusion without creating new walls to imprison its opponents. Injustice invariably wears a mask of legitimacy that covers the will to dominate, and nonviolent actors *do* tear it off. Those whose power is eroding frequently resort to violence to impose their will and in so doing forfeit their authority. The Southern sheriffs' posses, with their horses and cattle prods, confronting the civil rights marchers demonstrated only the impotence of violence in defense of entrenched power.

Dr. King did not need to read Reinhold Niebuhr's *Moral Man and Immoral Society*, as he did in graduate school, to recognize the recalcitrance of entrenched "power." Jim Crow taught that painful lesson every day. Nonviolence does more than unmask the violence hiding behind the prevailing legitimating frame. Fusing love, power, and justice, Dr. King offers his own justice frame. In his earliest writings, King argued that nonviolence embodied love as *agape*. *Agape*, one of several Greek terms for "love," is not to be confused with romantic love, with "liking," or even with friendship. Agape is unconditional love for every person. It is the unassailable sense of the intrinsic worth of all human beings and it is embodied in actions premised on this understanding. Throughout his writings and sermons, King stresses that agape is love in action.[18] Agape in action breaks through the armored skin of established power.

In words that seem to echo the *Dhammapada,* Dr. King argues that violence perpetuates itself in a chain reaction of hate begetting hate. Agape is the one force that can break the chain: "In the final analysis agape means a recognition of the fact that all life in interrelated. All humanity is involved in a single process." Agape is also the one force that can mend a broken community; it can create community from the dry bones of our hatreds. "When I am commanded to love," Dr. King said, indicating that agape is not so much a matter of feelings as of a responsive will, "I am commanded to restore community, to resist injustice and to meet the needs of my brother."[19]

Despite the emphasis on love and reconciliation, Dr. King never denied the presence of an element of coercion in nonviolent action.[20] For example, a boycott, while nonviolent, does financially harm a merchant. Nonviolent actors would organize a boycott only after other tactics had been met with resistance. Given a spirit shaped by agape and with the intention of achieving eventual reconciliation, the element of coercion was justifiable. Dr. King went further in suggesting that nonviolent pressure was the most effective politics for an oppressed minority. It had the potential—in the aftermath of a successful campaign—to create a community based on mutual respect and "complete equality."[21] And then Dr. King added a key qualification: "Men are not easily . . . purged of their prejudices and irrational feelings. . . . So the nonviolent approach does not immediately change the heart of the oppressor. It first does something to the hearts and souls of those committed to it. It gives them self-respect; it calls up resources of strength and courage that they did not know they had. Finally, it reaches the opponent and so stirs his conscience that reconciliation becomes a reality."[22]

In the aftermath of the landmark civil rights legislation of 1964 and 1965, four contextual factors, argues Harvard scholar, Brandon Terry, led Dr. King to deepen his understanding of the relationship of love and power: the structural violence of urban poverty, the virulence of the white backlash of the mid-1960s, the crisis created by the war in Vietnam, and "the visceral challenge of Black Power."[23] Especially in relation to the young men and women who had suffered greatly working in the trenches of the civil rights movement, and to the youth in the Northern ghettos, Dr. King's Christian rhetoric of self-sacrificing goodwill rang hollow.

To his credit, Dr. King took each of these challenges to the efficacy of nonviolent action seriously.[24] As always, he sought to create a dialectical synthesis, in this case between his understanding of agape and the necessity to exercise power to reach just goals. In *Where Do We Go from Here: Chaos or Community?*, Dr. King defines power initially in neutral terms as "the ability to achieve purpose." African American efforts to achieve political and economic power, like any other social group, are legitimate expressions of power put to a good purpose. Then Dr. King pushes more deeply. "One of the greatest problems of history," he suggests, "is that love and power are usually contrasted as polar opposites." Viewing nonviolence as a *powerless* effort at purely moral persuasion versus violent "power" reflects this false understanding. "What is needed," he continues, "is a realization that power without love is reckless and abusive and love without power is sentimental and anemic. *Power at its best is love implementing the demands of justice. Justice at its best is love correcting everything that stands against love*" (italics added).[25]

I have struggled over the meaning of the last two sentences for a long time. I see them as expressing something similar to what Buddhist scholar and practitioner John Makransky calls "fierce compassion."[26] What stands in the way of love is not only the obduracy of individuals but also oppressive institutions, ideologies, laws, and policies that together constitute structural violence. Power, gained through unified, strategic action on multiple fronts, is necessary to break apart these cemented structures that warp all our lives while traumatizing some in significantly more violent ways. Love is the spiritual energy to act powerfully to create new just structures replacing the existing power structure.

"The Negro," King concludes, "has not gained a single right without persistent pressure and agitation. . . . White America will never admit [the Negro] to equal rights unless it is coerced into doing it."[27] Neither Gandhi nor Dr. King suspended their efforts when conversion did not occur. They moved ahead with nonviolent actions to bring about change in spite of the recalcitrance of entrenched power. Nonviolent methods in contrast to violent methods create the possibility that mutual recognition may occur *at some point*. Speaking to striking sanitation workers in Memphis less than a week before he was murdered, Dr. King urged them not to despair and not to go back to work until their demands were met. "If we are going to get equality, to get adequate wages, we are going to have to struggle for it." It won't be served up on a silver platter. It might be necessary, he continued, to call for a "general work stoppage." "We need power," he concluded. "What is power? Walter Ruether said once that 'power is the ability of a labor union like the UAW to make the most powerful corporation in the world—General Motors—say yes when it wants to say no.' That's power."[28]

In the face of widespread hostility locally toward the striking sanitation workers and nationally toward Dr. King and his movement, both power and love were given a tougher meaning. In the aftermath of civil rights successes but facing the immense challenges of social and economic injustice, Dr. King was clear: his Poor People's Campaign would not be fully effective in altering the basic political and economic structures of runaway capitalism "until it has achieved the massive dimensions, the disciplined planning, and the intense commitment of a sustained direct-action movement of civil disobedience on the national scale."[29] This "testament of hope" is, to say the very least, a far cry from the domesticated voice of the sanctified Martin Luther King of our civil religion. More than fifty years later, Dr. King's hope remains as distant as ever.

Justice

"Seek Justice. Rescue the oppressed" (Isa 1:17). From Isaiah to Dr. King the central theme of the prophetic tradition is justice. Engaged Buddhists have an ambivalent relationship to justice discourse. Some decline to use the concept at all. The ambivalence arises from assuming that retribution for misdeeds is what justice seeks. The Hebrew prophets, speaking about justice, frequently employ the adversarial rhetoric of the courtroom. That language implies a clear-cut distinction between who is right and who is wrong.[30] Retribution flows from a determination of guilt. When "justice" is seen as what the courts do, Buddhists demure. From a Buddhist standpoint, a sharp delineation between guilt and innocence ignores the reality of interdependence. We all have a hand in shaping those whom we label "criminals." Moreover, retributive justice increases the amount of suffering in the world. It is a clear break with the intent of the Four Noble Truths to end both individual and collective dukkha.

In the pursuit of justice, social movements frequently employ dualistic rhetoric that may well be another source of Buddhist ambivalence. The contemporary refrain of activists, "No justice, no peace," rings false to Buddhists' ears. It sounds like a declaration of war.[31] "All violence," counters Thich Nhat Hanh, "is injustice."[32]

Engaged Buddhists's approaches to the concept of justice are more complex than a simple rejection of retributive justice. Most Engaged Buddhists, such as the Dalai Lama, are forthright in their use of rights language that, arguably, forms the conceptual core of theories of justice in the Western liberal tradition. Likewise, virtually all Engaged Buddhists work with some understanding of *distributive* justice. Thai Engaged Buddhist Sulak Sivaraksa argues, "As a Buddhist, I cannot consider economic efficiency as the ultimate value for a social order. I am constrained to evaluate a system of social organization in terms of its capacity to address human suffering, to promote distributive justice and allow for individuals within society to realize their full potential."[33] When he was told of the rapid growth of billionaires in the United States, the Dalai Lama said much the same thing only with overtones of prophetic denunciation: "This I consider to be completely immoral. . . . While millions do not have the basic necessities of life—adequate food, shelter, education and medical facilities—the inequity of wealth distribution is a scandal."[34] Sri Lanka's Sarvodaya movement pursues its version of distributive justice by facilitating the creation of "no poverty/no affluence" village republics in which basic physical and health requirements and educational, cultural, and spiritual needs are met.[35]

The concept of "social justice" is both more capacious and more fluid. It goes beyond while including negative rights, that is, the individual's immunities from unjust interference with personal liberty, and beyond the distribution of basic goods. It is closer in meaning to Sarvodaya's core needs, which include access to an enriching culture and moral and spiritual development. Despite being host to a plethora of interpretations, we can point to some overlapping meanings of social justice. First, it implies that the prevailing social system is not simply maladjusted, it is oppressive, at least for key members of the society. Direct or structural violence, overt or hidden violence, is asserted to dominate some groups to ensure benefits for those who claim power. Second, social justice takes its shape in the minds of those who resist abusive power. They recognize that another world is possible. Third, as such, social justice is intrinsic to movement politics. It is not a fixed state of collective existence but a collective process. Never at rest, it pushes toward a future in which all are freed from domination and can enact power democratically. Each person is enabled to flourish. As a process, it is periodically reinvigorated by prophetic fire. Finally, recall Dr. Ambedkar's understanding of justice as involving a persistent tension between equality and liberty that can be mediated only through loving-kindness (*maitri*). In the context of a collective movement, *maitri* is better understood as solidarity. Movements toward social justice rely on participants enacting the solidarity that they envision as key to a just future. When solidarity wanes, the movement fizzles.

Most Buddhist models of justice do not focus on *collective* action in pursuit of social justice. I also miss in these Buddhist theories what was very clear in Dr. King's model, namely, a dialectical relationship between justice and love in which each depends upon and transforms the other. Sallie King's summary of Engaged Buddhist ambivalence about the language of justice is worth juxtaposing to Dr. King's. For the Buddhist thinkers whom we have studied, justice is ultimately inadequate: "Justice must be interpreted with compassion and mercy, non-negotiable Buddhist values that . . . may sometimes be in conflict with the rhetoric of justice. If there is a conflict, it seems, we should hang on to compassion and mercy and let ideas of justice go."[36] To the contrary, I would rather hold on to the possibility that further thought and practice might lead to a genuine dialectic between seemingly conflicting ideals, letting go of fixed ideas about both justice and compassion.

Power Embodied in Social Organizations

Undoubtedly the strongest form of countervailing power in the lifetime of many of us was the African American struggle for civil rights—and later for social and economic rights. We generally focus on the civil rights movement and its use of a quiverful of nonviolent tactics (marches, boycotts, sit-ins, and freedom rides, among others). However, that is only part of the story. Without the support, both spiritual and logistical, of the Southern Black churches there would not have been a civil rights movement. Nurturing communities, such as the Black churches, create solidarity. They empower activists, spiritually ground their commitment to social change, and heal the wounds inevitable in any political struggle. Likewise, the role of the NAACP working through the federal court system was crucial. We forget that it was a Supreme Court decision in a case brought by the NAACP, not the capitulation of the City of Montgomery authorities, that crowned the bus boycott with success. In previous writings, I have argued that examples of successful resistance to oppression such as the Montgomery bus boycott resulted from a "working of the linkages" among supportive communities, courageous movements, and "countervailing institutions." The latter were well-established and often well-funded supporters working through the system.[37]

Let's look at Thich Nhat Hanh's claim about power as craving viewed in the light of these multiple types of expressing power nonviolently. "Community building is our true practice," Thich Nhat Hanh insists.[38] From the point of view that we have been developing, community building is an expression of transformative power. Thich Nhat Hanh takes a long-range view in seeing how such communities can build a culture of peace: "When we protest against a war, we may assume that we are a peaceful person . . . but this might not be the case. If we look deeply we will observe that the roots of war are in the unmindful ways we have been living. We have not sown enough seeds of peace and understanding in ourselves and others, therefore, we are co-responsible. . . . To prevent war, to prevent the next crisis, we must begin right now. . . . If we and our children practice ahimsa in our daily lives, . . . we will begin to establish real peace and, in that way, we may be able to prevent the next war."[39] Engaged Buddhists all seem to affirm that—in Thich Nhat Hanh's words—making peace depends upon being peace. From this point of view, we all have the seeds of both peace and violence within ourselves. Cultivating seeds of peace requires training in ahimsa (nonharming). In Western ethical terms, ahimsa is a virtue to be cultivated in body, speech, and mind; it becomes a pervasive way of relating to the world. Recognizing the roots of violence within ourselves, we must shed all illusions of moral superiority. Seeing the causes and conditions underlying the current personal and collective reality, we learn to live in ways that are truly peaceful.[40]

Thich Nhat Hanh, in short, has outlined a process of transformation through nurturance (growing seeds of peace) that is its own form of power-without-craving that is fully appropriate for spiritual communities. But entrenched oppression, most often masquerading as beneficent authority, will not simply melt away under the sunlight that sprouts seeds. It will repress fledgling shoots, like King's vision of a Beloved Community, treat them as something sinister or as fantasies to be scorned. Spiritual communities that nurture ahimsa are not enough.

Here is where engaged Buddhists should reflect carefully on Reinhold Niebuhr's and Dr. King's dictum that entrenched power rarely reforms itself without being forced to do so. We have already seen that social movements using nonviolent methods exercise power to shatter the aura of legitimacy that undergirds unjust and entrenched power. This can involve dislodging those who hold such power.

In addition to nonviolent movements for social change expressing prophetic power, countervailing institutions, such as the NAACP, use institutionalized levers of power to transform the establishment.[41] Power as nurturance, power as resisting injustice, and power as reforming the system—each has a role to play in bringing about a more just society. Dr. B.

R. Ambedkar was that rare person who employed multiple skillful means to attack the injustice of the caste system. He established hostels—that later evolved into colleges—as housing and refuges for Dalits seeking higher education. He donned the mantle of a prophet in his attack on the caste system and espousal of radical equality. This included symbolic acts of resistance such as burning the *Manusmriti*. He led *satyagraha* campaigns and created a movement among Dalits for conversion to Buddhism. Finally, he worked with the British, the Congress Party, and within the new, postindependence government to secure basic rights for Dalits. Each of these actions expressed a different type of power.

Social movements are an obvious locus for the expression of prophetic power. Another social source of power that Buddhists can access is that of the voluntary association, especially those that act in concert with other NGOs to advocate for particular causes and for oppressed or underserved groups. As early as the 1830s, Alexis de Tocqueville saw associations created by ordinary people as a prominent feature of American society.[42] These myriad associations together constitute civil society as a source of power that can be a counterweight to the market and the state. In the era of the internet, a new form of countervailing power has emerged. Transnational advocacy networks (TANs) have exploded in numbers. Many of these NGOs function with an edge, with fierce compassion. Combining their resources, they do not primarily seek a harmonious society but rather to shake things up through advocacy on behalf of those whom established power ignores or oppresses.

From my viewpoint, the best example of a TAN revolution was the International Campaign to Abolish Landmines. It began in 1992 with a coalition of six small NGOs but grew to include more than one thousand organizations, including such well-institutionalized giants as the International Committee of the Red Cross. The Landmine TAN first created a social norm that stigmatized the deployment of landmines as a pernicious weapon that continues to wreak havoc on the lives of civilians long after the cessation of hostilities. As this network grew into a movement, it was able to bring together an unprecedented alliance of NGOs with United Nations agencies and some midrange nations led by Canada to convene the "Ottawa Process." This, in turn, produced a UN treaty in 1997 initially signed by 122 nations. While some of the most heavily militarized nations did not sign the treaty, the power of shame led the United States, for example, to foreswear the use but not the stockpiling of this weapon.[43] The campaign that most had labeled a quixotic endeavor became a new type of countervailing power.

Mindfulness Trainings as Koans

One last time let us examine Thich Nhat Hanh's understanding of power, but now by looking at the Fourteen Mindfulness Trainings for the Order of Interbeing. Thich Nhat Hanh goes well beyond the prophetic denunciations of the destruction of his homeland. His mindfulness trainings provide forms of practice that lead persons to act in pursuit of social justice. He makes it very clear that Engaged Buddhist practice focuses on outward action as well as on inner work. These trainings present a nuanced understanding of power. The first eight trainings focus on freeing the mind of fixed ideologies, on creating inner peace and compassion, transforming anger, and reconciling conflicts.[44] Each of these trainings cultivates ahimsa. The later trainings focus on collective as well as individual transformation. I see several of these trainings as forming contemporary koans for Engaged Buddhists to reflect and act upon. Casting some of these trainings in the form of a koan, I suggest, is an important injunction. Koans are not so much meant to be solved as they are to be lived. Let your vigorous work for social justice be subjected to persistent questioning, challenging all forms of fanaticism and self- or collective aggrandizement.

So, in the Ninth Training we are to avoid uttering "words that might cause division or hatred" but also "to speak out about situations of injustice."[45] In the Tenth Training we are to avoid turning the sangha "into a political instrument" but also told that a spiritual community should take a clear stance against oppression "without engaging in partisan conflicts."[46] The Twelfth Training urges us "not to kill" but also "not to let others kill," which presumably could involve a variety of exercises of power, ranging from electoral politics to nonviolent direct action to rein in the war machine.[47] Finally, in the Thirteenth Training we are not to possess things that rightfully belong to others. This is interpreted within a broad scope because we are also called to "prevent others from profiting from human suffering or the suffering of other beings."[48] This training, presumably, would entail not only personal engagement but also collective efforts to bring about a thoroughgoing transformation of global capitalism, what Joanna Macy calls "the Great Turning."[49]

Commenting upon the Tenth Training, Thich Nhat Hanh tells us to follow the method of the Four Noble Truths in putting the training into practice. First, clearly expose the situation of injustice that imposes suffering, naming it for what it is. Second, be specific in detailing the causes of social suffering. Third, plainly describe the goal as removing the suffering, that is, not to gain political power for oneself or one's group. Finally, propose measures that can end the unjust suffering.[50] As makes eminent sense from a Buddhist standpoint, each of these engaged Noble Truths focuses on suffering. This Buddhist way of tackling injustice could also be applied to the other trainings that focus on some form of oppression. To take the measure of this way of addressing each "justice koan" we may juxtapose Thich Nhat Hanh's four steps with the steps that a nonviolent campaign must follow as Dr. King outlined them in the Birmingham letter: (1) gather facts and analyses of the injustice; (2) negotiation; (3) self-purification (i.e., training in and commitment to nonviolent action); and (4) direct action. The aim of King's four steps is to bring the parties back to the negotiation table to resolve the injustice.[51] Thich Nhat Hanh's model nicely dovetails with Dr. King's steps 1 and 2. The Fourteen Trainings themselves provide an excellent approach to cultivating nonviolent discipline, that is, Dr. King's step 3. What is missing is King's step 4 and an understanding of how Buddhists ought to engage with social movements, TANs, and countervailing institutions with their distinctive expressions of nonviolent power that differ from those of spiritual communities. Also, Thich Nhat Hanh stops short of suggesting what the Eightfold Path would look like beyond presenting proposals for addressing injustice.[52] What happens when your proposals for moving toward justice are dismissed out of hand or, worse, ignored entirely? There still would remain the injunction, for example, "not to let others kill" or, to give one more example, "to prevent others from profiting from human suffering." Buddhist social activism requires a much broader repertoire of skillful means.

As we saw in our discussion of King's Birmingham letter, negative peace, the peace of law and order without justice, is not true peace. Nonviolent action creates a crisis because it unburies unjust suffering. Certainly, the nonviolent actors may experience the suffering of repression from opponents who have cemented their identity within unjust structures. To some degree, everyone experiences the suffering of a disrupted society. Nevertheless, nonviolent agents refuse to allow unjust suffering to be reburied. This is the trauma of change. Dr. King did not shy away from a determined exposure of the cancerous body politic as a prerequisite to healing. Nonviolent agents who are motivated by agape, unconditional love, hold open the possibility that through their respect for the humanity of the oppressor healing will occur.

Like most other religious traditions, Buddhist sects have not been exclusively committed to nonviolence. During the invasion of China and

World War II, many Japanese Zen priests strongly supported Japan's imperialistic violence. More recently, some Buddhist monks in Myanmar and Sri Lanka have strongly supported government violence directed at ethnic minorities. Yet virtually all those practitioners who identify themselves as "Engaged Buddhists" see, as Gandhi did, a clear link between means and ends. In practice, this means a principled commitment to nonviolent methods of social change.[53] For these Buddhists the tension between Thich Nhat Hanh's cultivation of ahimsa and Reinhold Niebuhr's position on the need for power to effect social change represents a koan that demands action tempered by wisdom and compassion.

Conclusion

We are now in position to offer several principles to guide a distinctively Buddhist form of social engagement.[54]

- *No outer revolution without an inner revolution.* This is a cardinal principle in the thinking of all Engaged Buddhists. Apart from a spiritual practice, action becomes an exercise in greed, ill will, and delusion.

- *Disobedience.* Gene Sharp makes the case that the first task of a movement for social change is to liberate the mind of potential activists from acquiescence to authority. Thich Nhat Hanh's first three mindfulness trainings function as an ideology solvent by challenging us to guard against dogmatism in any ideology, to open our minds to alternative points of view, and to avoid imposing our ideologies on others.[55]

- *Agape.* We practice unconditional good will toward all beings. Agape seeks a recognition of the infinite worth of all beings. Macy's Council of All Beings is an example of a ritual to develop agape. We cultivate agape in all our actions to liberate all beings. Agape creates solidarity beyond tribal loyalty. Dr. King's Beloved Community is the utopian vision grounded in agape that guides collective action.

- *Nonviolent action.* Nonviolent action is a corollary to agape. It fuses love and power. Nonviolence includes cultivating nondualism in the actions of body, speech, and mind. Nonviolence is never absolutely pure. It is both difficult and necessary to fuse love and power.

- *Power.* Buddhists develop and employ skillful means to carry forward the fusion of love and power, recognizing that the means and the ends are one. Different types of social groups have an affinity for different skillful means. Communities nurture and heal. Advocacy networks and movements are the preferred locus for the exercise of prophetic power that calls into question entrenched, unjust authority. Countervailing institutions use the system's levers of power to reform the power structure. They support and defend movements and communities.

- *Justice.* Compassion is not enough. This principle recognizes that the three poisons take collective forms. A just society requires structures—institutions, laws, policies, and norms embedded in the culture—that stabilize and undergird communities. Justice demands liberation from structural violence.

- *Democratic structures.* Large organizations require built-in checks and balances. This applies not only to governments but also to the governance structures of other large-scale institutions such as corporations. Prophetic criticism is necessary to unmask the claims of those who have arrogated power that they are only serving the "will of the people" or the demands of the market. Stated positively, provisions for participatory democracy should be in place for all institutions as well as conflict resolution processes.

- *Radical equality and collective liberation.* Radical equality demands that provision must be made that is tailored to the needs for each person to thrive. Seen from a prophetic perspective, a just distribution of a society's resources should embody a preferential option for the poor, the marginalized, and those who have been historically oppressed. Who has been left behind? The liberation, social as well as spiritual, of each is dependent on the liberation of all.

Hannah Arendt's theory of action-in-concert, Dr. King's prophetic understanding of the relationship of agape and power, Thich Nhat Hanh's koans for Buddhist activists, and the guiding principles for Buddhist activists offer a new slant on nonviolent action. We can call numerous expressions of power "craving," but not all. We are surely required to use the levers of power available to us as nonviolent activists to effect change in a violent society. Anything less appears to be a willful blindness to the reality that those in power seldom reform themselves unless forced to do so. As we act, we cultivate loving-kindness and fierce compassion. We train ourselves to avoid falling prey to pernicious dualisms, knowing all the while that purity is not an option.

Chapter Nine

From Prophecy to Praxis
Thinking Strategically about Action

I believe . . . that the condition of truth is to allow the suffering to speak. It doesn't mean that those who suffer have a monopoly on truth, but it means that the condition of truth to emerge must be in tune with those who are undergoing social misery—socially induced forms of suffering.

—Cornel West, *Prophetic Thought in Postmodern Times*[1]

There is no true word that is not at the same time a praxis. Thus, to speak a true word is to transform the world. . . . When a word is deprived of its dimension of action, reflection automatically suffers as well; and the word is changed into idle chatter, . . . into an alienated and alienating "blah."

—Paulo Freire, *Pedagogy of the Oppressed*[2]

In *Earth Household*, a collection of essays published in 1969, Gary Snyder, poet and Buddhist practitioner, called for a fusion of the theory and practice of social revolution with the multifaceted Buddhist wisdom traditions. "We need both," Snyder insisted. Traditional Buddhism, Snyder argued, excelled in the liberation of "a few dedicated individuals from psychological hangups and cultural conditioning. Institutional Buddhism has been conspicuously ready to accept or ignore the inequalities and tyrannies of whatever political system it found itself under. This can be death to Buddhism because it is death to any meaningful function of compassion."³ More than a half century later and despite the impressive record of Engaged Buddhism across the globe, the hybrid species of Buddhism envisioned by Snyder fusing in thought and practice, two histories and two trajectories of emancipation, remains more promise than reality.

David Loy, who has worked diligently to develop such a synthesis, agrees with Snyder. Traditional Buddhism, he says, lacked any "explicit social theory," a theory that might advance a "meaningful function of compassion." To be sure, there were many stories and sutras that touched upon the social institutions of their age but nothing like a normative analysis of prevailing social structures.⁴ The strategic use of power shaped by agape depends upon some grasp of the collective shape of dukkha in our historical context, or what Cornel West calls "social misery." In other words, a prophetic critique requires a social theory if it is to lead to strategic action or praxis. Social theory, in turn, arises out of the transformative actions emerging in our time. It draws upon multiple forms of Engaged Buddhist practice in promoting social change and the numerous theoretical discussions that shape those forms of practice.

As we have repeatedly seen, the vision of social revolution, as it developed in Western culture, was metaphorically mapped in the biblical story of Exodus. With the Hebrew prophets, Rabbi Ward-Lev has insisted, this story became a framework for an ongoing struggle. Again and again, the narrative trajectory of leaving Egypt, traveling through the wilderness, creating a covenanted community, and reaching the Promised Land has resurfaced to shape the politics of the West.⁵ Always the story has catalyzed critical reflection on the prevailing forms of oppression. In the late 1960s this story became the catalyst for emerging Christian base communities in Latin America seeking liberation from regimes that exploited the poor, and it gave rise to a new form of theology—liberation theology—that quickly spread globally. Liberation theologians appropriated Marx's famous dictum in his Eleventh Thesis on Feuerbach—"The philosophers have only *interpreted* the world in various ways; the point is to *change* it"—and saw it as constituting an "epistemological break" with preceding ways of reflecting theologically.⁶ Their break can be expressed in a single phrase: *praxis* is the key to any social revolution. The efforts of these theologians to map a religiously based, systematic theory of oppression and its overcoming will provide direction to similarly engaged Buddhists. Throughout this chapter I will draw comparisons with liberation theology to elucidate the development of a Buddhist social theory.

Praxis Defined

The term "praxis" has become so widely used as to be virtually evacuated of any shared meaning. It has been used, variously, as synonymous with "action," with acts that bring about any sort of transformation, and with practice as well as with actions seeking some form of social revolution. While in ancient Greek *praxis* was used to refer to action in general, with Aristotle it took on a distinctive meaning. Besides its general meaning, Aristotle "also uses 'praxis' to designate all of the ways of life open to a free man, and to signify the sciences and arts which deal with the activities characteristic of man's ethical and political life."[7] Christian theologian David Tracy offers a helpful clue to a more precise understanding of praxis: "Praxis is correctly understood as the critical relationship between theory and practice whereby each is . . . influenced and transformed by the other."[8] This understanding of praxis is widely confirmed by Latin American liberation theologians, for whom praxis gives rise to critical reflection that, in turn, sharpens and shapes further world-transforming action.[9]

The rapid rise of theologies of liberation rooted in various religious traditions and in different social contexts has led some Engaged Buddhist thinkers to ask what Buddhists can learn from their Christian counterparts. John Makransky focuses on epistemological issues in his reflections on the import of liberation theology for Buddhist social thought. Makransky sees the epistemological core in the liberation theologians' attempt to articulate God's "preferential option for the poor":

> [Latin American liberation theology] seeks to awaken the consciences of all who participate in unjust structures and to empower the poor to recognize their special place in God's care, to move from the margins to a new position as historical subjects, and to imagine a world of justice in which the social order can be remade. The epistemology of this approach, informed by the prophetic tradition culminating in Jesus's identification with the oppressed, points our attention intensively to the . . . poor and socially marginalized, and, through them, to the oppressed structures that mediate their suffering, a social analysis that goes beyond what Buddhist epistemology, in its classical forms, has attempted to do. This perspective . . . has significantly informed elements of engaged Buddhism today and . . . should further inform many aspects of Buddhist thought and practice.[10]

Makransky's critical appropriation of liberation theology's preferential option is thoughtful and robust. Gustavo Gutiérrez's classic formulation of theology as "Critical Reflection on (Christian) Praxis" takes us more deeply into the methodological heart of liberation theology.[11] Opting for the poor in the Latin American context meant allying oneself with Christian base communities, and their reflective process coined in the directive "See. Judge. Act." Liberation theologians worked with this embryonic praxis to develop their own fusion of theory and practice implied in Gutiérrez's trenchant phrase.

The pieces of the puzzle of an adequate, Buddhist critical reflection on praxis exist but have yet to be put together into a Buddhist theory of social and spiritual, political and economic, transformation akin to any number of liberation theologies. To this end, I offer a definition of praxis as a heuristic device for teasing out the elements of a Buddhist understanding of liberating social change: *Praxis is action that is symbolically constituted, historically situated, critically mediated by a social theory, and strategically and politically directed.* Examining various Buddhist forms of engagement in light of these four components will enable us to see how a fully developed Buddhist social theory can guide action for social transformation.

Symbolically Constituted Action

In bringing forth the new, action is intentional and as such both strategic and communicative.[12] Movements for social change at their deepest level frame actions by drawing upon symbols and symbolic actions that are deeply rooted in our psyche. They are emotionally freighted forms of cognition that draw upon a culture's symbolic repertoire but do so in order to reframe its view of reality.[13] Gandhi's Salt March to the Sea, Rosa Parks's refusal to move to the back of the bus, the United Farm Workers grape boycott, and, more recently, the Black Lives Matter campaign framed action with powerful symbols. Among the Buddhist examples of symbolic acts that we have examined are Rita Gross's evocative act of "borrowing a prophetic voice," Thich Nhat Hanh's unmasking the depravity of war in his "The Lonely Watchtower" poem, B. R. Ambedkar's public burning of the *Manusmriti*, and Joanna Macy's Council of All Beings, ritualizing the movement from grief about the extinction of species to commitment. These examples are potent symbolic acts of resistance operating on multiple levels. Such symbolic actions are already an embryonic praxis. Here is where we begin to reflect.

Another example of symbolic reinvention generating new forms of Buddhist praxis comes from the Sarvodaya movement in Sri Lanka's reimagining of the Four Noble Truths. Sarvodaya is a rural development organization that has transformed over fifteen thousand villages in Sri Lanka. It seeks the awakening of all as a dual revolution, first, within each person's mind and, second, within each village through empowering villagers to work together and to rely upon their own collective action.[14] The First Noble Truth in Sarvodaya's reinterpretation becomes "There is a decadent village." The focus is immediately placed on collective dukkha. The Second Noble Truth identifies the causes of this form of dukkha as including materialism, disunity, ethnic hatred, and competition. These modern forms of the three poisons, Sarvodaya argues, are exacerbated by the Western model of development that has been imposed on Sri Lanka. The Third Noble Truth, focusing on the overcoming of dukkha, is exemplified in the *shramadana*, or work camp, in which villagers of all ages come together, meditate, and discuss in order to reach consensus on a work project. Finally, each component of the Eightfold Path is reinterpreted. For example, a Sarvodaya trainer explained right mindfulness as staying "open and alert to the needs of the village. . . . Look to see what is needed—latrines, water, road. . . . Is anyone getting exploited?" Right understanding of the systemic causes of villagers' suffering, right speech in building village consensus around basic needs, right action in which everyone contributes (*dāna*)—all of these reinterpretations open up a vision of a "no poverty/no affluence society" in which basic needs, including cultural and spiritual needs, are met.[15] Symbols and symbolic acts are powerful catalysts of social movements. Their power, in part, comes from invoking a history, in Rosa Parks's case a history of tired bodies humiliated and forced to give up their seats for decades.

Historically Situated Action

The epistemological revolution at the heart of Latin American liberation theology upheld the axiom that all theology geared toward praxis is contextual. Praxis is not the expression of abstract, universal norms. It arises within particular communities in particular places and at particular points in time. These communities have a history, and praxis represents the cutting edge of that history, its emancipatory thrust. Liberation theologians such as Gustavo Gutiérrez are quite clear that critical reflection must focus not only on the history of one's own culture but also on the religious tradition that structures one's own practice.[16] To say that praxis is historically situated is both a fact and a challenge. A genuine emancipatory thrust entails a critical appropriation of the past that has brought a society to a present crisis. This critical historical interpretation is, first, a *diagnosis* of a culture's developmental pathology and that of the tradition (in this case Buddhism) that claims transformative power. Second, it entails a *retrieval* of emancipatory possibilities from both within the culture and within the tradition that would transform that culture. If a culture were completely without emancipatory possibilities, it would be impossible for those within it to even imagine that—in the Zapatistas's phrase—"another world is possible." So, Rita Gross's *Buddhism after Patriarchy* is, first, a diagnosis of patriarchy as a pathology infecting all major schools of Buddhism. Second, her uncovering of an "indigenous Buddhist feminism" is a retrieval of an emancipatory thrust within the tradition itself.

Likewise, Brian Victoria's landmark historical research culminating in *Zen at War* is a prime example of how critical analysis of the past can transform how we approach religiously based action in the present.[17] This courageous work examines the dark side of one branch of Buddhism manifested in its self-serving, blind support for Japanese imperialism leading up to and during World War II. Victoria describes the writing of this book as falling down a rabbit hole: "Down below, warfare and killing were described as manifestations of Buddhist compassion."[18] The vision that he had absorbed as a Soto Zen priest was turned inside out. Key doctrines were twisted to serve a martial ideal. So the Bodhisattva's vow to save all beings became in Soto Zen master Iida Toin's words "the willingness to sacrifice one's life seven times over to repay the debt of gratitude owed to the sovereign. . . . Are you at this moment," he concluded, "prepared to die or not?"[19] Zen, numerous Zen masters insisted, was best positioned to prepare young men to make this sacrifice. Army major Okubo Koichi agreed and, for his part, reinterpreted the teaching of the no-self. The soldier, he said, "must become the order he receives. That is to say, his self must disappear."[20]

This inversion of Zen Buddhist teachings was not simply the product of uneducated priests. No less of a Buddhist luminary than D. T. Suzuki lent his voice to a wedding of Zen and militarism. Writing in 1938, he addressed the issue of how a Buddhist practice devoted to "love and mercy" could justify killing. Through a convoluted argument Suzuki distinguished between the sword that kills and the sword that gives life. For one who has been trained in self-sacrifice "the sword comes to be identified with the annihilation of things that lie in the way of peace, justice, progress and humanity." So long as Japan's aims were devoid of any thirst for personal gain, war was in the service of humanity. For the Zen trained soldier, it is not he but the sword that does the killing: "The enemy appears and makes himself a victim. It is as though the sword performs automatically its function of justice, which is the function of mercy."[21]

Those who resisted the imperial flood tide during the Meiji period were few and scattered. They appear as tiny nuggets of gold buried in the surging, muddy waters. One resistor was Uchiyama Gudo, a Soto Zen priest in an area of rural poverty. He came in contact with a socialist newspaper and soon became a regular contributor. "As propagator of Buddhism I teach that 'all sentient beings have a Buddha Nature' and that 'within the Dharma there is equality, with neither superior nor inferior,'" he wrote in 1904. "Having taken these golden words as the basis of my faith, I discovered that they are in complete agreement with the principles of socialism. It was thus that I became a believer in socialism."[22] When the newspaper was censored and its editors jailed, Gudo took the audacious step of setting up a secret press in his temple with which he published socialist tracts. In them, he attacked the emperor system, the reduction of rural peasants to tenant farmers, and the auctioning off of plum temple posts to the highest bidder.[23] While Gudo absorbed a prophetic voice through his encounter with socialism, it was the core teachings of Mahāyāna Buddhism that grounded his commitment and provided norms for judging the current social order. In May 1909, Gudo was arrested and convicted of terrorism. He was executed in January 1911.

By the 1920s institutional Buddhism was wholly in support of Japan's imperial aggression. Then in 1931 a new locus of resistance emerged, the Youth League for Revitalizing Buddhism led by Seno Giro, a lay activist. "This is an age of suffering," proclaimed the newly born organization. "The masses of people seek bread but are fed repression. . . . In such an age what should Buddhists be aware of, what contribution should they be making to society?" Despite possessing "the highest principles for the guidance of human beings," institutional Buddhism functions as an opiate. And is cursed by the masses.[24] "Carry the Buddha on your backs and go out into the streets," the Youth League charged its followers.[25] They did just that, teaching that self-centered nationalism, acquisitive capitalism, and a self-serving Buddhist establishment were incompatible with the Buddhist principle of selflessness. In December 1936, Seno Giro was arrested and charged with treason. In 1937 police conducted mass arrests of members of the league and broke its back.[26]

"I have sought to illuminate, as brightly as I could," Victoria concludes, "a dark and frightening passageway in Buddhist history, in the belief that Buddhists . . . must accept responsibility for both the best and the worst of their faith. . . . It is difficult to know who we ought to be if we cannot recognize who we have been."[27] Although Victoria does not adopt the rhetoric of a jeremiad, his careful scholarship works from within the Zen tradition to critique the tradition. Given the darkness of this past, the glimmers of resistance that he also excavates take on outsized significance. In the very teeth of authoritarian rule, Uchiyama Gudo and the Youth League offered interpretations of Mahāyāna teachings, especially that of Buddha Nature, to ground their visions of a society of radical equality. Victoria offers a challenge to all Buddhists. No tradition is immune to corruption when nations stoke war fever. We too, like the resistors, are forced to decide which interpretation of core Mahāyāna teachings represents a path forward.

Action Critically Mediated by a Social Theory

Rita Gross's reading of Buddhist history is informed by her feminist reading of the present. Our reading of the present situation, argues liberation theologian Clodovis Boff, is informed by some "socio-analytic mediation."[28] The real question is whether we can develop a *critical* mediation, that is, a systemic social analysis developed in a dialectic with the messy historical course of human affairs. Such a critical mediation takes three forms: a social-psychological critique (Robert J. Lifton's treatment of psychic numbness is a good example of this), an ideology critique (I have argued that Thich Nhat Hanh's first three mindfulness trainings function as an ideology solvent), and a critical analysis of systems of power and alienation (Dr. Ambedkar's *Annihilation of Caste* exemplifies this third form of critical analysis).

David Loy's extensive work in developing a Buddhist social theory is built upon his consistent use of a psychological-existential understanding of the sense of "lack" as the root source of both individual and collective misery. Loy first presented his theory in *Lack and Transcendence: The Problem of Death and Life in Psychotherapy, Existentialism, and Buddhism*. The subtitle captures the synthesis that Loy created. We can think of this theory as Loy's reflection on the myth of Gautama's trips outside the gates of the pleasure palace, where he witnesses the existential universals of old age, sickness, and death. Ernst Becker argues that we are haunted by our awareness of our own mortality, a haunting that leads us to endless *immortality* projects.

Underlying each of Gautama's experiences is the suspicion that this finite self is lacking in self-sufficient substance. Loy, extrapolating from Becker, argues that it is a pervasive sense of lacking a ground that leads us to endless *reality* projects.[29] "The basic difficulty is a sense of lack, which originates from the fact that our self-consciousness is not something self-existing but a mental construct. Rather than being self-sufficient, the sense of self is more like the surface of the sea: dependent on depths it cannot grasp because it is a manifestation of them. . . . Problems arise when such a conditioned consciousness seeks to ground itself, that is, wants to become unconditioned and autonomous, which is to say *real*."[30] Our "reality projects" are never sufficient. The realization that there is no "self" that needs to be grounded disentangles this existential Gordian knot. The release of the self that hankers after self-sufficiency opens us up to unlimited possibilities, opens us, that is, to authentic freedom.

In *The Great Awakening: A Buddhist Social Theory* and in *Money, Sex, War, Karma*, this understanding of "lack" performs the work of a "socio analytic mediation." The alienation produced by the self's sense of lack leads us to take refuge in a group that itself experiences a "collective dukkha." The group ego becomes the site of a "collective reality project." But the process of alienation does not stop there: "We not only have group egos; there are institutionalized egos."[31] The megainstitutions of modern life are the objectification of a collective effort to escape an unbearable sense of lack. These large institutions mimic the self's dukkha: "The history of the nation-state system demonstrates that they are externally unstable and internally self-aggrandizing. Economically GNP is never big enough, corporations are never profitable enough, consumers never consume enough."[32] These institutions take on a life of their own and impose their ideologies on the human beings whose lives coarise with them. Simultaneously responsibility for how these large institutions impose their will in shaping a global society is diffused: "I can satisfy my coffee and chocolate cravings without knowing about the social conditions of the farmer who grew those commodities for me and without any awareness of what is happening to the biosphere."[33] Institutionalized greed, ill will, and delusion may last for generations, socializing each of us into submission to the "will" of these large institutions.

Given the impermanence and emptiness of all phenomena, the collective reality project is as doomed to failure as our individual efforts. Loy's social psychology approach is very productive because it traces our seemingly intractable dilemmas, for example, mushrooming economic inequality, to the dukkha at the core of the human heart and to its desperate stratagems manifest as greed, hatred, and delusion. It also aligns with the way in which Buddhism in the West has entered into a dialectical relationship with humanistic schools of psychology and psychotherapy. It is a distinctively Buddhist analysis developed in a Western idiom. Given the virtually unanimous assertion by Engaged Buddhists that there can be no outer transformation without inner transformation, this genre of social-psychological analysis takes on central importance. Without inner transformation, social change will simply result in replacing one structure of domination with another.

While I was working on this chapter, millions of people became convulsed in outraged protests against police brutality. The image of a policeman's callous knee on the neck of a Black man struggling to breathe was engraved in our consciousness. If we hadn't known it before, the protests brought the "boil"—racism as structural violence manifesting itself as physical violence—to the surface. Racism cannot be reduced to a product of universal lack. It has a distinct genealogy. The primary form of dukkha experienced by most people of color in the United States and by socially marginalized people the world over is not the existential universals revealed in the Buddha's mythical journey outside the palace gates but oppression, the social misery to which Cornel West refers. B. R. Ambedkar's alternative myth of the Buddha's leave-taking to discover the sources of conflict and violence and their cure is more of a skillful means directed to these multitudes than the classic myth. It encapsulates Ambedkar's own preferential option for the Dalits. Moreover, human beings undergo a long process of socialization as intrinsic to our survival. The surrounding culture inscribes its own particular forms of alienation and its dehumanizing ideologies on nascent psyches. Psychological-existential anxieties arise within such a historical context. We face a classic chicken-and-egg paradox. Because Engaged Buddhists have generally defaulted to the psychological-existential interpretation of dukkha, I suggest that we complement the kind of analysis that Loy performs so well with one that focuses on the social-historical forms of oppression. In other words, a critical social theory requires more than a social psychology. It requires both an ideology critique and a critical analysis of systems of power and alienation.

Ideology Critique

"The very heart of critical theory," argues Raymond Geuss, "is its criticism of ideology. Their ideology is what prevents the agents in the society from correctly perceiving their true situation and real interests."[34] Modern societies are thoroughly shaped and guided by ideologies that they themselves construct. At their most deeply rooted level, we call these social constructs "reality." We are socialized into a "consensus reality," but one that leaves us unsatisfied.[35] From a Buddhist standpoint, ideologies inevitably foster delusions that need to be cut through. Engaged Buddhists have developed practices to challenge the grip of ideologies. A case in point is the first three of the Fourteen Mindfulness Trainings of Thich Nhat Hanh's Order of Interbeing, which can be read as ideology solvents. The first training warns against the fanaticism and intolerance that arise from being bound to an ideology. With a gun you can kill dozens of people, Thich Nhat Hanh insists, but to kill millions you need an ideology. The second training recognizes that impermanence marks all knowledge. Attachment to a particular view inevitably impedes openness to new truth. The third training eschews all forms of propaganda or indoctrination as forms of imposing suffering on others.[36]

Contemporary societies mine our consciousness the way industrial society mined the earth. They colonize our consciousness using what David Loy calls "weapons of mass distraction and mass deception." At their worst, as in the case of the war in Iraq, the weapons of mass deception led to war with Iraq to keep us safe from (nonexistent) weapons of mass destruction. A consumer society uses mass deception to cultivate a false sense of an inadequate self. It then offers some commodity to heal our every sense of lack. We become addicts, trapped in a sense of our impoverishment. This colonization of the mind begins at birth, long before we develop the skills necessary to cut through delusions: "While half of four-year-old children do not know their own name, two-thirds of three-year-olds recognize the golden arches of McDonald's."[37]

Practicing these trainings and decolonizing our thinking is no simple task. Ken Jones quotes a saying attributed to the Buddha that expresses both the difficulty and the importance of this endeavor: "The world in general grasps after systems and is imprisoned by dogmas and ideologies." The wise, however, "do not go along with that system grasping" (*Samyutta Nikāya* XII).[38] Not grasping at systems is no easy task, particularly when we recognize that strategic action involves systemic analysis. What sort of systemic thinking avoids grasping? There is a clear distinction between an airtight, self-reinforcing doctrine, canonized as dogma, and an open, reflective, and revisable teaching that welcomes dialogue.

Not "going along," to be sure, involves a thorough reorientation of our basic inclinations. Compelled by our sense of lack, we seek self-affirmation through collective belonging. Group identity is solidified when we bind ourselves antithetically, that is, over against a group that we project as an evil "other." "Antithetical bonding," Jones argues, is the cement that turns ideologies into "subjectively freighted articles of faith." Ideologies, in turn, provide bonded communities with ready-made "identi-kits."[39] The critique of ideology is not simply an intellectual task. Quite a bit of emotional work must go into dissolving the enmity that metastasizes with antithetical bonding. Prying the hand of the mind loose from grasping at systems requires spiritual discipline.[40]

We tend to forget that the Hebrew prophets' messages were contested by others who claimed the mantle of prophecy. Hananiah, a court prophet, challenged Jeremiah in the temple and broke the wooden yoke that Jeremiah wore to symbolize imminent captivity. Jeremiah, in response, donned an iron yoke (Jer 28). This raises the question now as then: Who is the true prophet?

If we grant that modern societies are ideologically shaped, we cannot simply assert that my (Buddhist) view is a critical theory while your ideology exhibits false consciousness. As the examples of Thich Nhat Hanh and Ken Jones illustrate, Engaged Buddhism can draw upon a wide range of Buddhist teachings and practices in performing its ideology critique. Engaged Buddhists, reflecting on the Hebrew prophets' unflinching confrontation with those who oppressed the widow, the orphan, and the stranger in their midst, can take to heart Cornel West's dictum that the condition of truth is allowing the suffering to speak. By no means are these multiple forms of ideology critique foolproof, as the fusion of Buddhism with extreme forms of ethnic nationalism in Sri Lanka and Myanmar attest.

Confronting Alienation

If ideology critique is one area where Buddhists can make a distinctive contribution to a critical social theory, alongside a social psychological analysis of lack, the third contribution to a critical social theory is not well developed by Engaged Buddhists. "My perception," suggests David Loy, "is that Buddhists have become much better at pulling drowning people out of the river, but—and here is the problem—we aren't much better at asking why there are so many more people drowning."[41] In other words, we need to examine the forms that collective dukkha is taking in this time and place. If persons create systems, the converse is also true. We cannot assume that if enough people seek emancipatory wisdom, that systems will change. "The social forces that mold the ways we think, feel and act today—especially the state and the mass media, both largely corporate controlled—are so powerful that they cannot be ignored as we try to create a more generous, compassionate and wise society within the shell of institutionalized greed, ill will and delusion."[42] Loy's example of three-year-olds' recognition of the golden arches when they may not know their own name is a case in point. What resources do three-year-olds, or their parents for that matter, have to filter the messages of multinational corporations? Yet here we run up against what is both a strength and a limitation of Loy's own social theory: Loy always leads back to the self's sense of lack that leads us to band together to create institutions that invariably alienate us. But we can flip the order that gives priority to this deluded sense of self and assign it to our social alienation. This is what Marx does in his Sixth and Seventh Theses on Feuerbach": "The essence of man is no abstraction inhering in each single individual. In its actuality it is the ensemble of social relationships. . . . Feuerbach does not see, consequently, that 'religious feeling' is itself a social product and that the abstract individual he analyses belongs to a particular form of society."[43] So, from this perspective, the self's experience of "lack" is not so much human beings' universal sense of dis-ease in the face of old age, sickness, and death or the haunting sense of impermanence and lack of an enduring substance but a particular form of alienation spawned by the institutions of the modern world. Marx claims that through productive work, humans create objects that because of the existing social structures assume a hostile stance toward their producers. For example, in producing food, tenant farmers create a farm and themselves as farmers, but under given historical conditions they do not control the products of their work, the work itself, or the farm. Alienation is not an ontological concept nor, primarily, a psychological concept but a historical condition residing within the institutions (tenant farming) that structure social existence. Alienated action that reinforces the social structures must be overcome by revolutionary praxis for which consciousness raising is a necessary pedagogy.[44]

Several points are worth considering here. Marx's understanding of social existence coheres nicely with the Buddhist understanding of dependent coarising. We are shaped by historical causes and conditions. More precisely, in Marx's vision there is an internal relation between self and world.[45] Each is the reflex of the other. Or, as Thich Nhat Hanh puts it, we inter-are with all others, with the institutions that we create as they shape us, and with the natural world. The structures to which we are internally related are impermanent. We are socialized into a karmic reality, but by awakening to its full complexity we can begin to unmake it and, in the process, remake ourselves. Marx says as much in his Third Thesis on Feuerbach: "The coincidence of change of circumstances and of human activity or self-change can be comprehended and rationally understood only as revolutionary practice."[46]

So, what elaborations of Engaged Buddhism might correspond to Marx's understanding of alienation and its overcoming? As we saw in chapter 5, B. R. Ambedkar, above all, gave priority to collective dukkha in his social analysis. His analysis of caste, his appropriation of Dewey's concept of democracy as unfettered association and communication within and across all spheres of society, and his comparison of Buddhism and Marxism do add up to a systemic understanding of alienation and oppression and their overcoming. If we look for something on a par with Loy's social-psychological analyses or at the level of Ambedkar's critique of caste as collective dukkha, I don't believe we will find it yet in the corpus of contemporary Engaged Buddhist analyses. To be sure, there are scathing criticisms of the Western model of development with its institutionalized expressions of greed, ill will, and delusion in, for example, the jeremiads of Thai Buddhist Sulak Sivaraksa. Individual essays in *Mindful Politics: A Buddhist Guide to Making the World a Better Place* and *Hooked: Buddhist Writings on Greed Desire and the Urge to Consume* sparkle with insights.[47] However, they do not offer a systematic critique of the structural violence of the dominant political and economic institutions.

Strategically and Politically Directed Action

Representing a new generation of liberation theologians, Ivan Petrella provides a diagnosis of the eclipse of the first generation of liberation theologies. That demise coincided with the fall of the Berlin Wall. Latin American liberation theologians had committed themselves to a Marxist critical theory that saw capitalism as a monolithic force whose destructive power could be overcome only through a revolutionary politics leading to a socialist state.[48] Socialism, Petrella argues, was the "historical project" of the first generation's liberation theology. With the downfall of state socialism in Eastern Europe, Latin American liberation theology lost its historical project. Petrella defines a historical project by quoting José Míguez Bonino, one of liberation theology's founding generation: "Historical project is . . . a midway term between an utopia, a vision which makes no attempt to connect itself historically to the present, and a program, a technically developed model for the organization of society. . . . A historical project is defined enough to force options in terms of the basic structures of society. . . . It is in this general sense that we speak of a Latin American socialist project of liberation."[49] Despite the loss of its historical project, Latin American liberation theology was able to rescue its core theological concepts: the preferential option for the poor, God's reign, and liberation/salvation. These concepts retained their symbolic power in the new historical context. But rescue came with a price: without a new historical project to provide strategic guidance for praxis it became unclear what these key theological concepts meant in terms of social action and to what kind of alternative society they pointed. Liberation theology's key terms are not simply principles for judging society, "they are to be developed as alternative social forms, that is, political, economic and social institutions that can be enacted on society's many levels."[50]

Petrella takes us back to Aristotle, for whom praxis was "that form of truly human activity manifested in the life of the *polis*."[51] Political life is about more than ruling and being ruled. It is about creating in concert with others a just and livable society. Petrella recognizes that social movements and communities geared toward praxis need to act based on some vision of an alternative society that, to be truly transformative, must be a viable option and not a utopian fantasy. Praxis is not truly praxis unless it is strategically and politically directed action.

Among the various Engaged Buddhist movements, the movement that comes closest to defining and pursuing a historical project is Sri Lanka's Sarvodaya movement. Sarvodaya's project is building a "no poverty/no affluence society" that meets basic needs, including developing spiritual and cultural capacities. "Development," says its founder, A. T. Ariyaratne, "is an awakening process." This entails nothing less than a total revolution, beginning with the transformation of the human personality.[52] The *shramadana* camps, with their ethos of self-reliance, are exercises in consensus-based, participatory democracy. They create a social infrastructure within the formerly "decadent village." Organized villages evolve through a five-stage process that culminates in their designation as pioneering villages. Such villages take responsibility for facilitating and supporting the development of several nearby villages. This developmental process is supported by the Sarvodaya Economic Enterprises Development Services, which provides initial capital, technical and entrepreneurship training, and education about innovative agricultural practices. Villages are networked together through this process and power is decentralized, giving birth to "a commonwealth of village republics."[53] From these practices, villagers "build their own economic 'theory' supportive of the life they really live and aim to live," in contrast to professional economic theories whose top-down models ignore the multiple challenges that villagers confront.[54]

Sarvodaya's approach to integral human development is strategic. It offers a clear alternative to Western models of development that concentrate power in the hands of an elite, which exacerbate ethnic conflicts, and which foster an unsustainable consumer economy that sacrifices the poor for the sake of the affluent. Sarvodaya works from an integral vision of basic human needs and capacities and presents a method for fully engaging rural communities to meet self-defined needs, unlike movements that impose a vision of total revolution that ignores local issues. Sarvodaya's form of praxis is contextually appropriate in its strategic use of power to foster the evolution of a "commonwealth of village republics." In contrast, Western, urban Engaged Buddhists have yet to develop a strategic, historical project that might unify their proliferation of efforts to transform different aspects of society.

Vehicles of Liberation

Keeping in mind that praxis is collective action, we must ask a final question: In the American context, what kinds of Buddhist groups might engage in strategic, political action? For the first generation of liberation theologians in Latin America, the carriers of liberation were clear. They were the Christian base communities where priests, nuns, and peasants reading and reflecting on scripture together performed the process called "See. Judge. Act." They acted with support from the institutional church. For Sarvodaya the answer is equally clear: the local villages and their networks with the institutional backing of the Sarvodaya Economic Enterprises Development Services are the vehicles of liberation. In the American context we need to keep in mind that Engaged Buddhists are a minority within a minority religion. Right now, the predominant model of engagement is a centrifugal strategy: sanghas provide spiritual nourishment and support while individual members find their own areas of engagement. This model maximizes individual freedom, but it means that a specifically Buddhist approach to social change does not come to the surface. Individual Buddhists have only a small voice within the movements they join or the institutions they work in or support. At best, individual Buddhists will find engaged groups whose missions bear a family resemblance to a Buddhist vision of social change. An initial step beyond centrifugal engagement toward action in concert would be peace and justice committees within sanghas, a model that already exists in many Catholic parishes and Protestant congregations. Sangha members remain free to join or not, but the committee can work toward consensus on a few areas where the committee members will act together and invite other sangha members to join them.

Thich Nhat Hanh has suggested that Buddhist monasteries and retreat centers could function as laboratories in ecological living.[55] They could take a step further and incorporate experiments in both service and nonviolent direct action as integral to their mindfulness training programs. These communities might then function as a leaven within American Buddhism.

Sanghas are rightly concerned with preserving their spiritual focus as they increase their engagement. We have multiple examples of religious communities that have created organizations to foster nonviolent engagement *as a spiritual practice* within movements for social change. The Southern Christian Leadership Conference is an obvious example. The American Friends Service Committee as the strategic action arm of the Quaker community is another. In the Buddhist context, the Buddhist Peace Fellowship, the Zen Peacemaker International (zenpeacemaker.org), and the Buddhist Action Coalition might serve this function. If Engaged Buddhists are serious about not just participating in but also shaping peace and justice movements, then we will have to go beyond ad hoc individual involvements to create advocacy networks of Engaged Buddhist peace and justice committees.

Conclusion

Engaged Buddhists have developed many of the theoretical components that are useful in shaping and guiding praxis. These efforts are illuminating, but they are also scattered and piecemeal. To be truly effective, such efforts need to draw on multiple disciplines developed in a coordinated fashion. The analysis in this chapter gives us a way to move in this strategic direction.

- *Symbolically constituted action.* Praxis does not offer abstract, universal norms. It arises in particular contexts. A final illustration of Buddhist symbolic action comes from Thailand, where old growth forests have been decimated to feed an export economy. With this heedless clear-cutting came floods polluting rivers and streams. Villagers, dependent on the forest for food, fuel, and fodder, have suffered greatly. In response some Thai monks have invented a ritual of "tree ordination," designed to protect the forest. The ordination becomes the occasion to raise ecological awareness and to teach the villagers new sustainable methods of agriculture.[56] The Thai Environmental Monks are a particularly good example of religious activists who have stayed in close touch with the collective dukkha, the social misery of their historical and cultural context. "Tree ordination" recognizes that the forest sustains the villagers with food, fuel, and fodder, while the villagers protect the forest. This symbol unites Buddhist thought and action with an ecological consciousness.

- *Historically situated.* Brian Victoria stated the importance of this key component of praxis succinctly: "It is difficult to know who we ought to be if we cannot recognize who we have been." Like human beings, no tradition fully escapes illness. Diagnosis discerns when both religion and culture have developed cancerous formations. Retrieval uncovers the emancipatory thrust of one's tradition, the bud at the tip of the living branch.

- *Social psychology.* One hallmark of Engaged Buddhism is its sophisticated understanding of the psychological dynamics that shape our actions. Thinker-activists such as David Loy and Ken Jones have provided models that trace collective dukkha to its roots in our individual dis-ease. Mindful practices that create an inner revolution are essential to any truly Buddhist praxis.

- *Ideology critique.* This is another strength of Engaged Buddhism. Mindful practices help us (a) to detach from fixed social teachings that resist challenge, (b) to recognize dualistic thinking that furthers "antithetical bonding," (c) to avoid either succumbing to or promoting propaganda that closes off the ongoing exploration of social reality, and (d) to recognize and resist "weapons of mass deception" that stigmatize the other and employ rhetoric that induces fear and then claims the authority to erase it.

- *Understanding alienation and oppression.* This is a weak point in Engaged Buddhist contributions to strategic practice. It is also a downside to American Buddhism's creative synthesis with various schools of psychotherapy. This synthesis leads to an emphasis on individual dukkha. At its worst, Buddhist practice is reduced to one more method of self-help. A truly complete understanding of interdependence will emphasize not only how individual dukkha gives rise to group fixed identities that reinforce the individual's dukkha. It will also recognize how we are socialized by alienated and oppressive social formations. Social misery is systemic. Designed to reinforce the power of some over others, it is historically invented (e.g., racism). As such, it can be ended.

- *Strategic action.* Mindful behavior is essential, but it is not enough. We are confronted with entrenched social formations that socialize us in ways that we find difficult to discern. Strategic action becomes much more effective if Engaged Buddhists go beyond centrifugal engagement to coalesce around a historical project that can be pursued using a variety of skillful means that make room for individual and group creativity. Sallie King quotes a Quaker leader who calls his spiritual community to think strategically in terms of a one-hundred-year struggle for peace and justice. That is a challenge to Engaged Buddhists well worth taking to heart. What distinctive impact upon the direction of American society would Engaged Buddhists seek to have as the years, then the decades, unfold?[57]

Chapter Ten

Facing Up to Evil, Abolishing Our Racial Caste System

> Race is the ultimate delusion in that it both does and does not exist.
>
> —Rev. angel Kyodo williams, *Radical Dharma*[1]

> Any upheaval in the universe is terrifying because it attacks one's own reality. Well, the black man has functioned in the white man's world as a fixed star, as an immovable pillar, and as he moves out of his place, heaven and earth are shaken to their foundations. . . . But these men are your brothers. . . . We, with love, shall force our brothers to see themselves as they are, to cease fleeing from reality and begin to change it.
>
> —James Baldwin, "My Dungeon Shook"[2]

> How do you expect to leave everything behind when you enter a meditation center? The kind of suffering that you carry in your heart, that is society itself. You bring that with you, you bring society with you. You bring all of us with you. When you meditate, it is not just for yourself, you do it for the whole society.
>
> —Thich Nhat Hanh, *Being Peace*[3]

Just as the COVID pandemic was starting to wane, I sat in on a Zoom webinar focusing on Engaged Buddhism. A Chinese American Buddhist whose grief-stricken face appeared as fine porcelain lined with veins of pain spoke calmly about her sense of abandonment. It was a few weeks after a mass shooting in Atlanta targeted Asian Americans. This woman was struck by the silence of the American Buddhist community (although with some exceptions). If Buddhists had denounced this latest upsurge in hate crimes directed at Asian Americans, it was not forceful enough to reach her ears. She felt exposed. Those whom she expected to have her back were not on the scene.

Weeks later, she is still on my mind. I read an account of a 2012 Pew Research Center survey that finds that two-thirds of Americans call themselves Buddhists are Asian Americans.[4] The convert sanghas that I am familiar with lament their lack of diversity despite a strong commitment to inclusivity. Yet we who are labeled white have not connected the dots: the majority of our coreligionists are targets of racism ranging from microaggressions—that never feel micro—to active discrimination, to hate crimes. Engaged Buddhists who would act against racial injustice need to confront what is swirling around us. We ought to begin at home.

"I find myself, not for the first time, in the position of a kind of Jeremiah," James Baldwin said in a debate before a group of Cambridge University students in 1965.[5] I first read James Baldwin more than fifty years ago. I thought then that he had revealed the reality of racism—both interpersonal and institutional—in Northern cities. His jeremiad hit home. Now, rereading Baldwin after all this time, I am aghast that his pointed diagnosis seems as accurate as before. "The great force of history comes from the fact that we carry it within us, are unconsciously controlled by it in many ways . . . , People who imagine that history flatters them . . . are impaled on their history like a butterfly on a pin and become incapable of seeing or changing themselves, or the world. This is the place in which it seems to me most white Americans find themselves. Impaled."[6] After each moment in our collective awakening to and denunciation of embedded racism, promises are made, laws are passed, but the underlying disease mutates and metastasizes. Why after all the struggles of the past fifty plus years are we still trying to get at the DNA of this virus? I don't know.

According to Zen master Bernie Glassman, maintaining a "don't-know-mind" is the first step in coming to terms with collective suffering. Don't-know-mind dissolves all isms.[7] Thich Nhat Hanh adds that mindfulness is the opposite of retreating into a cocoon to comfort ourselves. We bring our world poisoned with racism with us when we meditate. No innocence; no room for that delusion. We recognize our interbeing and take responsibility for all the needless suffering. So, as an admonition to myself to abandon any dualistic ideology that separates our collective reality into "children of light and children of darkness," I paraphrase the key ("sea pirate") stanza in Thich Nhat Hanh's signature poem "Please Call Me by My True Names" that we examined earlier:

> I am the Black teenager.
> running from the police
> My crime? Wearing a hoodie.
> And I am the white police officer
> my heart welded shut
> who fires into the back
> of the unarmed child.

I will keep the challenge of the Chinese American Buddhist and the prophetic denunciation of James Baldwin close as I work on this chapter. What follows is provisional and inevitably marred by my own blind spots. Moreover, the magnitude of the disease, its permeation of our whole culture, defies the efforts of any single person, much less an older white man. I have tried to listen to others and to reflect their prophetic wisdom as best I can. What I have to offer is a sketch of a prophetic praxis for illustrative purposes. It is an invitation to dialogue.[8]

Racism Defined

Racism is the parent of race, not the reverse. "Race" is a particularly problematic term because, as angel Kyodo williams put it, "Race is the ultimate delusion." In constructing race, racism presumes that differences among different groups are both "permanent and unbridgeable" and correlated with specific inner qualities. Arbitrary external differences are embedded in a system of—in Dr. B. R. Ambedkar's terms—"graded inequality" that is held in place through violence ranging from social discrimination to genocide.[9]

We can get a more nuanced and complex understanding of racism by comparing activist Fania Davis's and historian George Frederickson's definitions. Davis argues that racism operates within three dimensions. Individual and interpersonal racism involves embedded psychological frameworks expressed in explicit or implicit bias. It includes a whole range of attitudes, stereotypes, and fears that warp our human interactions. It mostly operates below the level of conscious awareness.[10] Frederickson is wary of describing racism in interpersonal terms. Racism, he insists, is always about an unequal distribution of power.[11] Davis agrees. She calls her second dimension "institutional racism." It includes social practices and policies within all social institutions that disadvantage some socially constructed groups (people of color) and privilege others (whites). These social practices and institutions shape us from birth to death.[12] Frederickson adds, "[Racism] either directly sustains or proposes to establish a *racial order*, a permanent group hierarchy that is believed to reflect the laws of nature or the decrees of God."[13] This last phrase leads us to Davis's third dimension, which she calls "structural racism" but which I prefer to call racism as a social framework. It is "the normalization and legitimation of white supremacy enacted from [America's] beginnings by vast historical . . . cultural . . . educational . . . and psychological forces."[14] At times this framing process is manifested in explicit terms, that is, as an ideology; in others, as coded language ("law and order"). Most dangerously, it is, as Davis says, normalized, simply "the way things are." Just as fish are hard put to be conscious of water, those who inhabit the upper levels of the hierarchy of graded inequality infrequently realize how thoroughly racism permeates the air that we breathe until now and again the blunt force of white supremacy shatters our complacency.

If anything embedded in American culture and institutions demands a moral chemotherapy, it is the disease of racism. Again and again, it has metastasized. Burned out in one social organ, it invades another. To be sure, there were thousands of examples of resistance during the eras of oppression. Prophets such as Ida B. Wells, in her relentless exposure of the evil of lynching, provided beacons of light in such eras. Nevertheless, viewing the sweep of American history, the periods of breakthrough were all too fleeting.

Prophetic Forbearer

Jan Willis is a Buddhist practitioner, a professor at Wesleyan University, and a scholar of Tibetan Buddhism. She is an African American who grew up in a small town, Docema, Alabama, where cross burnings by KKK members in hoods and robes were a persistent form of psychological terrorism practiced by her neighbors. As a young teenager, she marched with Dr. Martin Luther King Jr. in Birmingham. "White people no longer held my spirit in chains," she affirms.[15] Admitted to Cornell University, she arrived at the height of student activism both for real inclusion of Black people in the university and for an end to the war in Vietnam. At Cornell she read Buddhist thinkers such as D. T. Suzuki. "I heard Buddhist doctrines long before I knew about Buddhism," she said later. "I heard them from King."[16] Willis points to one of Dr. King's sermons that seems to echo the *Dhammapada:* "Returning hate for hate multiplies hate, adding deeper darkness to a night already devoid of stars. Darkness cannot drive out darkness; only light can do that. Hate cannot drive out hate; only love can do that. . . . Hate multiplies hate, violence multiplies violence . . . in a descending spiral of destruction."[17] A trip to Nepal where she met Lama Thubten Yeshe changed her life. She was his student for fifteen years.[18] The Tibetans too had experienced historical trauma. Tantric Buddhism, with its deity yoga, visualizing the self as divine, dissolved the self that was haunted by the memory of slavery and the specter of racism. Willis began to see herself as a lion, roaring.[19]

Willis speaks out against the implicit bias in the way Buddhism in America is categorized, dividing it into immigrant Buddhism and convert Buddhism. Buddhists of Chinese and Japanese ancestry were here building temples and practicing long before the ancestors of many convert Buddhists arrived as immigrants. All too often Buddhists of color have been rendered invisible. "We are here!" she roars. African American Buddhists can share with their fellow Buddhists reservoirs of spiritual resilience and the example of tenaciously holding on to their humanity in a hostile world.[20]

Willis more explicitly borrows a prophetic voice in several articles published in *Lion's Roar*. In December 2014 she gave a profound meditation on breathing and on the police-inflicted choking to death of Eric Garner. For Buddhists breathing is more than life-sustaining; it is the most intimate teaching aid. It teaches us that we are in no shape or form independent. It transcends Black or white or any other polarity. We breathe the same air, and "if Eric Garner cannot breathe, then we cannot breathe." Something must be done, she cries, "because at this moment, none of us can breathe."[21]

And yet. And yet. Once more we had to witness the choking out of George Floyd's life, minute by excruciating minute. So once more, Willis, like one of Jeremiah's keeners, cries out, "Where is justice?" Her cry seems futile, a sparrow's call in the midst of a thundering storm. Why is it so difficult to see young men and women as human beings and not prejudged and summarily executed as criminals? How does the conceit that "I am better than the other" take such deep roots in us? Compassion is not enough. We, each of us, must equalize each other. "Not better. Not worse."[22]

There are many groups in America with a long tradition of practice—five generations of practice in the case of the Chinese Americans in California who constructed the first Buddhist temple in the United States in

1853—who have been rendered invisible until fairly recently. In the inaugural issue of *Tricycle* in the winter of 1991, the editor, Helen Tworkov, made the regrettable comment that "so far" Asian Americans "have not figured prominently in the development of something called American Buddhism."[23] Reverend Ryo Imamura, an eighteenth-generation member of the Jodo Shin sect, responded to the Tworkov editorial with a letter to the editor. Reverend Imamura praised the white Buddhists for introducing an exciting new form of Buddhism, but he took *Tricycle* to task for historical amnesia. He reminded readers that the first Buddhist communities in America were formed by his grandparent's generation, that his parent's generation preserved Buddhist traditions in the face of racist hostility toward Japanese Americans who were forced into US concentration camps during World War II, and that his generation welcomed convert Buddhists into their temples and helped them establish their own sanghas.[24] To dismiss these contributions and the unflagging persistence of Asian American Buddhist communities in the face of pervasive racism is a grave mistake.

Thirty years later, a new generation of Asian American Buddhists echoes Reverend Imamura's words but with a more strident tone. Chenxing Han has interviewed dozens of these young adults. They are not to be mollified by some progress in creating more welcoming homes for Buddhist people of color. They insist that the marginalization of Asian American sanghas by a middle-class Buddhist establishment is a violation of the dharma. "I am constantly frustrated," professes one woman interviewee, "by the invalidation of my Buddhist experience by the mainstream American Buddhist powers. . . . I am hurt, and more than that I am angry, but even more than that I am tired. Nothing I say as a woman of color ever seems to be of any consequence to the all-knowing white Buddhist establishment, who remains determined as ever to tell me, how I'm 'doing Buddhism wrong.'"[25] So it is not just the "outer world" that is shot through with racism but our Buddhist sanghas as well that must wake up to racism.

The Inner Work for Racial Justice

Engaged Buddhists affirm that there can be no outer revolution that truly liberates without an inner revolution. A collective of unawakened egos taking over the apparatus of power is not a genuine revolution. Although prophetic wisdom focuses upon the shaping role of social systems, inner transformation must work in tandem with collective action.

Rhonda Magee is an African American professor of law at the University of San Francisco. She is also a mindfulness trainer who has modified a whole range of mindfulness exercises designed in order to get at the inner roots of racism. Traditionally Buddhists have focused on the delusion of a separate self and the suffering that arises from this misperception. Our lives are warped as we confront sickness, old age (if we are fortunate), and death. Magee, however, works with suffering that is not inherent in finite human existence but that is historically and socially constructed. This disease warps both our psyches and our relationships in myriad ways. This suffering is both "unnecessary and unequally distributed."[26] Training in mindfulness in the West, she argues, is largely directed toward an individual's personal improvement. What she calls "ColorInsight practice" goes further: "At the heart of the work of mindful racial justice is a commitment to doing no harm, to healing the wounds of injustice through caring—through a fierce, courageous and far-sighted love."[27]

Magee, who as a child experienced multiple forms of abuse, exemplifies the teacher as a healed healer. "We have all suffered enough," she maintains, but, as Baldwin insists, it is only when we name the suffering that is racism that we can end it. Magee trains her groups to develop seven "foundational traits" that are clearly rooted in Buddhist practices, including nonjudgmentalism, loving-kindness, patience, and don't-know-mind. For Magee compassion is not just a feeling but the will "to actually do something to assist in alleviating suffering." Steadfastness is the ability to endure the discomfort we feel in cutting through our delusions of innocence. Finally, we need to develop the courage to "act for justice."[28]

Where others discuss "white fragility," which warps our conversations about race and racism, Magee provides simple but effective mindfulness techniques. Recognizing how deeply embedded racial bias is in "our brains, our perceptions, our thoughts, our interactions and our communities," Magee offers more than two dozen mindfulness training exercises that we can adopt.[29] For example, Magee teaches us to **STOP** when we are confronted with racism. **Stop**. Check your reactivity. **Take** a few deep breaths. **Observe** what is happening in your body. What emotions are triggered by the situation? Finally, **proceed** by liberating yourself and others from fixed patterns of response. Practicing STOP develops our "emotional intelligence and psychological flexibility" when we engage with racism.[30] Magee also teaches a version of loving-kindness meditation to ground the inner work in care for ourselves and others. These simple exercises serve to reduce "fear-based reactivity" and to create a sense of security and mutual compassion.[31]

Given the strong emotions that can be triggered by examining both our implicit biases and the deep suffering that people of color have experienced as targets of racism, mindfulness techniques are necessary skillful means to avoid a sudden derailing of the process of interrogation. ColorInsight practice eschews spurious claims to be free of racism or to be "more woke than thou."[32] There is hard work to be done by all of us in unveiling how we have been absorbed into a culture of white supremacy:

> The ColorInsight approach emphasizes that we develop the habit of turning *toward*—not away—from aspects of our embodied experience that deal with race. We look at the psychological aspects of our experience—what our minds do with social identity cues. And we look at what the cultural aspects of our experience—the surroundings, context and power dynamics in which we find ourselves—do to us and our sense of our social identities. If we keep looking, we see how our sense of ourselves is constructed by our sense of the so-called Other and the constructs that keep re-creating the sense of separation and impassable difference fall away.[33]

We are works in progress. To be serious about confronting racism requires a persistent effort to see whiteness as a determining factor in our culture that affects all of us. Having acted upon the will to cut through the delusions of racism, developed a nuanced understanding of how it works in our culture and ourselves, and deepened our capacity to relate to others with compassion, we investigate the strengths that we can contribute to the transformative work for the liberation of all of us.[34]

Mourning and Memory

Rhonda Magee is clear that this work will require dealing with difficult emotions. Perhaps a very shameful memory. Perhaps the sense of pain that arose because of someone's abusive action toward you. We saw in chapter 1 that for the Hebrew prophets grief was the expressive signal that things had gone terribly wrong. "The condition of Black life is one of mourning," proclaims Claudia Rankine, poet and Yale University professor. She, however, speaks not of mourning as an emotion that remains trapped within victimhood. In African American communities, mourning is a flag of resistance and resilience. She points to the mother of Emmett Till, who wielded mourning as a weapon. Till was the fourteen-year-old boy who was beaten and murdered in Mississippi in 1955 for allegedly flirting with a white woman. Where Black bodies were left hanging where they were lynched to further terrorize the Black community, Mami Till Mobley turned the tables by revealing to the whole world the monstrous injustice mapped on her son's battered face. Her refusal to cower, her defiance of a system that brutalized Black bodies with impunity, was a catalyst for the civil rights movement.[35] Those who in a feat of arrogance wonder why African Americans cannot get over slavery would do well to think about its 246 years of daily violence inflicted on Black bodies. More importantly, all of us need to reckon with the fact that the violence has never ceased. The all-too-brief years of the civil rights movement were marked by brutal beatings of nonviolent demonstrators, by the bombing of homes and churches, and by numerous murders. Black lives remain precarious. "The unarmed, slain black bodies in public spaces," continues Rankine, "turn grief into our everyday feeling that something is wrong everywhere and all the time, even if locally things appear normal. Having coffee, walking the dog, reading the paper, dropping the kids off at school, all of this good life is surrounded by the ambient feeling that at any given moment, a black person is being killed in the street or in his home by the armed hatred of a fellow American."[36] Listening to those who have been oppressed, says Rabbi Ward-Lev, leads to mourning.[37] Mourning shatters the psychic numbness that Robert J. Lifton diagnosed; it banishes complacency. So much has been lost; so many lives destroyed; so much of the American dream disfigured beyond recognition. This is not the world we want for all of us. Lean into your grief and be released into action.

Transforming Sanghas

"Community Building is our true practice," Thich Nhat Hanh insisted.[38] Part of the interpersonal work for racial justice, community building requires reforming sanghas and their practices. Larry Yang, Buddhist teacher and one of the founders of the East Bay Meditation Center in Oakland, California, has made that injunction his calling. East Bay Meditation Center was founded in 2007 as a culmination and expression of earlier retreats for women, for people of color, and for LGBTQ practitioners. The community that the founders built is diverse both in its teachers and its practitioners, as well as multicultural in its practices. It is a community that creates a zone of safety while working through issues of race, gender, and sexual orientation. If Rhonda Magee's inner work enables individuals to sit together while they cut through the delusions of racism, Yang does the complementary work of creating inclusive communities where transformative Buddhist practices can flourish. Recall how central the southern Black churches were to sustain the civil rights movement and you get a sense of the potential of inclusive Buddhist sanghas to sustain justice work. Clearly this is hard work. It is hard for white converts who need to examine their own biases, who need to move over to allow those on the margins to exercise a prophetic voice, and to introduce new practices.[39]

Some have argued that integrating investigation of one's identity as it is shaped by the surrounding culture, including racism, sexism, and homophobia, into sangha practice is at odds with the teaching of the non-self. Offering special forms of practice for certain groups, they say, creates divisiveness and fractures the sangha. To the proponents of a generic dharma Yang's response is blunt: "This is a reflexive reaction of the culturally unconscious."[40] Using softer language, Yang points to the six or seven hundred years that it took Buddhism to adapt to Chinese culture and in the process give birth to new schools of Buddhism. We, all of us, carry our cultures in our body, speech, and mind. Not only that but we are the embodied intersection of multiple cultures. Joseph Goldstein, one of the founders of the Insight Meditation Society, said, "When we came back from Asia and started teaching, we kind of infused the teachings with our white, educated, middle-class perspectives."[41] There is no leaving our culturally shaped identity with our shoes as we enter the meditation hall. Yang says that the path to enlightenment does not require that we transcend our cultural background. We shine the light of mindfulness and compassion on the cultures that have shaped us.[42] The problem arises when a dominant group identifies its culturally shaped appropriation with "authentic" Buddhism. Others need space to sort through their own appropriation of the dharma. The dominant group needs to step back and look carefully at its own take on Buddhism. Skillful means need to be devised if the dharma as practiced in largely white convert communities is to become more inclusive, and East Bay Meditation Center has become boldly experimental. New forms of practice embody prophetic wisdom in bringing a diverse crowd to the other shore.[43]

Radical Dharma

In the introduction I acknowledged that the term "prophetic wisdom" had earlier been used by Reverend angel Kyodo williams, Lama Rod Owens, and Jasmine Syedullah in *Radical Dharma*. The authors situate their work within the Black prophetic tradition. They suggest that this prophetic fire has sputtered in the aftermath of the social and political changes embedded in the civil rights laws of the 1960s.[44] Crisscrossing the country, they revealed the legacy of the Black prophetic tradition to Buddhist communities. *Radical Dharma* is the distillation of their conversations. Prophetic wisdom emerges collectively. "The prophets called for in these times," williams argues, "necessarily arise from . . . organic (post, trans and) multi-religiosity. . . . Rather than adherence to or containment by a particular ideology, its starting point is that fundamental wisdom and basic goodness are inherent. As a result, it pivots away from salvation toward liberation."[45] Like Moses, the authors welcome all sorts of prophets, ranging from spiritual warriors to political organizers. "Wisdom prophets" will emerge when Buddhists launch themselves into a "third space as yet unknown," a space where inner liberation and social struggle fuse.[46] Such prophets form a "constant pole signaling . . . who remain on the outside" not to bring them in but to expand the reach of the sangha so that the oppressed are at the center. Such prophets "must be fierce believers in possibility . . . motivated by a deep, unwavering love of all of life, and committed to seeing that love expressed as justice."[47] These prophets will break down the doors of the prison that williams calls the "mind of whiteness."[48]

The radical dharma that these prophets will teach, argue the authors, is a "mash up" of teachings from many of the major religious traditions and the worldviews of indigenous peoples. Even a cursory look at the history of Buddhism tells us that it has opened itself to local cultures, incorporating other traditions.[49] Williams says that queerness prepared her to practice the dharma as practicing the choice to be free, exercising the will to accept herself. A queer dharma is one that goes beyond binary oppositions not just of sexuality but of all other binaries that "yoke ourselves into a system of control." This includes the separation of inner and outer practice.[50]

Radical acceptance pushes beyond loving-kindness expressed in interpersonal relations. What prevails in this society is a privatized concept of love restricted to interpersonal relationships. By contrast, radical love is "an earthy grounding power to be wielded for justice, sometimes with attending fire that burns through whatever may obscure the truth."[51] This "burning through" is required to purge the delusion of race; it is a form of love that williams sees as part of her African American legacy. Burning love challenges the Buddhist emphasis on equanimity. Lama Rod Owens sees this fierce love not as aggression but as the embodiment of Black prophetic fire. As a teacher, Lama Owens insists that his role is not to make people comfortable but to tell the truth about the suffering that we bring to the sangha.[52] If you go to any place seeking spiritual sustenance and don't feel uncomfortable at times, Reverend williams chimes in, then "you are not doing the work."[53]

As with the Hebrew prophets, there is a sense of urgency, an urgency that gives birth to an insurgency. Fifty some years after the civil rights victories of 1964 and 1965 it is clear that clinging to these past accomplishments provides cover for new forms of systemic racism. White people's reluctance to face their collective impact on people of color, their willful ignorance about the past and present, leaves a wound that festers. Buddhist communities are in crisis too. By and large, we have failed to shine the light of collective wisdom on systemic social suffering. The authors of *Radical Dharma* level a prophetic challenge to Buddhist communities in America: "This is the time when we will actually embody our practice and teachings or not." To do so, sanghas must abandon a "hyper-individualized salvation model" and overcome their "persistent resistance to playing an appropriate societal role."[54]

America's Racial Caste System

Prophetic fire is indispensable if Buddhist communities are to play a social role. Effective, strategic action also requires a critical social theory. Isabel Wilkerson's thesis that America has a racial caste system enables us to understand systemic racism on a deep level where religious traditions like Buddhism can provide an antidote.[55]

"America is an old house," Wilkerson declares near the beginning of *Caste: The Origins of Our Discontents.* Some of us know exactly what she means. A gutter has come loose and the water from a heavy rain is trickling into the basement. There is a discolored stain on the ceiling of one of the bedrooms. Does that mean that there is a leak in the roof? And most troubling of all, some sawdust has collected at the bottom of one of the original wooden pillars that hold up the house. Termites? "Ignorance is no protection from the consequences of inaction." This old house is a living organism. It breathes, coughs, and gasps. We the occupants are dependent upon it. Claiming that I was not here when the house was built so it is not my fault does not repair the damage. We are its current occupants, "and any further deterioration is, in fact, on our hands."[56] Those who believe we live in a postracial society deliberately turn a blind eye to the sawdust in the basement. We occupants have plenty to be discontented about. Some of the damage to the old house came from shoddy construction.

Wilkerson's analogy is not about guilt but about responsibility for that which has sustained us for many years. Wilkerson claims that the old house was built as a racial caste system. Like other caste systems, this building rests upon Eight Pillars. The First Pillar, "Divine Will and the Laws of Nature," grounds the system in a transcendent reality.[57] Religious scripture and/or secular "science" reveal an innate hierarchical order. In the American context the Bible, and particularly the story of the curse of Ham (Gen 9:20–27), were used to justify the enslavement of millions. In the early twentieth century a pseudoscience of eugenics provided a secular rationale for the dominance of the white, Anglo-Saxon race over all other ethnic groups, placing those of African descent at the lowest rung of the ladder. Dr. Ambedkar, we recall, argued that a caste system can be annihilated only when its core justification is challenged.

The Second Pillar, "Heritability," ensures the permanence of caste divisions.[58] Unlike the category of class, caste does not allow for social mobility. Again, we saw Dr. Ambedkar's metaphor for a caste system as a multistory building with no doors or windows and, most importantly, no staircase. In Virginia a series of laws were passed beginning in the mid-seventeenth century and consolidated in the early eighteenth century that created the categories of white and Black persons. They declared that the race of a child was determined by the race of the child's mother, not the father as in British practice. A child of an enslaved woman would also be enslaved. This law, Wilkerson notes, "converted the black womb into a profit center."[59]

The Third Pillar, "Endogamy and the Control of Marriage and Mating," built a "firewall" between castes.[60] In India, America, and Nazi Germany love across caste lines was prohibited. Permitting legal unions only between persons of similar physical traits reinforced the fiction of "race." Forty-one of the states in the United States passed laws forbidding intermarriage, statues that were overthrown by a Supreme Court decision, but not until 1967. While love was forbidden, rape by upper-caste males of lower-caste women was not only tolerated but was one more method of controlling the bodies of the lower castes.[61]

The Fourth Pillar, "Purity versus Pollution," anchors the system in primitive fears of contagion.[62] Such fears are deeply embedded in unconscious reactions of disgust and abhorrence.[63] Immigrants have often been stigmatized as dirty, smelly, and disease-ridden, a danger to the health of the body politic. Water seems to be a primary conduit of both purity and pollution. Recall the Dalit *satyagraha* campaigns that were focused on gaining access to public water wells and reservoirs. Lakes from which the livestock of Dalits could drink freely were considered polluted if a Dalit were to take one sip. In 1919 an African American boy swimming in Chicago's Lake Michigan crossed an invisible line separating the African American beach from the white beach. This led to several days of rioting across Chicago in which thirty-eight people were killed. For someone like me who grew up swimming in public pools, Wilkerson gives a disturbing plethora of examples of white mobs forcing African Americans out of public pools. Authorities forbade access to African Americans on the grounds that they would have to empty the pools in order to disinfect them if African Americans entered them. In the aftermath of the civil rights legislation of 1964, many municipalities emptied their pools and, in some cases, filled them with concrete to avoid having to integrate them.

The Fifth Pillar, "Occupational Hierarchy," confines the lower castes to the most menial occupations.[64] In the case of India, occupations considered as inherently polluting—cleaning latrines, tanning animal hides, and handling the dead—were assigned to Dalits. After the Civil War, South Carolina passed a law requiring African Americans to purchase an expensive license annually to pursue any trade except agricultural and domestic work. In 1890, 85 percent of Black men and 96 percent of Black women were employed in one of these two categories. Throughout the nineteenth century and far into the twentieth in the North, unions restricted access of African Americans to the skilled trades.

The Sixth Pillar, "Dehumanization and Stigma," is key to manufacturing an outgroup. It is, says Wilkerson, "a monumental task. It is a war against truth, against what the eye can see and what the heart could feel if allowed to do so on its own."[65] The Greek word *stigma* referred to tattoos or brands engraved mostly on the face of criminals—an ancient scarlet letter—that made permanently visible a person's shame.[66] In a society with a four-hundred-year history of racism, a person's very face itself, its color and various features, have been stigmatized. No need for a yellow star to brand one as an outcast. The stigmatized other becomes the scapegoat of the fears, resentments, and hostilities of the larger society.

Stigmatizing functions on a deep unconscious level. One way to understand it is by examining what gets labeled "normal" in society. It refers to traits of the dominant group even when—in the case of white heterosexual males—the group is a minority. It overlooks the ways in which so-called normal people deviate from the norm. I deviate from the norm of 20/20 vision and need corrective lenses. But this is not seen as a stigma. What is coded as normal slides almost imperceptibly into what is normative. It is seen as that which conforms to the nature of things. Stigmatizing displaces my shame at not adhering to the norm, my forbidden desires, and, most of all, my fears onto a vulnerable group. "Thus shame in the self often leads to the wish that others feel shame, and to practices of humiliation or active shaming that inflict stigma on vulnerable people and groups."[67] When performed collectively, stigmas seem to be projections no longer but how the other actually is. This understanding of stigmatization adds a collective delusion to what Ken Jones discussed as "antithetical bonding." Stigmatization is a form of dualistic thinking that is deeply rooted in our social psyche.

The Seventh Pillar, "Terror as Enforcement, Cruelty as a Means of Control," hides behind the manufactured illusion of the bucolic plantation and the happy, childlike slave.[68] At every moment of every day slavery was kept in place by violence and the threat of violence. Historian Edward Baptist details how torture was systematically used in forced labor camps to increase the enslaved person's productivity.[69] After the country abandoned Reconstruction in 1877, the KKK conducted a terror campaign that targeted any Black person who attempted to vote. Lynching carried out with impunity from the late nineteenth century through mid-twentieth century became the preferred terrorist weapon, especially when Black bodies were left hanging for the Black community to recognize just how little their lives mattered to white supremacy.

The Eighth Pillar, "Inherent Superiority versus Inherent Inferiority," is less of an independently standing pillar than it is the net result of the other seven.[70] It is the socially constructed platform that rests upon these pillars. It has been given the lie by the accomplishments of hundreds of thousands of African Americans and other persons imprisoned in the lower castes who have broken through the walls of the caste hierarchy, broken the barriers forbidding entrance to universities and sports teams, lunch counters and the presidency. And yet it would be a bitter delusion to hold that the caste system has been destroyed.

The metaphor of pillars is one way of conveying the strength of a caste system. It conveys the power of a caste system to endure over four hundred plus years in this land, and over centuries in India. We can point to numerous ways in which people of color and their allies have chipped away at some of these pillars. I believe that the two most resistant pillars are purity/pollution and dehumanization/stigmatization. As we have seen, both work on unconscious and conscious levels. Despite the difficulty of dealing with the fears that underly both pillars, I believe that Buddhism has a tool chest full of skillful means for addressing the delusive foundations on which they are cemented. First, as we discussed in chapter 3, the first three of Thich Nhat Hanh's Fourteen Mindfulness Trainings function as an ideology solvent. Practicing them, we become aware of our own patterns of dualistic thinking. Probing more deeply, we recognize how coded language (for example, "law and order" rhetoric) serves to discredit protest movements and how the "War on Drugs" served to criminalize addiction instead of treating it as a public health issue. We become aware of our own emotional attachment to stigmatizing labels and our own propensity to antithetically bond.

To get at the unconscious levels of shaming others and projecting them as the source of our fears, Rhonda Magee's "inner work of racial justice" would need to become a recurrent part of sangha practice, not simply a single event. Creating a space of respect and compassion, a space that makes room for expressing strong emotions, her exercises encourage us to mindfully examine our own fears and grasp how we stigmatize others as their source.[71] Mindfulness of the body, for example, can lead us to become aware of how our bodies and those of people that we meet have been racialized. We begin to be aware of how the images of our bodies and those of others have been socially conditioned. Through the various ColorInsight exercises we develop the emotional intelligence that takes us beyond sanitized conversation on race and fosters the will to act for a better world.

Mindfulness practices that nurture prophetic wisdom would no longer focus solely on the spiritual and psychological well-being of individuals in isolation. Instead, they would support a collective effort connecting inner work and outer revolution. For this to happen, sanghas across the spectrum of Buddhist traditions would need to recognize, as did Dr. King, that systemic racism is a deadly poison and that, so long as it persists, we court spiritual death. Wilkerson's critical social theory enables us to see why systemic racism endures; it is less specific, however, about how we go about dismantling it. Michelle Alexander's metaphor of a "bird cage" offers one way of moving forward strategically.

The Bird Cage

One of the features of the American caste system, argues Wilkerson, is its ability to "shape-shift" in each era to preserve it basic hierarchal structure. It has done so repeatedly. For example, numerous groups, such as the Irish, who initially were categorized as not-white were eventually incorporated and labeled as white.⁷² Michelle Alexander develops this thesis. She argues that there is a pattern to this shapeshifting. Each time African Americans and their allies make a breakthrough to secure greater freedom and equality, a white backlash heralds a new form of oppression. She sees the major shifts as evolving from slavery to Jim Crow and then to mass incarceration. A rough chronology can help to visualize this pattern:

1619–1865	246 years of slavery
1865–1877	12 years of Reconstruction and Black freedom
1877–1954	77 years of Black Codes and Jim Crow
1954–1968	14 years of the civil rights revolution
1968–1980	12 years of "law and order"
1980–2024	44 years of mass incarceration
2014–2024	10 years of Black Lives Matter
2024–?	???

Again, this is a rough chronology (I double counted the last ten years), but the main lines are incontrovertible: 379 years of intensified oppression, with 36 years of revolutionary change. This chart gives the lie to any rosy view of progress toward a "postracial" future. To be sure, throughout the darkest periods courageous resistance by ordinary Black and white people, and uncompromising challenges by prophets lit up the sky. Incremental change also occurred. Nevertheless, the math is devastating. We are trapped in the era of mass incarceration. While we may think that mass incarceration was designed to fight an increase in crime, Alexander insists that

> the term mass incarceration refers not only to the criminal justice system but also to the larger web of laws, rules, policies and customs that controls those labeled criminals both in and out of prison. Once released, former prisoners enter a hidden underworld of legalized discrimination and permanent social exclusion. . . . The system operates through our criminal justice institutions, but *it functions more like a caste system than a system of crime control.* . . . [italics added] Although this new system of racialized social control purports to be colorblind, it creates and maintains a racial hierarchy much as earlier systems of control did. Like slavery and Jim Crow, mass incarceration operates . . . collectively to ensure the subordinate status of a group defined largely by race.⁷³

Alexander uses the metaphor of a bird cage to explain how systemic racism works. If we look at a single wire, we wonder why the bird does not fly away. Only when we see multiple wires linked together do we begin to understand why the bird is trapped. Mass incarceration may seem to be a single wire, but in reality, it is a label for thousands of laws, policies, and practices that together constitute the criminal justice system and enable it to enforce caste subjugation. "Every system of control depends for its survival," Alexander maintains, "on the tangible and intangible benefits that are provided to those who are responsible for the system's maintenance and administration. This system is no exception."[74] Under the umbrella of the "War on Drugs" launched by President Ronald Reagan, a whole regime of discriminatory practices was created with incentives and rules designed to solder the multiple wires of the criminal justice system together. Drug use as a public health issue was shrouded in the fog of this war. Incentives were provided to police to increase drug arrests, which led to targeting users and low-level dealers. In 2005 only one in five drug arrests was for selling drugs. Media portrayed Black and Latinx communities as war zones. Black and Brown men were "rounded up" for crimes routinely ignored in predominately white communities. SWAT teams serving no-knock warrants ran roughshod over citizens' basic rights. Prosecutors gained reelection by being tough on crime. Public defenders were overwhelmed with cases. Mandatory sentencing guidelines handcuffed judges. Plea bargaining created instant felons without the benefit of a trial, and a prison industrial complex was born. A huge network of prison managers and workers, the rural communities where new prisons were located, and investors in prisons run by private firms had a strong incentive to keep the system in place. Finally, in the absence of alternative ways to deal with troubled children, a school-to-prison pipeline was created. Teenagers, stigmatized as criminals, were burdened with an arrest record before they graduated from high school.[75]

Once prisoners are released from prison, they enter what Alexander calls a "parallel universe" that looks remarkably like Jim Crow. They move from being "locked up to locked out." It is perfectly legal to discriminate against ex-offenders for having once committed a felony. Not only are they barred from public housing, access to food stamps, and—in many states—deprived of the right to vote and serve on juries, but it is not illegal for landlords to reject them or for business not to hire them. Branded with the stigma of a felon, they undergo a "civic death." Having done their time, they are, in effect, sentenced to a lifetime of exclusion. Sentenced with the prisoners are their impoverished families and devastated communities.[76]

A Historical Project

When Latin American liberation theologians talked about socialism as a historical project, they were pointing to a shared goal formed in solidarity with oppressed peoples throughout the continent. Religious leaders worked with "base communities" applying the prophetic teachings of the Jewish and Christian scriptures to the everyday experiences of injustice. Their historical project lay between a utopian vision and a practical blueprint for systemic change. A historical project offers a concrete focus to enable strategic action. Engaged Buddhists in the West, however, are far from developing a shared historical project rooted in dialogue within sanghas. My conviction is that if Engaged Buddhist were to develop a historical project, they would need to immediately confront the issue of systemic racism. To do so would require engaging in conversation with and following the lead of Buddhist teachers and practitioners who are people of color. What follows is simply an attempt to think with Engaged Buddhists who are people of color as a way of illustrating how prophetic wisdom could be brought to bear as a moral chemotherapy targeting systemic racism. An illustration, I hasten to add, is not a program or project. That requires collective work. Consider it, if you will, as an appeal—flawed and by no means free of blind spots—to Buddhists across all traditions within American culture to seek solidarity, within our own communities and in alliance with other groups, as a prelude to the work of the transformative imagination.

For purposes of this illustration, I suggest that working to transform mass incarceration as "the new Jim Crow" might be an appropriate historical project for Engaged Buddhists. Michelle Alexander argues forcefully that overcoming mass incarceration would tear out one crucial wire in the Bird Cage. Those of us who are Americans must remove the shameful stigma of being the nation with both the most incarcerated persons and the most prisoners per capita. That mass incarceration has racialized criminality and has disproportionately affected those who are poor or grappling with mental illness only adds to our collective shame.

There are also reasons internal to the teachings and practices of Buddhism that recommend this historical project. First, Buddhists have a history of offering mindfulness training for prisoners. Think of that as providing an inner revolution for both prisoners and their Buddhist collaborators. To work only on the inner revolution, however, is to be blind about how the prison industrial complex works, how those governing in our name have created pipelines to feed new recruits into its maw. Second, I argued above that Buddhist practices can be very helpful in dealing with stigmatization and antithetical bonding. This is a particularly pernicious form of dualistic thinking. Judith Tannenbaum, a Buddhist practitioner who has worked with prisoners for over thirty years, gives the clearest insight into prisons as stigmatizing machines: "For a moment, think of the worst thing you've ever done. Whatever it is, Remember it well. Now imagine that everything in your world is designed to treat you as a person defined by that act. Any other fact of your life—any act of love, kindness, compassion, intelligence, creativity, joy, humor—is irrelevant. You are only a person who has done this worst thing. That's it, that's you, from now till forever. This is the reality of a person in prison."[77] Third, the teaching that all beings have a Buddha Nature makes it clear that all people are capable of transformation. No one is to be equated with their worst action. Likewise, the teaching that birth as a human being is precious also makes it clear that no one is disposable, having a life that does not matter.

From a Buddhist standpoint those who have committed crimes have damaged their community and themselves. They have torn Indra's Net. The task of the community in cooperation with the offender is to repair the torn net, to disentangle the knotted nodes. Retribution only tears the net further. Those who have proven to be a danger to themselves and others may need to be restrained for a time, but the community should see this as a demand to bring to bear all of its healing arts. Finally, Dr. Ambedkar came to realize that religious traditions must play a crucial role in overcoming caste hierarchies. Religions, including Buddhism, need to foster a collective realization of the shamefulness of America's system of mass incarceration. They need to generate the motivation, the political will to change.

Restorative Justice

Guiding the praxis of ending mass incarceration requires a shift from a punitive mindset expressed in the theory and practice of retributive justice to restorative justice. "Restorative justice" is a term applied to a variety of experiments in over a half century (over millennia in the case of numerous indigenous peoples) to develop alternatives to arrest, trial, and imprisonment. These alternatives share a common focus on healing victims, insisting that offenders take responsibility for their actions, and on restoring what has been damaged in the community. Engaged Buddhists' ambivalence regarding reliance on a concept of justice to guide praxis leads to one clear conclusion: there should be no ambivalence about retributive justice. I take it as axiomatic that retributive justice is incompatible with Buddhist teachings because it increases rather than diminishes suffering.[78] Punishment is the coercive imposition of suffering. Prisons, even if they maintain the fiction of rehabilitation, are designed to victimize the one who has broken the law, to rob a person of any sense of agency. That person must "pay" for the crime committed. Prisons are places where violence is the daily norm. In most cases imprisonment exacerbates a complex entanglement of poverty, poor schools, lack of jobs that pay a living wage, and mental illness. However, we have seen that there are alternative approaches to justice that Engaged Buddhists might consciously embrace.

Restorative justice offers a clear alternative. It shifts the focus from a binary frame (guilt/innocence, crime/punishment) to a wholistic approach that addresses the needs of the victim—something that the criminal justice system largely ignores—and the community, as well as requiring that the offenders take responsibility for their actions. Howard Zehr, a pioneer in the development of the theory and practice of restorative justice, defines restorative justice as "an approach to achieving justice that involves, to the extent possible, those who have a stake in a specific offense or harm to collectively identify and address harms, needs and obligations in order to heal and put things as right as possible."[79] Where the criminal justice system treats the offender as violating the state and its laws, restorative justice sees an offense as harm to an individual and as a tear in the social fabric.

Given restorative justice's commitment to address the needs of all parties to an offense, participation in every stage of the process is consensual. There must be no coercion of either the victim or the offender. This requires careful preparation. Trained facilitators play a critical role in establishing a safe space where all parties can share what they are going through.[80] The heart of the process is an event in which all involved are present in a circle. Victims articulate the harm that they have experienced and its ongoing effects; offenders must listen and take responsibility for their actions and indicate their willingness to fulfill collectively determined obligations. Family members and community representatives can speak of their failure to provide adequate guidance to the offender in the past and pledge their future support. Those gathered in the circle come to an agreed set of obligations that the offender must fulfill to repair the harm that has been done. Offenders are closely monitored and mentored as they go through a lengthy process of meeting the agreed-upon obligations.

Through its inclusiveness, restorative justice reveals a broader truth, not just a determination of guilt but a contextual truth, the tear in the social fabric.[81] The degree of restoration depends upon the commitment of all parties to the process and to carrying out ensuing obligations to put things right.[82] According to its proponents, restorative justice is one facet of a "deliberative democracy," one way of creating grassroots institutions that treat all members of the community with dignity and respect. Offenders are not stigmatized. The community pulls together to support efforts to heal the torn social fabric.[83] Zehr summarizes the differences between retributive justice and restorative justice:

Retributive Justice:	**Restorative Justice:**
Crime is a violation of the law and the state.	Crime is a violation of people and relationships.
Violations create guilt.	Violations create obligations.
Justice requires the state to determine blame (guilt) and impose pain (punishment).	Justice involves victims, offenders and community members in an effort to repair the harm, "to put things right."
Central focus: offenders getting what they deserve.	*Central focus: victim's needs and offender's responsibility for repairing harm.*[84]

This approach to criminal justice has been employed by indigenous peoples for centuries. For small societies a rent in the social fabric can have disastrous consequences if not quickly repaired, and they cannot afford to dispose of potentially productive members of their societies. For at least the last half century restorative justice approaches have taken a variety of forms, ranging from one-on-one conferences between victims and offenders to Truth and Reconciliation processes in postconflict situations. They have been widely used in schools and as diversionary programs of court systems in lieu of expelling or arresting children.[85]

At every level of the criminal justice system, argues Danielle Sered, the founder and director of Common Justice, a restorative justice organization in the Bronx and Brooklyn, we have as a society become more and more punitive: more aggressive policing, more suspensions and arrests of school children, greater criminalization of addiction and mental illness, longer prison sentences, mandatory minimum sentences and three strikes laws, and greater surveillance of parolees. Mass incarceration is only the tip of a relentlessly punitive system. "We control each other," Sered laments, "punish each other and throw each other away."[86] Bluntly stated, mass incarceration needs to be seen as horrific violence carried out by the state against its own people.

Sered approaches the ripple effects of mass incarceration in a spirit of not-knowing. We do not know what the long-term effects will be on neighborhoods stripped of potentially productive members. How can those communities cope with so much pain and trauma? We do not know what the intergenerational effects of mass incarceration will be. We do not know what will happen to the children whose caregivers are taken away. Above all, "we do not know what happens to the psyche and character of a nation that surpasses all others in its use of confinement." Not-knowing is no excuse. "We know enough to know that incarceration generates devastating and often lasting negative repercussions and that it has an intergenerational effect." We face a national reckoning.[87] It will be painful. It will entail grieving for the people thrown away. It is necessary if we are to break the hold of a cruel spirit that has taken hold of our psyches.[88]

Set within this cancerous context, restorative justice functions as a moral chemotherapy. Except for Truth and Reconciliation processes in postconflict war zones, restorative justice processes are, for the most part, elected when the infraction does not involve violence. Violent actions, however, are the acid test for this alternative to retributive justice. Unless we deal with more serious crimes, Sered argues, we will not achieve the 50 percent reduction in incarceration that reformers seek.[89] Common Justice is one model that has successfully and directly met this test. It is a court diversion program based on four core principles: it is "survivor-centered, accountability-based, safety-driven and racially-equitable."[90] Common Justice's practice of restorative justice begins with this dictum: "Violence rips something in the social fabric."[91] The existing criminal justice system does nothing to repair that tear. So Common Justice centers on the survivors, on their trauma and needs for healing.[92] Above all the restorative process flows from the acknowledgment that what has been done to the survivor was wrong. To restore trust, it must be made clear that the world does not accept violence as the norm.[93] Consequently, the survivor's explicit consent is necessary to begin the process and at each subsequent step. Healing both the survivor and the community takes time and attention to restore a sense of safety.

"Accountability-based" is the crux of the matter. Forgiveness and mercy may arise, but they are not the goals of the process. Rather the responsible parties are recognized as moral agents, persons of moral worth who are responsible for their actions. An accountability-based process is fundamentally different from a court's finding of guilt and subsequent punishment. The responsible parties must listen to the survivors' narratives of the harm that they have experienced and, without excuses or evasion, acknowledge their responsibility and indicate their remorse for what they have done. Responsible parties, survivors, and the community must come to agreement on a course of action to repair the harm as much as possible. Finally, the responsible parties must avoid any recurrence of their violent behaviors. Only after the process is complete will the felony charge be vacated.[94]

Engaging in an accountability process takes months of preparation just to begin. It can take years to complete stipulations, ranging from taking the GEDs to writing letters of apology to those harmed, from finding and keeping a job to joining an organization dedicated to violence prevention, from keeping a journal tracking one's process to speaking about the violent act and its aftermath with a group of peers.[95] Donnell is one responsible party who went through such a process over several years after attacking another person with a knife. He clearly expresses the impact of the process:

> It's like I had to go through something to feel a connection to anybody being hurt. I had to go through my own hurt too. . . . When you do, you watch the magic of something happening where you start to give that same care back to the person that you harmed. That's what meeting that person has done. . . . We've [Donnell and the survivor] been in different places sharing our story. I'm sitting here looking at this person, like, you're so similar to me. You're so much of who I am. Your dreams are like mine. . . . We are so connected, and we didn't even know this thing.[96]

Restorative justice has proven to be especially effective as an alternative to expulsion and arrest in the school context. But for it to be scaled up would require close ties between teachers and school officials with parents and the community the school serves. Social workers would replace police officers in the schools. It would need cadres of trained facilitators, and the willingness of the community to provide mentorship and volunteer support as the responsible students fulfill their pledges and the survivors heal.

Religious communities are particularly able to provide such support. Many, including Buddhists, already offer support to prisoners. Compassionate care extended to victims enabling them to regain a sense of security, a sense of worth and an affirmation that the harm they have suffered was wrong, is one step further. Another step in expanding compassion is the ability of religious communities to destigmatize offenders, while supporting their taking responsibility for their actions. Religious communities can enable the offenders' families to overcome their sense of shame. Practical help to reintegrate ex-offenders also is well within the capacity of sanghas.[97] Buddhists could be particularly helpful in a number of these roles given their mindfulness training and the centrality of the practice of compassion.

We already practice a form of restorative justice, insists Sered, namely in our treatment of white, middle-class adolescents. First, we treat them as adolescents and not as protocriminals. We offer assistance and resources. We do not see their acting out as predictive of their future. We work around the legal system when they are accused of possessing or selling small amounts of illicit drugs. "We provide pathways out of the idiocy and chaos of adolescence into adulthood." We breathe a sigh of relief when they follow such a path. All children, Sered concludes, deserve such support.[98]

Conclusion

Restorative justice practices are only one strategy for disentangling the mass incarceration wire in the bird cage. The criminal justice system, as we saw, is a network of laws, policies, and practices fostered by a fear-based punitive ethos in the culture. It ties together the school-to prison-pipeline, overpolicing of Black and Brown communities, the lack of mental health services, district attorneys who run for office promising to get tough on crime, and the criminalizing of drug addiction. Each of these entangled wires needs to be dealt with. Some Buddhist groups might feel called to work in electoral politics in alliance with progressive movements to elect district attorneys and judges who see the effectiveness of restorative justice and are willing to create diversion programs for youthful offenders. Buddhists might be especially helpful in addressing the "punishment mind-set" that manifests itself in increasingly punitive measures, including arresting young students, that is, the criminalization of children; longer prison sentences; and legalized discrimination against ex-convicts.[99] Integrating mindfulness practices that bring to the surface and heal the fears that underlie this mindset with a commitment to the political work of ending mass incarceration could be especially useful.

Granted, dismantling an entire criminal justice system is a multigenerational task. We have seen, however, in Eastern Europe in the 1980s and 1990s and, for that matter, in the American civil rights movement that at certain points trickles of change coming together create a cascade. Meanwhile, if a sangha as a group were willing to take on a historical project, that would almost surely lead to deep discussion of the dharma and new forms of mindful practice.

The beauty of the bird cage metaphor is that it does not require every wire to be pulled out for there to be liberation. Pull up several interlocking wires and the bird will leap free and the cage will rust. The civil rights movements labored mightily on some concrete projects (bus boycotts, desegregating lunch counters, registering voters) until in a remarkably short space of time the pillars supporting Jim Crow were torn down. To be sure, these victories were hardly unambiguous. The racial caste system continued (and continues) to mutate.

The strategic pragmatism of a historical project is imperative, but, in the midst of struggle, it must hear the prophetic voice. The Hebrew prophets of the Exile of the sixth century BCE did not settle for half measures. They offered a vision of an alternative future in which, as Isaiah put it, there will be a new heaven and a new earth in which one will not build and another inhabit, one will not plant and another eat (Isa 65:21–23; 66:22). The eschatological vision of the Hebrew prophets tapped into hopes that had persisted for ages like an underground aquifer. These hopes transcended any particular historical project. What kind of a community must we build in which Maitreya the Buddha of the future will be born? What kind of world will facilitate all persons' realization of their Buddha Nature? Have we even begun to have that discussion? Toward what future do the many projects of Engaged Buddhists point?

Prisons, argues Mariame Kaba, are the microcosmic mirror of the system that requires prisons and a society given over to racialized policing and control. We have so internalized a punitive, stigmatizing mindset that if mass incarceration were to end at dawn, we would likely replicate it by day's end. "It's time to imagine what it would look like to see justice done without relying on punishment and the barbarity of carceral systems. . . . It's time," Kaba demands, "for a jailbreak of the imagination."[100]

Conclusion

At the core of each life's journey is one question that we are born to pursue. For me, that question has been How can I be fully present to my world—present enough to rejoice and be useful—when we as a species are destroying it? The query was clearly my life koan. I learned then in a circle of colleagues, that expressing our pain for the world can uncover a wellspring of solidarity and creativity.

—Joanna Macy, *A Wild Love for the World*[1]

For whenever I speak, I must cry out, I must shout, "Violence and destruction! . . . If I say, "I will not . . . speak any more in his name," then within me there is something like a burning fire shut up in my bones; I am weary with holding it in, and I cannot.

—Jer 20:8–9

Moses said . . . Would that all the Lord's people were prophets and that the Lord would put his spirit on them.

—Num 11:29

Moses, Jeremiah, and Joanna Macy. We began with them, so it is fitting that we end with them. We would be hard-pressed to find three more temperamentally different personalities. Yet we have explored how aspects of the thoughts, speech, and actions of Engaged Buddhists, like Macy, bear a family resemblance to key traits that characterize the prophetic ethos. This ethos is robust. It is much deeper than social criticism. Its wellsprings can be tapped into from many different angles, from within many different traditions, both religious and secular.

The Hebrew prophets are their voice, and through that voice they turned the wheel of truth and justice. Through their words, symbolic acts of resistance, and visions of an alternative future, they prefigured a just community. The prophetic texts are classics that retain the power to spark new readings and, more importantly, new forms of action. Like the Qumran community, we inserted ourselves within the prophetic tradition, drawing strength and direction from their example of revisioning the prophetic texts. To be sure, this reading of the prophets has been highly selective. The Buddhist teachings of dukkha, impermanence, interdependence, and Buddha Nature have filtered what we borrowed. So, for example, the prophetic texts' frequent misogynistic metaphors, dualistic theology, and warrior god are inconsistent with any reimagining of Buddha Nature and with Engaged Buddhism's commitment to nonviolent action.

The Prophetic Ethos

The prophetic classics embody numerous traits that are potentially transformative. We focused on eight such traits.

1. *Polyphonic texts and ethical interpretation.* Having been redacted extensively, the prophetic texts do not speak with a single voice. We are forced to ask which of the many voices in these texts represent an emancipatory thrust. Similarly, Rita Gross called upon all Buddhists to engage in an ethical interpretation of which strands within patriarchal Buddhism represent both the deepest understanding of core Buddhist teachings and a way forward. In her case, fundamental teachings, such as Buddha Nature, and the Buddha's own admission that women are fully capable of achieving enlightenment served as guidance in a critical retrieval of one continuous strand affirming human equality weaving its way through history, albeit frequently as a maligned minority view.

2. *Subversive memory.* Brian Victoria's *Zen at War* is a classic model of critical historical research that unveils the dark side of his own Soto Zen tradition. Diagnosis entails discovering just where one's own tradition veered off the rails. From a Buddhist standpoint we look for the moments when the bearers of a tradition rationalized collective actions that increased suffering. Victoria retrieves examples of individuals and groups who resisted the flood tide of imperial aggression and fortified their resistance by uncovering core Buddhist ideas and practices that embodied an emancipatory thrust. Lacking such a subversive memory, a tradition comes to a dead end.

3. *Practice of grief. Prophetic Wisdom* began by recounting the anguished cry of a nameless woman in a Montgomery jail. Her grief and that of others in this book testified that "something is terribly wrong." The Hebrew prophets' enactment of grief broke through the collective denial that a way of life was about to be destroyed. Grief is not a "negative" emotion to be quickly resolved so that one can "move on." Treating it as such denies the reality of suffering. Rather grieving is a practice. Reckoning with trauma is necessary for the rebirth of hope. Repeatedly we have seen the importance of grief as a spiritual as well as a psychological process in, for example, Rita Gross's "leaning into grief" or Joanna Macy's workshops designed to break through psychic numbness about the perils of nuclear weapons and nuclear waste.

Chapter 10 opened with the lament of a Chinese American Buddhist. "Where are you?" she seemed to demand of her fellow Buddhists. Where are you when Asian Americans are the targets of hate crimes? In Jan Willis's article "We Can't Breathe," grief gave birth to a jeremiad directed at Buddhist sanghas.

4. *Alternative narrative.* The Hebrew prophetic texts offer an alternative to the royal consciousness that proclaimed a sacred, cosmic order with a fixed hierarchy of king and priests ruling over a chosen people in God's holy city of Jerusalem. The prevailing narrative suggested that this order would be eternal until in the sixth century BCE its pillars were destroyed. The prophets also saw the empire du jour for what it was: a collective delusion bristling with weapons but as impermanent as the societies it conquered. Dr. B. R. Ambedkar similarly attacked the sacred Hindu texts that sanctified the caste system. He argued relentlessly that democracy and caste, as a ruthlessly enforced system of graded inequality, are incompatible, but the annihilation of caste requires dealing with its religious roots. In contrast to caste ideology, his alternative narrative offered a vision of democracy as free and equal association within all spheres of social existence bound together by loving-kindness.

5. *Ideology critique.* Engaged Buddhism is particularly well suited to carry out the prophetic task of ideology critique. Thich Nhat Hanh's first three mindfulness trainings, for example, are focused on resisting what David Loy calls "weapons of mass deception." These include fixed ideas, particularly those that involve dualistic thinking, propaganda, dogmas that cut off the search for truth, and rhetoric that stirs up fears while claiming authority to overcome them. Fixed, emotionally rooted identities become superglued through "antithetical bonding" over against a stigmatized other. The Other becomes an evil that must be eradicated.

Buddhists committed to the abolition of mass incarceration should look to the roots of the punishment mindset as exhibiting a similar pattern. The more that persons can be stigmatized as evil, the more they can be confined and exposed to constant pain and humiliation. Ignoring the social context of offenses, viewing them as solely the responsibility of the offender, and defining offenders in terms of their worst actions justifies the state's arrogation of the power to punish. Reason alone will not suffice to resist the increasing criminalization of social conflicts. Mindfulness training can enable us to be aware of these connected processes.

6. *Justice.* Understandably, Buddhist thinkers shy away from the Hebrew prophets' use of justice discourse because they see *retributive* justice that ferrets out guilt and justifies punishment as a pervasive strain within the prophetic tradition. Retributive justice in these texts sanctifies an increase of suffering. However, retributive justice is only one of several models of justice that we have viewed, some of which accord more closely with Buddhist teachings. Early Buddhist sutras, for example, strongly affirm *distributive* justice as preventing a society's descent into poverty and spiraling from there into violence and chaos.[2] For the Hebrew prophets, justice demanded a preferential option for the widow, the orphan, and the stranger, those who had no place within the patriarchal clan structure. Jeremiah offers a utopian vision of justice as a covenant that will be written on each person's heart. In this revision of the covenant on Mount Sinai there will be no need for hierarchical authority as intermediary between a god and her people, an authority that inevitably governs through coercion.

Our discussion of mass incarceration as one wire in the bird cage of systemic racism led to a model of justice that, arguably, fits most tightly with Buddhist social ethics and contrasts most sharply with retributive justice. *Restorative* justice offers an alternative to retribution in dealing with wrongdoing. It addresses the suffering of the victim and the offender and knits the tear in the social fabric by including all relevant parties in a process of accountability, reflection, and determination of reparative actions. It actualizes the principle of interdependence in a concrete way that preserves the agency and responsibility of all participants. It is a way of reconciling justice with loving-kindness and compassion while preserving moral accountability. Engaged Buddhists could make a helpful contribution to a variety of restorative justice projects.

7. *Practice of hope.* The Hebrew prophets were neither fortune tellers nor political strategists. They did envision a radical social transformation, the inauguration of a "new heaven and a new earth" (Isa 65:17). "The task of the prophetic imagination," Walter Brueggemann insists, "is to bring to

public expression those very hopes and yearnings that have been denied for so long and suppressed so deeply that we no longer know that they are there."[3] Joanna Macy's call for "the Great Turning" similarly offers a radical hope against hope. Such hope, we argued, is not wishful thinking, nor a delusive distraction from the present moment, with all of its complications. Racism has been so baked into the policies and practices of our institutions that many Americans recoil from even acknowledging its reality. Hopelessness is contagious. Working to dismantle the bird cage wire by wire is an act of hope that harbors no illusions but inspires others to act.

8. *A call to action.* In the midst of an imperial invasion of Judah, Jeremiah followed God's command to buy a field and plant it. This symbolic act embodied hope. Each of our elders was set in motion by what Dr. Martin Luther King Jr. called "the fierce urgency of now." Rita Gross demanded that all Buddhists lay to rest patriarchal Buddhism and ferret out the androcentric biases in Buddhism. Thich Nhat Hanh called for a cessation of hostilities on all sides in the Vietnam War and trained young people to enter burned-out villages and rebuild them. Joanna Macy devised workshops that prepared participants to take on the work of ushering in the Great Turning. B. R. Ambedkar used all manner of skillful means—including rhetoric resembling the jeremiad—to annihilate the caste system in India. Numerous Engaged Buddhists of a younger generation have also responded to the fierce urgency of now. The authors of *Radical Dharma* see the present as the time when Buddhists will either take on the task of overcoming systemic racism or, like Dr. King's Rip Van Winkle, will sleep through a revolution.

From Prophecy to Praxis

The jeremiad has long been a compelling discourse within American reform movements calling the nation to recognize the danger of a collective spiritual death. Used sparingly, it functions as a moral chemotherapy. *Prophetic Wisdom* concentrated on the role of African Americans in igniting prophetic fire. We can see a line stretching from Frederick Douglass to Ida B. Wells to Martin Luther King Jr. Wildfires are rarely contained within conventional boundaries. Prophetic fire leaped across boundary lines and sparked Buddhists such as Jan Willis, who leveled her own jeremiad.

New prophetic voices are emerging from those sanghas that have created a younger, multicultural, multiracial community. They challenge sanghas to adopt a variety of skillful means to attract and meet the needs of a diverse group of practitioners. No one way of being Buddhist can claim to be the authentic way. We need to listen deeply to every voice.

Jeremiads are not enough. In confronting the three collective poisons identified by Dr. King (poverty/economic exploitation, militarism, and racism), Engaged Buddhists need to move from exercising a prophetic voice to strategic action, to praxis. However, most sanghas in the American context have not thought through how confronting collective poisons could be an intrinsic part of their practice. Nor have they begun the dialogue that might lead to a shared project of social transformation.

The Bodhisattva path sees the liberation of each as dependent upon the liberation of all. This includes liberation from historically and socially conditioned dukkha. The earlier generation of Engaged Buddhists represented by our four elders and the many voices that we have listened to in earlier chapters used prophetic wisdom to turn the Dharma wheel. Christopher Queen says that in the process they created a new vehicle of liberation, a Navayāna.[4] They offered Buddhist teachings with an emancipatory thrust. They and others leave a precious legacy in our hands.

One way of continuing that legacy is for sanghas to provide spiritual nurturance to sustain individuals in their professional life, in volunteer efforts, and in social activism. This we called a centrifugal strategy, spinning out individuals to follow as best they can the path of right action. A centrifugal strategy maximizes individual liberty but at the expense of collective action in which Buddhists might make a visible and distinctive impact on fields of action. Without coercing their practitioners' commitments, individual sanghas and networks of sanghas should offer the opportunity for Buddhists to act in concert, offering Buddhist insights and modes of action to larger communities and movements for social change. Such action requires strategic thinking to be maximally effective.

Engaged Buddhism has been shaped and reshaped by those who have drunk from the waters of the prophetic ethos. Multiple streams constitute our cultural watershed. To recognize our multiple sources of wisdom and the ways in which specific streams nourish us is to invigorate our continuing struggle for social justice and complete liberation. Our elders' innovations in Buddhist practices, like Joanna Macy's Council of All Beings, and Rhonda Magee's ColorInsight exercises, prefigure an alternative future in which agape, power, and justice achieve a dynamic and ever-changing equilibrium.

As I write, I have just returned from leafleting at our local farmers' market. The flyer announces a rally to commemorate the bombings of Hiroshima and Nagasaki seventy-eight years ago. It calls on all of us to join the Union of Concerned Scientists in stepping "back from the brink."[5] The Chicago chapter of the Buddhist Peace Fellowship has been cosponsoring this event with local peace organizations for the last seven years. It is a bright sunny day. Last night's downpour has moderated temperatures. The prospect of a nuclear holocaust is the last thing on people's minds. They walk happily from the market with their baskets and reusable bags full of green vegetables, peaches, sunflowers, and the season's first corn. Others stream into the market, purposeful and intent. They too crave the earth's abundance. Both groups take my flyer with only a pause when they glance at the rally's title: "Hiroshima: History or Prelude?" And then they move on. The title puzzles me: History is aways a prelude. The question is, What kind of prelude? Is this what Robert J. Lifton meant by "psychic numbness"? Jeremiah was sentenced to death and thrown into a cistern for his version of leafleting in the temple precincts, for challenging the royal consciousness of a sacred order that would last forever. Whatever terror he experienced, at least he knew that his words stung deeply. Today the military industrial juggernaut rolls on, spending our national treasure to the tune of 1.7 trillion dollars over thirty years to upgrade nuclear weapons that must be left to rust forever. So many rallies, so many pebbles bouncing off its armor plates.

I don't begrudge the crowd's unfeigned happiness. After I have handed out my flyers, I, too, go shopping in the market. How many are mindfully shopping today? How many have found their own ways of demanding a nuclear-free future? Jeremiah, cursing the day he was born, is not a good model of a prophet who combines joy in the good things of this earth with firm resistance to all those forces that would obliterate this earth and its living beings.

Dr. King's experience in formally opposing the war in Vietnam comes closer to Jeremiah's calling out the keeners than to the happy shoppers. As we saw in chapter 7, "A Time to Break Silence" is a lament, a lament for the loss of life but also for the derailing of a revolution on American soil. Vilified by the erstwhile liberal establishment, accused of treason by his detractors, and abandoned by his fellow civil rights leaders, King prophesied an endless series of wars unless the United States would carry out a revolution of values. King's own version of a Great Turning involved addressing the collective ills of racism, militarism, and economic exploitation. Failure to do so, he insisted, would mean spiritual death. "Over the bleached bones . . . of numerous civilizations," he lamented, "are written the pathetic words 'Too late.'"[6] Those words were preached over fifty-six years ago. Can a people court spiritual death for that long without succumbing? So many signs point to spiritual death: endless wars and preparations for wars, obscene economic inequality, the growing aggression of the white supremacist movement, the inability to mount an all-out vigorous, multipronged, and global response to the climate emergency, to state only a few signs of a metastatic social cancer.

Yet our engaged elders and the many others whom we have studied insist that a Great Turning is possible. Ezekiel's dry bones shall live again (Ezek 37). Dr. King offered a moral chemotherapy with a large dose of loving-kindness to heal the trauma. We honor his legacy and that of our Buddhist elders by borrowing a prophetic voice ourselves, by choosing to be here fully engaged in this time of peril for all sentient beings. Thich Nhat Hanh offers a koan—one not to be solved but to be lived—that best describes the task before us:

> "The work of building will take ten thousand lifetimes
> But dear one, look—
> That work has been achieved ten thousand lives ago."[7]

Notes

Introduction

1. Joanna Macy, "Our Life as Gaia," in *Thinking Like a Mountain: Towards a Council of All Beings*, ed. John Seed, Joanna Macy, Pat Fleming, and Arne Ness (Philadelphia, PA: New Society, 1988), 63–64.

2. Thich Nhat Hanh, "Discourse on Love," https://plumvillage.org/library/sutras/discourse-on-love.

3. Some scholars have suggested that we should not capitalize "Engaged." Others have argued that prevailing definitions are too narrow. The premise of this book is that "Engaged Buddhism" is a distinct international movement that has emerged within various schools of Buddhism. It has identifiable leaders and distinctive themes and concepts. To be sure, it manifests itself in multiple forms of engagement, and the boundaries of the movement are fuzzy. There is no orthodoxy or orthopraxis apart from the Buddhist commitment to work for the liberation of all living beings. Capitalizing "Engaged" orients the reader to this identifiable movement. Compare this with the use of capitals to identify the "Social Gospel movement" in the American context or the United Presbyterians, not the united Presbyterians. A more diffuse movement such as the "Proud Boys" is still capitalized. We do not say "proud boys." For a critical appraisal of different understandings of what falls within the broad tent of Engaged Buddhism, see Donna Lynn Brown, "Beyond Queen and King: Democratizing 'Engaged Buddhism,'" *Journal of Buddhist Ethics* 30 (2023): 7–58.

4. Sallie King, *Socially Engaged Buddhism* (Honolulu: University of Hawaii, 2009), 1.

5. Christopher Queen, "Introduction: A New Buddhism," in *Engaged Buddhism in the West*, ed. Christopher Queen (Boston, MA: Wisdom, 2000), 1–2. To clarify further what kinds of commitment Engaged Buddhism calls for, I suggest that there are three types of social engagement. First, social service represents organized compassion directed toward healing social suffering (e.g., Thich Nhat Hanh's School

of Youth for Social Service). Second, social development builds communities, networks, NGOs, and civil society to enable persons and groups to thrive. For example, Paul Farmer's organization, Partnership in Health, trains Haitian community health workers. See Paul Farmer, *Pathologies of Power: Health, Human Rights, and the New War on the Poor* (Berkeley: University of California Press, 2005). In some cases it offers a wholistic alternative to Western forms of economic educational, and cultural development (e.g., Sri Lanka's Sarvodaya movement). Third, social transformation pursues fundamental social change through collective, nonviolent action. This third form focuses on multiple forms of systemic, structural violence, institutionalized forms of the three poisons. Structural violence becomes normalized through ideologies that require deconstruction if society is to be reconstructed.

6. Johan Galtung pioneered the use of the term "structural violence" to describe how social institutions impose oppression in a way that does physical as well as mental harm. Johan Galtung, "Violence, Peace and Peace Research," *Journal of Peace Research* 6, no. 3 (1969): 167–91. The late Paul Farmer, a medical doctor and advocate internationally for health care for poor peoples, adds, "[Latin American liberation theologians] used the term broadly to describe 'sinful' structures characterized by poverty and steep grades of social inequality, including racism and gender inequality. Structural violence is violence exerted systematically—that is, indirectly—by everyone who belongs to a certain social order: hence the discomfort these ideas provoke in a moral economy still geared to pinning praise or blame on individual actors. In short, the concept of structural violence is intended to inform the study of the social machinery of oppression." Paul Farmer, "Anthropology of Structural Violence," in *Partner to the Poor: A Paul Farmer Reader*, ed. Haun Saussy (Berkeley: University of California Press, 2010), 354. For an illustration of how global economic development leads to premature death, see Farmer *Pathologies of Power*, 31–35.

7. Rita Gross, *Buddhism after Patriarchy* (Albany, NY: SUNY Press, 1993), 134, 169–70, 215; Rita Gross, *A Garland of Feminist Reflections: Forty Years of Religious Exploration* (Berkeley: University of California Press, 2009), 237; Rita Gross and Rosemary Radford Ruether, *Religious Feminism and the Future of the Planet: A Christian Buddhist Conversation* (New York: Bloomsbury Academic, 2001), 164–70.

8. Gross, *Buddhism after Patriarchy*, 134.

9. Rebecca Solnit, "How Buddhism Has Changed the West for the Better," *Guardian*, February 8, 2022, https://www.theguardian.com/commentisfree/2022/feb/08/buddhism-thich-nhat-hanh-death.

10. Gross, *Buddhism after Patriarchy*, 214, 218.

11. Paul Knitter, *Without Buddha I Could Not Be a Christian* (Oxford: One World, 2009).

12. Charles R. Strain, *The Prophet and the Bodhisattva: Daniel Berrigan, Thich Nhat Hanh, and the Ethics of Peace and Justice* (Eugene, OR: Wipf and Stock, 2014), 245–47.

13. Rita Gross, "Buddhism and Feminism Part II," *Eastern Buddhist* 19, no. 2 (1986): 62–63; Thich Nhat Hanh, *Living Buddha, Living Christ* (New York: Riverhead Books, 1995), 9–11. Interdependent coarising (*Pratītya samutpāda*) is the central Buddhist teaching that all that is comes to be because of an infinite chain of events, causes, and conditions. We lack any permanent, substantive reality. We are constantly changing, and we are changing the world around us. We are intrinsically bound up with all reality. Or, as Thich Nhat Hanh puts it, we interare with all beings. Thich Nhat Hanh, *Interbeing: Fourteen Guidelines for Engaged Buddhism*, 3rd ed. (Berkeley CA: Parallax Press, 1998), 6.

14. Gross, *Buddhism after Patriarchy*, 183).

15. The term "dukkha" is commonly translated in English as "suffering," as in the First Noble Truth: Life is suffering. Many scholars agree that this translation misses important nuances. Numerous alternatives have been suggested. Life is plagued by dis-ease. Life is out of whack, out of kilter, warped. Life is troubled by a sense of lack. Buddhism has, for the most part focused on the existential/psychological roots of dukkha. See David Loy *Money. Sex. War. Karma: Notes for a Buddhist Revolution* (Boston: Wisdom Publications, 2008), 15–23. I am tempted to add a verse from a Bruce Springsteen lyric as capturing the meaning of dukkha: "Everybody's got a hungry heart."

In this book we focus on collective dukkha and see it just as fundamental to our predicament as existential dukkha. Here the First Noble Truth might be phrased: Life is pervaded by and intertwined with oppressive forces, social structures, institutions, ideologies, laws and cultural mores. It is manifested in explicit thwarting of both individuals' and groups' possibilities for flourishing. It may also be enforced as a taken for granted "reality." It may be invisible to those who benefit from the status quo but painfully evident to those whom it excludes from sharing the resources, opportunities, and benefits that a society offers to those it includes. Collective dukkha is grounded in the discriminatory exercise of power.

16. All translations from the Hebrew scriptures are from the New Revised Standard Version.

17. Abraham Heschel, *The Prophets* (New York: Harper and Row, 1962), 204.

18. Gross, *Buddhism after Patriarchy*, 132–34.

19. Gross, *Buddhism after Patriarchy*, 183.

20. Rabbi Abraham Heschel as cited in Cornel West, "Hope and Despair: Past and Present," in *To Shape a New World: Essays on the Political Philosophy of Martin Luther King Jr.*, ed. Tommie Shelby and Brandon M. Terry (Cambridge, MA: Harvard University Press, 2018), 329.

21. I thought that this term was my own invention until I went back and reread *Radical Dharma*. The authors use the term frequently. Here is their capsule summary of the term: "Prophetic wisdom . . . transcends dualism or any frames that would limit the creative emergence of truth. Rather than adherence to or containment by a particular ideology, its starting point is that fundamental wisdom and

basic goodness are inherent. As a result, it pivots from salvation toward liberation. Collectively its practitioners are bound by an allegiance . . . to a new dharma." angel Kyodo williams and Lama Rod Owens, with Jasmine Syedullah, *Radical Dharma: Talking Race, Love, and Liberation* (Berkeley, CA: North Atlantic Books, 2016), 192.

Chapter One

1. Martin Luther King, "My Jewish Brother," in *The Radical King*, ed. Cornel West (Boston, MA: Beacon Press, 2015), 101–2.

2. Else K. Holt, "The Prophet as Persona," in *The Oxford Handbook of the Prophets*, ed. Carolyn J. Sharp (New York: Oxford University Press, 2016), 309.

3. Mid-twentieth-century scholarship on the prophets searched for the historical kernel in the heavily redacted prophetic books. More recently, scholars have interpreted the meaning of these texts as literary wholes. The Jeremiah and Isaiah that appear in the text, as well as their God, are literary inventions even when dealing with real historical events such as the Exile. This suspension of the quest for the historical Jeremiah does not undermine the power of the prophetic voice; it shifts it to the meaning disclosed in the text. So when we refer to "Amos" or "Micah" or certainly to "Jeremiah," it is always the text—often one redacted over several centuries—to which we refer as well as to the prophetic persona who appears in the text. Louis Stulman and Hyun Chul Paul Kim, *You Are My People* (Nashville, KY: Abingdon Press, 2010), 9–10; Holt, "Prophet as Persona," 299–310; Marvin A. Sweeney, *The Prophetic Literature* (Nashville, KY: Abingdon Press, 2005). Margaret Zulick gets at the heart of this process: "Just as later adoptions of the prophetic posture are a type of rhetorical strategy, so the prophetic persona at its inception is also a public and rhetorical act. The prophetic persona is, in short, a product of social invention. Margaret Zulick, "Agon of Jeremiah or the Dialogic Invention of Prophetic Ethos," *Quarterly Journal of Speech* 78, no. 2 (May 1992): 128.

4. Martin Luther King Jr., *Stride toward Freedom: The Montgomery Story* (New York: Harper and Row, 1958), 114. Of course, the ultimate reluctant prophet is Jonah, who wants no part in presenting God's offer of forgiveness to the Ninevites, the hated enemy and imperial overlord, so he runs away only to be swallowed by a (very) big "fish."

5. The women who are explicitly called prophets in the Hebrew scriptures include Miriam, Deborah, Huldah, No'adiah, and the unnamed wife of Isaiah. Wilda C. Gafney, *Daughters of Miriam: Women Prophets in Ancient Israel* (Minneapolis, MN: Fortress Press, 2008), 24–25, 28, 38–39, 120–22.

6. In *Varieties of Moral Discourse*, James Gustafson argues that there are multiple forms of moral discourse. Prophetic discourse is one of four types. The other three are rational deliberation, narrative ethics and policy formation. Each has

its own strengths. James Gustafson, *Varieties of Moral Discourse: Prophetic, Narrative, Ethical, and Policy* (The Stob Lectures Endowment, MI: Calvin College, 1988).

7. Julia M. O'Brien, "Metaphorization and Other Tropes in the Prophets," in *The Oxford Handbook of the Prophets*, ed. Carolyn J. Sharp (New York: Oxford University Press, 2016), 244; Barbara Green, "Genre Criticism," in *The Oxford Handbook of the Prophets*, ed. Carolyn J. Sharp (New York: Oxford University Press, 2016), 258–76.

8. Holt, "Prophet as Persona," 302; cf. Charles R. Strain, *The Prophet and the Bodhisattva: Daniel Berrigan, Thich Nhat Hanh, and the Ethics of Peace and Justice* (Eugene, OR: Wipf and Stock, 2014), 108–12, 126; Kristen Tobey, *Plowshares: Protest, Performance, and Religious Identity in the Nuclear Age* (University Park: Pennsylvania State Press, 2016).

9. Louis Stulman, "Prophetic Words and Acts as Survival Literature," in *The Oxford Handbook of the Prophets*, ed. Carolyn J. Sharp (New York: Oxford University Press, 2016), 328.

10. O'Brien, "Metaphorization and Other Tropes," 244; Brueggemann, *Prophetic Imagination*, 41–45, 47.

11. Stulman and Kim, *You Are My People*, 7, 10–11. While Buddhist scholars have engaged with prophetic traditions, notably in dialogue with liberation theologies, they have not, to my knowledge, similarly tackled the roots of those traditions in the prophetic texts of the Hebrew Bible. John Makransky, "A Buddhist Critique of and Learning from Christian Liberation Theology," *Theological Studies* 75 (2014): 635–57; "What Christian Liberation Theology and Buddhism Need to Learn from Each Other," *Buddhist-Christian Studies* 34 (2014): 117–34.

12. Stulman "Prophetic Words," 324.

13. See, inter alia, Martin Luther King Jr., "Beyond Vietnam: A Time to Break Silence," in *The Radical King*, ed. Cornel West (Boston, MA: Beacon Press, 2015), 217. Because many of the prophetic texts were redacted over centuries, they reflect multiple, often conflicting viewpoints. Likewise, no one prophet represents all of the distinctive elements of the prophetic ethos. As the prophetic dimension was tapped over time by new prophets, it became more complex and robust, adding new layers of meaning. Dr. King is as much a paradigmatic prophetic figure as Jeremiah. As we will see in chapter 7, King's fusion of an agapic theology with a commitment to nonviolent action gave a new meaning to the prophetic tradition. Because the thinking and action of the "elders" in this work bear a "family resemblance" to aspects of the prophetic tradition, they too are part of the expansion of the prophetic ethos. My analysis of the prophetic ethos also is a construct informed by the classic prophetic corpus with a view to its value to Engaged Buddhist thought and action.

14. David Tracy, *The Analogical Imagination* (New York: Crossroad, 1981), 102.

15. Margaret Zulick, "The Normative, the Proper and the Sublime: Notes on the Use of Figure and Emotion in Prophetic Argument," *Argumentation* 12 (1998): 481.

16. Tracy, *Analogical Imagination*, 105, 130.

17. Tracy, *Analogical Imagination*, 120–21, 132.

18. Kathleen O'Connor, "Terror All Around: Confusion as Meaning Making," in *Jeremiah (Dis)placed: New Directions in Writing/Reading Jeremiah*, ed. A. R. Pete Diamond and Louis Stulman (New York: T&T Clark, 2011), 67–69, 71–72, 79; Zulick, "Agon of Jeremiah," 144n23, 145n38.

19. Alex P. Jassen, "The Prophets in the Dead Sea Scrolls," in *The Oxford Handbook of the Prophets*, ed. Carolyn J. Sharp (New York: Oxford University Press, 2016), 362–65, 368–69.

20. Elizabeth Van Volde as cited in Julia M. O'Brien, *Challenging Prophetic Metaphor: Theology and Ideology in the Prophets* (Louisville, KY: Westminster John Knox Press, 2008) 108.

21. O'Brien, *Challenging Prophetic Metaphor*, 114.

22. Louis Stulman insists that the text does not present a monolithic presentation of this Deuteronomic theology. Jeremiah insists that his suffering at the hands of the authorities is undeserved. Louis Stulman, *Jeremiah, Abingdon Old Testament Commentaries* (Nashville, KY: Abingdon Press, 2005), 82–84, 266–67.

23. Cathleen Kaveny, *Prophecy without Contempt: Religious Discourse in the Public Square* (Cambridge, MA: Harvard University Press, 2016), 4, 126, 287, 312.

24. Kaveny, *Prophecy without Contempt*, 287–88, 312–13, 315, 331–32.

25. Gross, *Buddhism after Patriarchy* (Albany, NY: SUNY Press, 1993), 25.

26. O'Brien, *Challenging Prophetic Metaphor*, 33–34.

27. O'Brien, *Challenging Prophetic Metaphor*, 110, 38.

28. Stulman, "Prophetic Words," 320.

29. Rita Gross, *Soaring and Settling: Buddhist Perspectives on Contemporary Society and Religious Issues* (New York: Continuum, 1998), 13–14.

30. Juliana L. Claassens, *Mourner, Mother, Midwife: Reimagining God's Delivering Presence in the Old Testament* (Louisville, KY: Westminster John Knox Press. 2012), 7–8.

31. Claassens, *Mourner, Mother, Midwife*, 22–25.

32. Stulman and Kim, *You Are My People*, 73–74.

33. Claassens, *Mourner Mother, Midwife*, 11–12, 33.

34. We have already discussed why prophetic texts require an ethical interpretation. The other attributes of the prophetic ethos—revealing geopolitics as an exercise in self-deluding power and a call to action—are implicitly treated under these five rubrics.

35. Abraham Heschel, *The Prophets* (New York: Harper and Row, 1962), 198; Thomas Leclerc, *Yahweh Is Exalted in Justice: Solidarity and Conflict in Isaiah* (Minneapolis, MN: Fortress Press, 2008), 38, 89–91, 129.

36. Gail A. Yee, "Materialist Analysis of the Prophets," in *The Oxford Handbook of the Prophets*, ed. Carolyn J. Sharp (New York: Oxford University Press, 2016), 491–506.

37. Heschel, *Prophets*, 204.

38. The prophets' understanding of injustice attacks not only poverty with all its deprivations but also the grinding down of the poor that is its inevitable accompaniment. Cf. Michael Walzer, *Spheres of Justice: A Defense of Pluralism and Equality* (New York: Basic Books, 1983), 174–77, 274–78.

39. Daniel Berrigan, *No God but One* (Grand Rapids, MI: William B. Eerdmans, 2009), 71.

40. Michael Walzer, *Exodus and Revolution* (New York: Basic Books, 1985), 91.

41. Green, "Genre Criticism," 272.

42. Walzer, *Exodus and Revolution*, 115.

43. Nahum Ward-Lev, *The Liberating Path of the Hebrew Prophets, Then and Now* (Maryknoll, NY: Orbis Books, 2019), 22, 26–27.

44. Ward-Lev, *Liberating Path*, 113, 137–38.

45. Walzer, *Exodus and Revolution*, 133.

46. Walter Brueggemann, *The Prophetic Imagination* 2nd ed. (Minneapolis: Fortress Press, 2001), 40.

47. Brueggemann, *Prophetic Imagination*, 23, 28–30, 64.

48. Walter Brueggemann, *Reality, Grief, Hope: Three Urgent Prophetic Tasks* (Grand Rapids, MI: William B. Eerdmans, 2014), 89–91.

49. While the prophets challenge the royal consciousness, they also appeal to a model of sovereignty whose quintessential expression is the Divine Warrior. The "oracles against the nations" envision ultimate peace through a global war of vengeance (Ezek 25–30; Amos 1–2; Jer 46–51; Isa 34, 63:1–6); Steed Vernyl Davidson, "Postcolonial Readings of the Prophets," in *The Oxford Handbook of the Prophets*, ed. Carolyn J. Sharp (New York: Oxford University Press, 2016), 511, 520.

50. Brueggemann, *Prophetic Imagination*, 23; O'Brien Challenging Prophetic Metaphor, 25.

51. Brueggemann, *Prophetic Imagination*, 23. From an Engaged Buddhist standpoint, what constitutes a court of appeals to judge between just and unjust laws?

52. Stulman, "Prophetic Words," 322–23.

53. Brueggemann, *Reality, Grief, Hope*, 57–58.

54. Heschel, *Prophets*, 24, 26.

55. Stulman, *Jeremiah*, 24–25.

56. Stulman, *Jeremiah*, 198–200; Kaveny, *Prophecy without Contempt*, 355–356.

57. Stulman, *Jeremiah*, 110.

58. Brueggemann, *Reality, Grief, Hope*, 59–60; Gafney, *Daughters of Miriam*, 121–22.

59. Brueggemann, *Reality, Grief, Hope*, 82–83.

60. Kathleen O'Connor, *Lamentations and the Tears of the World* (Maryknoll, NY: Orbis Books, 2002), 85–86, 131.

61. Stulman, *Jeremiah*, 130, 198–200; Stulman and Kim, *You Are My People*, 115–22.
62. Brueggemann, *Prophetic Imagination*, 65.
63. Brueggemann, *Prophetic Imagination*, 39–41.
64. Walzer, *Exodus and Revolution*, 11–12, 21.
65. Rebecca Solnit, *Hope in the Dark* (New York: Nation Books, 2006), 5.
66. Michael Walzer, *Revolution of the Saints: A Study in the Origins of Radical Politics* (New York: Atheneum, 1969).
67. Michael Walzer, *In God's Shadow: Politics in the Hebrew Bible* (New Haven, CT: Yale University Press, 2012), 12–13, 15, 73, 79–80, 82, 210.

Buddhist Reflections in a Prophetic Key #1

1. Sallie King, "Right Speech Is Not Always Gentile: The Buddha's Authorization of Sharp Criticism, Its Rationale, Limits, and Possible Applications," *Journal of Buddhists Ethics* 24 (2017): 351; Bhikku Bodhi, ed., *The Buddha's Teachings on Social and Communal Harmony* (Somerville, MA: Wisdom 2016), 80.
2. Chi Kwang Sunim, "Old Woman, Zhaozhou, and the Tiger," in The Hidden Lamp: Stories from Twenty-Five Centuries of Awakened Women, eds. Florence Caplow and Susan Moon (Boston: Wisdom Publications, 2013), 135.
3. Eva Myoen Marko, "Ziyong's Earth," in *The Hidden Lamp: Stories from Twenty-Five Centuries of Awakened Women*, ed. Florence Caplow and Susan Moon (Boston, MA: Wisdom, 2013), 241.
4. Sallie King, "Right Speech," 351; Bodhi, *Buddha's Teachings*, 80.
5. King, "Right Speech," 353; John Makransky, "Confronting the 'Sin' Out of Love for the 'Sinner': Fierce Compassion as a Force for Social Change," *Buddhist-Christian Studies* 36 (2016): 87–96.
6. King, "Right Speech," 353, 356; Bodhi, *Buddha's Teachings*, 81.
7. King, "Right Speech," 351, 359.

Chapter Two

1. Jonathan Walters, "Gotami's Story, in *Buddhism in Practice*, ed. Donald S. Lopez, Jr. (Princeton, NJ: Princeton University Press, 1995), 126.
2. Rita Gross, "'Is the Glass Half-Empty or Half-Full?'" A Feminist Assessment of Buddhism at the Beginning of the Twenty-First Century," *Feminist Theology* 16, no. 3 (2008): 291–311.
3. Walters, "Gotami's Story," (v. 31–32), 121.
4. Walters, "Gotami's Story," 136.
5. Walters, "Gotami's Story," 117.

6. Rita Gross, *Buddhism beyond Gender: Liberation from Attachment to Identity* (Boulder, CO: Shambhala, 2018), 107–29.

7. Rita Gross, *Soaring and Settling: Buddhist Perspectives on Contemporary Social and Religious Issues* (New York: Continuum, 1998), 37–38.

8. Nancy Auer Falk, "Rita Gross as Colleague and Collaborator," *Buddhist-Christian Studies* 31 (2011): 63–67.

9. Rita Gross, *A Garland of Feminist Reflections: Forty Years of Religious Exploration* (Berkeley: University of California Press, 2009), 32–33.

10. Gross, *Soaring and Settling*, 14, 34–35.

11. Gross, *Soaring and Settling*, 26–27.

12. Gross, *Soaring and Settling*, 27, 29–31.

13. Gross, *Soaring and Settling*, 32–33.

14. Gross, *Soaring and Settling*, 41.

15. Gross, *Buddhism after Patriarchy*, 134, 169–70, 215; Gross, *Garland of Feminist Reflections*, 237.

16. Gross, *Buddhism after Patriarchy*, 134, 214, 218.

17. Judith Simmer-Brown, "Rita Gross's Contribution to Contemporary Western Tibetan Buddhism," *Buddhist Christian Studies* 31 (2011): 70, 72.

18. Gross in one other place also refers to the "prophetic method" as involving a deconstruction and reconstruction of Buddhism. Gross, *Soaring and Settling*, 25.

19. Gross, *Buddhism after Patriarchy*, 183.

20. Gross, *Buddhism after Patriarchy*, 134–35. Gross analyzes the mutual transformation of Buddhism and feminism as a representative of the prophetic tradition in "Buddhism and Feminism: Toward their Mutual Transformation, Part 1," *Eastern Buddhist* 19, no. 1 (1986): 44–58; and "Buddhism and Feminism, Part 2," *Eastern Buddhist* 19, no. 2 (1986): 62–74. *Buddhism after Patriarchy* focuses on the transformation of Buddhism. Here we are studying the impact on Engaged Buddhism of tapping into its prophetic dimension.

21. Gross, *Soaring and Settling*, 9.

22. Rita Gross, "The Suffering of Sexism: Buddhist Perspectives and Experiences," *Buddhist Christian Studies* 34 (2014): 69. For the fullest discussion of how any set of gender roles is a prison, how it conflicts with the Buddhist understanding of the no-self and offers a spurious essentialism, see Gross, *Buddhism beyond Gender*, especially chapters 3 and 4.

23. Gross, *Soaring and Settling*, 9.

24. Gross, *Soaring and Settling*, 14–16. This experience sheds light on Gross's contention that the prophetic voice needs to purify itself of elements that create deep wounds, in this case exclusive truth claims. Gross, *Soaring and Settling*, 16.

25. Gross, *Buddhism after Patriarchy*, 318–19. There is a thin line separating Gross's commitment to the interchange between Engaged Buddhism and feminism and the imperialist pretensions present in a quotation from an unnamed white convert Buddhist feminist: "If we had not spoken up, the Buddhist women's move-

ment . . . would not even exist. Things might not have changed for another 2500 years." The young Asian American Buddhist who repeats this quotation goes on to challenge the American white Buddhist establishment that claims the authority to tell her that she is doing Buddhism all wrong. Chenxing Han, *Be the Refuge: Raising the Voices of Asian American Buddhists* (Berkeley, CA: North Atlantic Books, 2021), 212. Prophetic wisdom claims that the prophetic tradition offers some distinctive concepts and practices to Engaged Buddhists, not that Engaged Buddhism is bereft of resources for self-transformation. Although it is not the subject of this book, it is certainly true that Engaged Buddhism also has distinctive gifts to offer to an evolving prophetic tradition. There is no room for self-aggrandizing. We scrape together whatever wisdom we can and share.

26. Gross, *Soaring and Settling*, 14–15.
27. Gross, *Buddhism after Patriarchy*, 32–34, 36–37.
28. Gross, *Buddhism after Patriarchy*, 19–20, 23.
29. Gross, *Buddhism after Patriarchy*, 18, 115–16.
30. Gross, *Buddhism after Patriarchy*, 209–10.
31. Gross, *Buddhism after Patriarchy*, 116.
32. Gross, *Buddhism after Patriarchy*, 36, 209–14.
33. Gross, *Buddhism after Patriarchy*, 142–45.
34. Gross, *Buddhism after Patriarchy*, 134–35, 145–46, 183; Gross, *Soaring and Settling*, 13.
35. Gross, *Buddhism after Patriarchy*, 299–301.
36. Emptiness is the teaching that all things are a product of causes and conditions. As such, they are impermanent and radically interdependent. There is no fixed, substantial reality that is impervious to change. The self too is empty of any enduring substance, for example, an immortal soul. We are the confluence of a myriad of causes and conditions, including our own thoughts and actions. Emptiness and interbeing are the one reality perceived from different angles. It may be helpful to think of emptying as a verb or gerund. I empty myself of the illusion that there is some substantial reality on which to anchor myself. Emptying myself, I simultaneously open myself to the infinite web of interacting beings that Buddhists call Indra's Net.

37. Gross, *Buddhism after Patriarchy*, 173–84. Rita Gross did not live to complete final edits on her manuscript of *Buddhism beyond Gender*. Evidently, she wished to add a section on transgender issues. Judith Simmer-Brown, "Introduction," *Buddhism beyond Gender: Liberation from Attachment to Identity* (Boulder, CO: Shambhala, 2018), xvi–xvii. Gross remained adamant that any prescribed gender roles are imprisoning: "No one of any identity is exempt from the implications of teachings about egolessness and the downside of clinging to identity." Gross, *Buddhism beyond Gender*, 12. This position raises some questions: What about lightly held identities that are an embodied resistance to culturally prescribed, gender-defined identities? Is there a way of fluidly evolving an identity that is consistent with Buddhist under-

standing of the no-self? How would Gross consider current understandings of gender fluidity and hybridity? See Julie Regan, "The Soaring and (Final) Settling of Rita Gross, 1943–2015," *Journal of Feminist Studies in Religion* 32, no. 2 (2016): 8–9.

38. Gross, *Buddhism after Patriarchy*, 188–89. The teaching of Buddha Nature arose in India with the earliest texts composed between 200 and 350 CE. As Gross mentioned, a literal translation of the Sanskrit *tathāgatagarbha* is "Buddha womb" or "Buddha embryo." Simply stated, all living beings have a Buddha Nature. More precisely, all are Buddha. As the terms "Buddha womb" and "Buddha embryo" make clear, Buddha Nature is not an underlying permanent substance such as a human soul. Nor is it an essence or a set of essential traits, as in the expression "human nature." Our Buddha Nature is obscured by deluded thoughts and our self-serving actions. We need to nurture that Buddha embryo so that it becomes manifest. We do not own our Buddha Nature; we actualize it moment after moment. This teaching spread throughout East Asia, becoming a "pivotal" part of the teaching of indigenous Buddhist schools. Sallie King, *Buddha Nature* (Albany, NY: SUNY Press, 1991), 1–4, 12. Several corollaries follow from this teaching: (1) All living beings as Buddha are equal in the deepest sense; (2) Buddha Nature offers a positive view of human capacities (this teaching is the antithesis of the idea that women are somehow defective and need to be reborn as men to become capable of liberation); liberation is within the grasp of all beings; and (3) "ordinary phenomena . . . are exemplars of ultimate reality," an idea that has profound implications for an ecological worldview and practice. King, *Buddha Nature*, 159–68.

39. Gross, *Buddhism after Patriarchy*, 48–54; *Therīgāthā: Poems of the First Buddhist Women*, trans. Charles Hallisey (Cambridge, MA: Harvard University Press, 2015).

40. Gross, *Buddhism beyond Gender*, 107–29.

41. Gross, *Buddhism beyond Gender*, 117–19.

42. Donald K. Swearer, "Bimba's Lament," in *Buddhism in Practice*, ed. Donald S. Lopez (Princeton, NJ: Princeton University Press, 1995), 541–52.

43. Gross, *Buddhism beyond Gender*, 119.

44. Gross, *Buddhism beyond Gender*, 34–35, 119–27.

45. Gross, *Soaring and Settling*, 161–62.

46. Gross, *Soaring and Settling*, 162–63.

47. Gross, *Soaring and Settling*, 164–65.

48. Gross, *Soaring and Settling*, 141.

49. Gross, *Garland Feminist Reflections*, 238.

50. Gross, *Garland Feminist Reflections*, 241.

51. Gross, *Garland Feminist Reflections*, 240–41, 243.

52. Gross, *Soaring and Settling*, 27.

53. Gross, *Buddhism after Patriarchy*, 225–55.

54. Rita Gross, "I Am Speechless," *Buddhist Christian Studies* 31 (2011): 97.

Buddhist Reflections in a Prophetic Key #2

1. *Therīgāthā: Poems of the First Buddhist Women*, trans. Charles Hallsey (Cambridge, MA: Harvard University Press, 2015), 111, 113, 115, 266–267n1.
2. Gross, *Buddhism after Patriarchy* (Albany, NY: SUNY Press, 1993), 53.
3. Reiko Ohnuma, "Mother-Love and Mother-Grief: South Asian Buddhist Variations on a Theme," *Journal of Feminist Studies in Religion* 23, no. 1 (2007), 97–98, 100, 103–4.
4. Ohnuma, "Mother-Love and Mother-Grief," 102; Gross, *Buddhism after Patriarchy*, 233–34.
5. Thich Nhat Hanh defines *bodhicitta* as "the mind of love": it is "the deep wish to cultivate understanding in ourselves in order to bring happiness to many beings. With bodhicitta as the foundation of our thinking, everything that we do or say will help others be liberated." *The Heart of the Buddha's Teaching: Transforming Suffering into Peace, Joy and Liberation* (New York: Broadway Books, 1998), 62.
6. Gross, *Buddhism after Patriarchy*, 181.
7. *Therīgāthā*, 73, 75, 260–61n18.
8. Paul Farmer, *Pathologies of Power: Health, Human Rights, and the New War on the Poor* (Berkeley: University of California Press, 2005), 143–44.
9. Walter Brueggemann, *The Prophetic Imagination*, 2nd ed. (Minneapolis, MN: Fortress Press, 2001), 11.

Chapter Three

1. Thich Nhat Hanh, *Vietnam: Lotus in a Sea of Fire* (New York: Hill and Wang, 1967), 76.
2. Thich Nhat Hanh, *"Call Me by My True Names": The Collected Poems of Thich Nhat Hanh* (Berkeley, CA: Parallax, 1993), 9.
3. Thich Nhat Hanh, "Twenty-Four Brand New Hours," in *Call Me*, 167.
4. Thich Nhat Hanh, *Love in Action: Writings on Nonviolent Social Change* (Berkeley, CA: Parallax Press, 1993), 136; Thich Nhat Hanh, *Living Buddha, Living Christ* (New York: Riverhead Books, 1995), 197.
5. Thich Nhat Hanh, *My Master's Robe: Memories of a Novice Monk* (Berkeley, CA: Parallax Press, 2002), 1–2, 14–15, 17, 19. These stories were written while Thich Nhat Hanh was still in his twenties. They were collected in a book titled *Humanity* in Vietnamese. Sr. Annabel Laity, "Foreword," in Nhat Hanh, *My Master's Robe*, ix.
6. Nhat Hanh, *My Master's Robe*, 77.
7. Thich Nhat Hanh, *Fragrant Palm Leaves* (New York: Riverhead Books, 1999), 7–9, 50; Sister Chan Khong, *Learning True Love* (Berkeley, CA: Parallax Press, 2007), 29.

8. Chan Khong, *Learning True Love*, 14–15, 25–26. Cao Ngoc Phuong later became Sister Chan Khong, Thich Nhat Hanh's principal associate.
9. Nhat Hanh, *Fragrant Palm Leaves*, 53, 56–57.
10. Chan Khong, *Learning True Love*, 48–50.
11. Nhat Hanh, "Peace," in *Call Me*, 27.
12. Nhat Hanh, *Love in Action*, 41.
13. Chan Khong, *Learning True Love*, 60–70.
14. Chan Khong, *Learning True Love*, 77.
15. Nhat Hanh, *Love in Action*, 49–56.
16. Nhat Hanh, *Lotus in a Sea of Fire*, 92–93.
17. Thomas Merton, "Foreword," in Thich Nhat Hanh, *Vietnam: Lotus in a Sea of Fire* (New York: Hill and Wang, 1967), x.
18. Nhat Hanh, *Lotus in a Sea of Fire*, 94.
19. Chan Khong, *Learning True Love*, 126–43.
20. Nhat Hanh, "Always the Same Mind," in *Call Me*, 80.
21. Nhat Hanh, *Call Me*, 7, 15, 17, 19, 27, 35; Nhat Hanh, *Love in Action*, 41–42, 60–61.
22. Thich Nhat Hanh, "Mudra," in *Call Me*, 8.
23. Thich Nhat Hanh saw the Buddhist peace movement in Vietnam as a cousin to Dr. King's nonviolent campaigns. Nhat Hanh, *Lotus in a Sea of Fire*, 107–8.
24. Thich Nhat Hanh, "The Fire That Consumes My Brother," in *Call Me*, 48–49.
25. Nhat Hanh, *Love in Action*, 43–45.
26. Not all actions in the peace campaign that eventually led to the downfall of President Diem were so extreme. Thich Nhat Hanh particularly applauds the courageous actions of those who brought their family altars—their most sacred treasure—into the streets to block the tanks sent to crush the demonstrators. He argues that these actions were not political. This problematic separation of politics from nonviolent actions to confront oppression will be taken up in chapters 7 and 8. For more on the "Buddhist struggle movement" and Thich Nhat Hanh's relationship to it, see Sallie B. King, "Thich Nhat Hanh and the Unified Buddhist Church," in *Engaged Buddhism: Buddhist Liberation Movements in Asia*, ed. Sallie B. King and Christopher S. Queen (Albany, NY: SUNY Press, 1996), 321–63.
27. Thich Nhat Hanh, "Condemnation," in *Call Me*, 37.
28. Thich Nhat Hanh, "Resolution," in *Call Me*, 21.
29. Cf. Jer 12:10–11, 14:1–6 on the correlation between ecological catastrophe and human beings collectively trapped in their greed, ill will, and delusion.
30. Thich Nhat Hanh, "Our Green Garden," in *Call Me*, 6–7.
31. Thich Nhat Hanh, "A Free White Cloud," in *Call Me*, 53. This poem was written in remembrance of Thich Thien Minh, a fearless lion in the Buddhist peace movement, who was imprisoned by the South Vietnam regime only to be

reimprisoned by the North after its takeover and tortured to death. Nhat Hanh, *Call Me*, 55.

32. Thich Nhat Hanh, "Those That Have Not Exploded," in *Call Me*, 22.

33. Thich Nhat Hanh, "Flames of Prayer," in *Call Me*, 28–31.

34. Nhat Hanh, *Love in Action*, 12, 16–17, 26, 29–32.

35. Nhat Hanh, *Love in Action*, 151.

36. Avalokiteshvara is known all over Asia as the one who listens to the cries of the world. She is known as Guanyin in China, Quan Am in Vietnam, and Kannon in Japan. Sometimes manifesting as male, sometimes as female, she is the embodiment of great compassion. See Taigen Dan Leighton, *Faces of Compassion: Classic Bodhisattva Archetypes and Their Modern Expression*, rev. ed. (Boston, MA: Wisdom Publications, 2003), 167–209.

37. Thich Nhat Hanh, "Those That Have Not Exploded," in *Call Me*, 22–23.

38. Thich Nhat Hanh, "Defuse Me," in *Call Me*, 142–43.

39. Thich Nhat Hanh, "The Sun of the Future," in *Call Me*, 38–39.

40. Thich Nhat Hanh, "The Lonely Watchtower," in *Call Me*, 42–43. I suggest that we couple "The Lonely Watchtower" with Thich Nhat Hanh's most-known and -quoted poem, "Please Call Me by My True Names" in *Call Me*, 72–73. That poem too takes us into the heart of darkness, but in that case it is a diagnosis of the kind of illness that those who see themselves as living a life of moral rectitude are vulnerable to: "I am the twelve-year-old girl/ refugee on a small boat, who throws herself into the ocean/ after being raped by a sea pirate. / And I am the pirate/ my heart not yet capable/ of seeing and loving." "I am the sea pirate!" That is enough to make any would-be-Jeremiah gag. The Buddhist prophet levels a prophetic critique on prophetic righteousness. For a more extensive analysis of the poem, see Charles Strain, *The Prophet and the Bodhisattva: Daniel Berrigan, Thich Nhat Hanh, and the Ethics of Peace and Justice* (Eugene, OR: Wipf and Stock, 2014), 69–70. For a nuanced critique of the poem that challenges Thich Nhat Hanh's understanding of complicity, see Sallie B. King, "Through the Eyes of Auschwitz and the Killing Fields: Mutual Learning between Engaged Buddhism and Liberation Theology," *Buddhist Christian Studies* 36 (2016): 58, 62; Sallie B. King, *Being Benevolence: The Social Ethics of Engaged Buddhism* (Honolulu: University of Hawaii Press, 2005), 99–104, 213–15.

41. Thich Nhat Hanh, *Interbeing: Fourteen Guidelines for Engaged Buddhism*, 3rd ed. (Berkeley, CA: Parallax Press, 1998).

42. Thich Nhat Hanh, *The World We Have: A Buddhist Approach to Peace and Ecology* (Berkeley, CA: Parallax Press, 2008), 1–2.

43. Nhat Hanh, *World We Have*, 40.

44. Thich Nhat Hanh and Daniel Berrigan, *The Raft Is Not the Shore* (Maryknoll, NY: Orbis Books, 2001), 52–53.

45. Nhat Hanh and Berrigan, *Raft*, 41–42, 46.

46. Thich Nhat Hanh, *Calming the Fearful Mind: A Zen Response to Terrorism* (Berkeley, CA: Parallax Press, 2005), 85.

47. Nhat Hanh and Berrigan, *Raft*, 42, 44.
48. Nhat Hanh and Berrigan, *Raft*, 1–2.
49. Nhat Hanh, *Living Buddha*, 171.
50. Thich Nhat Hanh, *Peace Is Every Step* (New York: Bantam Books 1992), 41–42.
51. Nhat Hanh, "Night of Prayer," in *Call Me*, 16–17.
52. Nhat Hanh, *Living Buddha*, 152–53.
53. Nhat Hanh, *Love in Action*, 41.
54. Thich Nhat Hanh, "Butterflies over the Golden Mustard Fields," in *Call Me*, 74, 77.
55. Thich Nhat Hanh, "The Good News," in *Call Me*, 169.

Buddhist Reflections in a Prophetic Key #3

1. Thich Nhat Hanh, "Please Call Me by My True Names," in Thich Nhat Hanh, *Call Me by My True Names: The Collected Poems of Thich Nhat Hanh* (Berkeley CA: Parallax Press, 1993), 72.
2. Thich Nhat Hanh, *Being Peace* (Berkeley, CA: Parallax Press, 2005), 65–68.
3. Nhat Hanh, *Being Peace*, 66–68, 111.
4. Sallie King, *Being Benevolence: The Social Ethics of Engaged Buddhism* (Honolulu: University of Hawai'i Press, 2005), 101.
5. Nhat Hanh, *Being Peace*, 66.
6. Pinning the blame on one individual or group leads to a theory of retributive justice. In this model, a crime must be balanced with a punishment proportionate to the offense. Most Buddhists recoil against retributive justice as increasing the amount of suffering in the universe. In chapter 10 we will discuss an alternative theory of justice, restorative justice, which preserves moral accountability while avoiding self-righteousness.
7. Sallie King, "Through the Eyes of Auschwitz and the Killing Fields: Mutual Learning between Engaged Buddhism and Liberation Theology," *Buddhist Christian Studies* 36 (2016): 59–60; Susan. Nieman, *Learning from the Germans: Race and the Memory of Evil* (New York: Farrar Straus and Giroux, 2019).
8. Sallie King, "Eyes of Auschwitz," 61–62, 65.

Chapter Four

1. Joanna Macy, "Afterword," in *A Wild Love for the World: Joanna Macy and the Work of Our Time*, ed. Stephanie Kaza (Boulder, CO: Shambhala, 2020), 358.
2. Joanna Macy, *Widening Circles: A Memoir* (Gabriola Island, BC: New Society, 2000), 161–62.
3. Macy, *Widening Circles*, 86–98.

4. Macy, *Widening Circles*, 162.

5. Joanna Macy and Molly Young Brown, *Coming Back to Life: Practices to Reconnect Our Lives, Our World* (Gabriola Island, BC: New Society, 1988), 61.

6. Joanna Macy and Chris Johnstone, *Active Hope: How to Face the Mess We Are in without Going Crazy* (Novato CA: New World Library, 2012), 3.

7. Macy, *Widening Circles*, 34–52, 64, 67.

8. Macy, *Widening Circles*, 71–72, 86–89.

9. Macy, *Widening Circles*, 102–3.

10. Joanna Macy, *Mutual Causality in Buddhism and Systems Theory* (Albany: State University of New York Press, 1991), 26, 39–40. For a defense of Macy's understanding of dependent coarising against her critics, see Charles Strain, "Engaged Buddhist Practice and Ecological Ethics," *Worldviews* 20 (2016): 191–97.

11. Macy, *Mutual Causality*, 72–73.

12. Macy and Brown, *Coming Back to Life*, 40–42.

13. Christopher Queen, "The Dharma of Natural Systems," in *A Wild Love for the World: Joanna Macy and the Work of Our Time*, ed. Stephanie Kaza (Boulder, CO: Shambhala, 2020), 166–71.

14. Macy, *Widening Circles*, 173.

15. Macy, *Mutual Causality*, 1–2.

16. Macy, *Widening Circles*, 170.

17. Macy, *Widening Circles*, 171.

18. Robert Jay Lifton, *Death in Life: Survivors of Hiroshima* (New York: Random House, 1967), 500–510.

19. Robert Jay Lifton and Richard Falk, *Indefensible Weapons: The Political and Psychological Case against Nuclearism* (New York: Random House, 1982), 76.

20. Lifton and Falk, *Indefensible Weapons*, 103–4.

21. Macy, *Widening Circles*, 173–74.

22. Joanna Macy, *Despair and Personal Power in the Nuclear Age* (Philadelphia, PA: New Society, 1983), 17–18.

23. Macy and Brown, *Coming Back to Life*; Macy and Johnstone, *Active Hope*. Shierry Weber Nicolsen argues that our pain for the world needs to be "communalized," held within a community of support if we are to embrace it. Shierry Weber Nicolsen, *The Love of Nature and the End of the World* (Cambridge, MA: MIT Press, 2002), 181.

24. Macy, *Despair and Personal Power*, 3, 19, 24; Macy and Brown, *Coming Back to Life*, 26–27.

25. Macy, *Despair and Personal Power*, 74; Macy and Johnstone, *Active Hope*, 37–39.

26. Kathleen Sullivan, "The Journey of a Nuclear Guardian," in *A Wild Love for the World: Joanna Macy and the Work of Our Time*, ed. Stephanie Kaza (Boulder, CO: Shambhala, 2020), 264.

27. Macy and Johnstone, *Active Hope*, 73–75. Shantideva was an eighth-century CE Indian monk. He is most noted as the author of *A Guide to the Bodhisattva Way of Life*.

28. Macy and Johnstone, *Active Hope*, 76.

29. Macy and Johnstone, *Active Hope*, 53–55, 76.

30. Arnie Naess, "Deep Ecology Movement: Some Philosophical Aspects," in *Environmental Ethics: An Anthology*, ed., Andrea Light and Homes Rolston III (Malden, MA: Blackwell, 2003), 264–68; Bill Devall and George Sessions, *Deep Ecology* (Salt Lake City, UT: Gibbs M. Smith, 1985), 65; Steve Odin, "The Japanese Concept of Nature, in Relation to the Environmental Ethics and Conservation Aesthetics of Aldo Leopold," in *Buddhism and Ecology: The Interconnection of Dharma and Deeds*, ed. Mary Evelyn Tucker and Duncan Ryuken Williams (Cambridge, MA: Harvard University Press, 1997), 93.

31. Elizabeth Kolbert, *The Sixth Extinction: An Unnatural History* (New York: Henry Holt, 2014).

32. Macy and Brown, *Coming Back to Life*, 151; John Seed et al., *Thinking Like a Mountain: Toward a Council of All Beings* (Santa Cruz, CA: New Society, 1988), 79–90, 97–113; Macy, *Widening Circles*, 222–23.

33. Macy and Brown, *Coming Back to Life*, 149–65; Macy, *Widening Circles*, 223.

34. Joanna Macy, *World as Lover, World as Self*, 2nd ed. (Berkeley CA: Parallax Press, 2007), 87.

35. Macy and Brown, *Coming Back to Life*, 46–47.

36. Macy and Johnstone, *Active Hope*, 3.

37. Rita Gross, *Soaring Settling: Buddhist Perspectives on Contemporary Social and Religious Issues* (New York: Continuum, 1998), 56–58.

38. Thich Nhat Hanh, *Living Buddha, Living Christ* (New York: Riverhead Books, 1995), 152–53.

39. Macy and Johnstone, *Active Hope*, 37–40.

40. Macy and Johnstone, *Active Hope*, 144–49.

41. Macy, *Widening Circles*, 243–44; Macy, *World as Lover*, 2nd ed., 169–70.

42. Robert J. Lifton as cited in Macy, *World as Lover*, 2nd ed., 174–75.

43. Thich Nhat Hanh and Daniel Berrigan, *The Raft Is Not the Shore* (Maryknoll, NY: Orbis Books, 2001), 2.

44. Macy and Brown, *Coming Back to Life*, 135–48; Macy, *World as Lover*, 2nd ed., 171–202; Joanna Macy "The Presence of the Future Beings," in *A Wild Love for the World: Joanna Macy and the Work of Our Time*, ed. Stephanie Kaza (Boulder, CO: Shambhala, 2020), 222–24.

45. For a more extensive discussion of "The Great Turning," see David C. Korten, *The Great Turning: From Empire to Earth Community* (Bloomfield, CT: Kumarian Press, 2006). Korten credits Macy with coming up with the term.

46. Macy, *World as Lover*, 2nd ed., 139–43; Macy and Johnstone, *Active Hope*, 13–33.

47. Turning the Wheel is a metaphor for introducing a new way of framing reality along with new forms of engagement. In Buddhist tradition, the first turning occurred when the Buddha preached for the first time in Deer Park. Macy sees the three forms of ecological action from a Buddhist standpoint as representing a new turning of the wheel. See Stephanie Kaza, "To Save All Beings: Buddhist Environmental Activism," in *Engaged Buddhism in the West*, ed. Christopher S. Queen (Boston, MA: Wisdom, 2000), 160.

48. Macy and Brown, *Coming Back to Life*, 17–24; Macy, *World as Lover*, 2nd ed., 143–47.

49. Macy, *World as Lover*, 2nd ed., 120–23.

50. Macy, *World as Lover*, 2nd ed., 201–02.

Buddhist Reflections in a Prophetic Key #4

1. Bernie Glassman, *Bearing Witness: A Zen Master's Lessons in Making Peace* (New York: Bell Tower 1998), 26, 33, 43, 188, 214–15.

2. Joanna Macy, *Widening Circles: A Memoir* (Gabriola Island, BC: New Society Publishers, 2000), 262–63.

3. Macy, *Widening Circles*, 264–67.

4. Macy, *Widening Circles*, 268–69.

5. Rob Nixon, *Slow Violence and the Environmentalism of the Poor* (Cambridge, MA: Harvard University Press, 2011).

6. Naomi Klein, *This Changes Everything: Capitalism vs. the Climate* (New York: Simon and Schuster, 2014), 378–79.

Chapter Five

1. B. R. Ambedkar, "What Way Emancipation?," in B. R. Ambedkar Writings and Speeches, ed. Nari Narake et al., 17, part 3 (Mumbai, India: Ambedkar Source Material Publication Committee, Higher Education Department, Government of Maharashtra, 2003), 145.

2. B. R. Ambedkar, The Annihilation of Caste: The Annotated Critical Edition, ed. S. Anand (London: Verso, 2016), 185.

3. Ambedkar, "What Way Emancipation?," 113. Arundhati Roy comments that the label "Untouchable" has been replaced by the term "Dalit" (Broken People). However, she insists, "Ambedkar used the word 'Untouchable' with cold rage, and without flinching, so must I." Arundhati Roy, "Introduction: The Doctor and the Saint," in B. R. Ambedkar, *Annihilation of Caste: The Annotated Critical Edition*, ed. S.

Anand (London: Verso, 2016), 20. I, however, do not fully grasp the impact of using this terrible term to convey the brutal reality that caste/outcaste continues to have on those who live under its oppressive force. As an American, I know how certain words are so evocative of traumatic history that their use causes suffering, so I will use the term "Dalits." Aishwary Kumar points out that Dalits themselves appropriated a term that originally conveyed being ground down to become a positive term for those who resist their subjugation. Aishwary Kumar, *Radical Equality: Ambedkar, Gandhi, and the Risk of Democracy* (Stanford, CA: Stanford University Press, 2015), 31.

4. Mohandas Gandhi as cited in B. R. Ambedkar, "Unfortunately I Was Born Hindu Untouchable but I Will Not Die a Hindu," in *Writings and Speeches*, 17, part 3, 94–97.

5. Christopher S. Queen, "Dr. Ambedkar and the Hermeneutics of Buddhist Liberation," in *Engaged Buddhism: Buddhist Liberation Movements in Asia*, ed. Christopher S. Queen and Sallie B. King (Albany, NY: State University of New York Press, 1996), 55–62.

6. Ambedkar as cited in Roy, "Introduction," 20, 95.

7. Ambedkar, *Annihilation of Caste*, 214, 216–17; Ambedkar, "What Way Emancipation?," 117.

8. Roy, "Introduction," 24.

9. Eleanor Zelliot, *From Untouchable to Dalit: Essays on the Ambedkar Movement* (New Delhi: Manohar, 2001), 155–56.

10. Roy, "Introduction," 23–25, 104. On contemporary violence directed at Dalits who seek to exercise the most basic of rights (e.g., the right to choose the clothes that you wear), see Roy, "Introduction," 21–22, 26–36, 99.

11. B. R. Ambedkar, "Conversion Is Necessary for Your Emancipation," in *Writings and Speeches*, 17, part 3, 109–10; Roy, "Introduction," 94–98.

12. Zelliot, *From Untouchable to Dalit*, 159.

13. B. R. Ambedkar as cited in Roy, "Introduction," 108–9.

14. Zelliot, *From Untouchable to Dalit*, 161.

15. Mohandas Gandhi as cited in Roy, "Introduction," 109.

16. Ambedkar, "What Way Emancipation?," 135.

17. Ambedkar, *Annihilation of Caste*, 265, 274n103, 290. B. R. Ambedkar, "Buddha or Karl Marx," in *The Essential Writings of B. R. Ambedkar*, ed. Valerian Rodrigues (New Delhi: Oxford University Press, 2002), 184.

18. Roy, "Introduction," 108–10. Looking back on twenty-five or more years of Gandhi's appealing to sweet reason, Ambedkar concluded that the appeals had achieved nothing. B. R. Ambedkar, *What Congress and Gandhi Have Done to the Untouchables* (Bombay: Thacher, 1945), 36–38, 247, 250.

19. Zelliot, *From Untouchable to Dalit*, 160–64; Kumar, *Radical Equality*, 4–5.

20. Ramachandra Guha, *Gandhi: The Years That Changed the World, 1914–1948* (New York: Alfred A. Knopf, 2018), 411.

21. S. Anand, "A Note on the Poona Pact," in Ambedkar, *Annihilation of Caste*, 361–68.

22. Ambedkar, *Annihilation of Caste*, 260–61. Roy, "Introduction," 48–50.

23. Guha, *Gandhi*, 157–58; Christophe Jaffrelot, *Dr. Ambedkar and Untouchability* (New York: Columbia University Press, 2005), 66–67, 71.

24. Guha, *Gandhi*, 498; D. R. Nagaraj, *The Flaming Feet and Other Essays: The Dalit Movement in India*, rev. ed. (Calcutta: Seagull Books, 2010), 35, 78. Gandhi's paternalism is evident in the very name he invented for speaking about Untouchables—Harijan, children of God. Kumar, *Radical Equality*, 277.

25. Within the four *varnas* (castes) were four thousand subcastes, each with its own hereditary occupation. Roy, "Introduction," 24.

26. Roy, "Introduction," 37. Ambedkar's rhetoric is itself a dramatic performance. Such rhetoric raises consciousness that has been buried under layers and layers of custom and tradition. Kumar, *Radical Equality*, 114. It rips away the layer added by Gandhi in patronizing Dalits while simultaneously leaving the caste system intact. "How pitiable as a people we would be . . . ," Roy exclaims, "if . . . this rage—this audacious denunciation—did not exist!" Roy, "Introduction," 48.

27. Ambedkar, *Annihilation of Caste*, 189–91, 194, 198.

28. Ambedkar, *Annihilation of Caste*, 286–88, 294–96; Roy, "Introduction," 50–51.

29. B. R. Ambedkar, *The Buddha and His Dhamma: A Critical Edition*, ed. Aakash Singh Rathore and Ajay Verma (New Delhi: Oxford University Press, 2011), 58. Cf. Gerald Berreman, *Caste and Other Inequities: Essays on Inequality* (New Delhi: Ved Prakash Vatuk Folklore Institute, 1979), 9–10. B. R. Ambedkar, "Prospects of Democracy in India," in *Dr. Ambedkar and Democracy*, ed. Christophe Jaffrelot and Narender Kumar (New Delhi: Oxford University Press, 2018), 242.

30. Ambedkar, "What Way Emancipation?," 128.

31. Ambedkar, *Annihilation of Caste*, 224, 231.

32. We will treat King's Letter in chapter 7.

33. Ambedkar, *Annihilation of Caste*, 288–89.

34. B. R. Ambedkar as cited in Roy, "Introduction," 21; "What Way Emancipation?," 127.

35. B. R. Ambedkar as cited in Jaffrelot and Kumar, *Ambedkar and Democracy*, 197.

36. B. R. Ambedkar, "Brahma Is Not Dharma. What Good Is Brahma?," in Jaffrelot and Kumar, *Ambedkar and Democracy*, 248. Ambedkar, "Prospects of Democracy in India," 241.

37. B. R. Ambedkar, "The Buddha Dhamma Will Be the Saviour of the World," in *Writings and Speeches*, 17, part 3, 541–42, 544.

38. Queen, "Dr. Ambedkar," 47.

39. Ambedkar, *Buddha and His Dhamma*, 118, 148–50. To be sure, Ambedkar's "liberties" were grounded in decades of study of primary sources in their original language to create his synthesis of the Buddha's Dhamma. See Christopher Queen,

"Ambedkar's Dhamma: Sources and Method in the Construction of Engaged Buddhism," in *Reconstructing the World: B. R. Ambedkar and Buddhism in India*, ed. Surendra Jondhale and Johannes Beltz (New Delhi: Oxford University Press, 2004), 132–50. "Kalama Sutta," *Angutara Nikaya* 3:66, trans. Thānissaro Bhikkhu, dhammatalks.org/suttas/AN/AN3_66.html.

40. Ambedkar, *Buddha and His Dhamma*, xxiii, xxvii.

41. Ambedkar, "What Way Emancipation?," 128.

42. The birth of Buddhism, Ambedkar insists, was as significant as the French Revolution in preparing for the emergence of democratic societies. B. R. Ambedkar, "Buddhism Paved the Way for Democracy and Socialistic Patterns of Society," in *Writings and Speeches*, 17, part 3, 407. Ambedkar shares with most, if not all, Buddhist modernists a rigorous method of demythologization. Ambedkar excises all mentions of supernatural agents and their interventions in the Buddha's life. Adele Fiske and Christoph Emmrich, "The Use of Buddhist Scripture in B. R. Ambedkar's *The Buddha and His Dhamma*," in *Reconstructing the World: B. R. Ambedkar and Buddhism in India*, ed. Surendra Jondhale and Johannes Beltz (New Delhi: Oxford University Press, 2004), 102–5.

43. Queen, "Dr. Ambedkar," 64–65; Queen, "Ambedkar's Dhamma," 141.

44. Ambedkar, *Buddha and His Dhamma*, xxi–xxx, 17–22, 41. I will examine this alternative narrative in more detail in the reflection that follows this chapter.

45. Ambedkar, *Buddha and His Dhamma*, 69–74, 126–29, 52–53, 168. Queen, "Dr. Ambedkar," 58; Fiske and Emmrich, "Use of Buddhist Scripture," 111.

46. Ambedkar, *Buddha and His Dhamma*, 57–58, 61–62, 178.

47. David L. McMahon, *The Making of Buddhist Modernism* (New York: Oxford University Press, 2008), 183–214.

48. Ambedkar, *Buddha and His Dhamma*, xxix–xxxi, 9, 65.

49. Queen, "Ambedkar's Dhamma," 141. I see Queen's distinction as an accurate description of Ambedkar's focus. Most Engaged Buddhists, however, would rather see an integration of the spiritual/sapiential and the prophetic/ethical. Both/and rather than either/or. It should also be added that the prophetic/ethical calls for an inner revolution as well as the spiritual/sapiential. The prophetic ethos in practice is a spiritual endeavor.

50. I have found two versions of a speech that Ambedkar gave to a conference of Buddhists in Kathmandu less than a month before his death. See Ambedkar, "Buddha or Karl Marx," in *Writings and Speeches*, 17, part 3, 549–58; Ambedkar, "Buddha or Karl Marx," in *Essential Writings of B. R. Ambedkar*, 173–92. Neither source explains the discrepancies between the two sources, whose arguments are substantially the same but whose explication differs considerably.

51. Ambedkar, "Buddha or Karl Marx," in *Essential Writings of B. R. Ambedkar*, 175–77. Clearly Ambedkar's comparisons are sketchy but the fact that he sees Buddhism as entering the arena to struggle with Marxism is itself indicative of a major shift in its soteriological orientation.

52. Ambedkar, *Buddha and His Dhamma*, 171. Cf. Karl Marx, "Theses on Feuerbach," in *Writings of the Young Marx on Philosophy and Society*, trans. and ed. Lloyd D. Easton and Kurt H. Guddat (Garden City, NY: Doubleday, 1967), 400–402.

53. Ambedkar, "Buddha or Marx" in *Writings and Speeches*, 552; Ambedkar, "Buddha Dhamma Saviour," 543; Ambedkar, "Buddha or Karl Marx," in *Essential Writings of B. R. Ambedkar*, 178–79.

54. Ambedkar, *Buddha and His Dhamma*, 73, 159–60. Ambedkar, "Buddha or Marx," in *Essential Writings of B. R. Ambedkar*, 183–89. Rajeev Kadambi, "Ambedkar's Framing of the 'Political' within Ethical Practice," *Studies in Indian Politics* 4 no. 2 (2016): 146–47, 149–50, 153–54. Kumar, *Radical Equality*, 59–61, 69.

55. Ambedkar, "Buddha Dhamma Saviour," 524, 533–34; Scott R. Stroud, "The Rhetoric of Conversion as Emancipatory Strategy in India: Bhimrao Ambedkar, Pragmatism, and the Turn to Buddhism," *Rhetorica* 35 no. 3 (2017): 330–31.

56. Ambedkar, "Buddha Dhamma Saviour," 530–32, 544. Stroud, "Rhetoric of Conversion," 334–36.

57. Kumar, *Radical Equality*, 114.

58. Ambedkar, *Buddha and His Dhamma*, 103–9. Berkeley sociologist Gail Omvedt, who has traced the history of the caste system in India, argues that the caste system was in an "incipient phase" during the Buddha's lifetime. There are clear confrontations between the Buddha and Brahmins recorded in early texts. Brahmanism was not dominant until midway through the first millennium CE, and the caste-based village social order was in place between the eighth century and the twelfth century CE. Gail Omvedt, *Understanding Caste: From Buddha to Ambedkar and Beyond* (Himayanagar, Hyderabad: Orient Blackswan, 2011), 11–12, 14.

59. B. R. Ambedkar, "Educate, Agitate, Organize, Have Faith and Lose No Hope," in *Writings and Speeches*, 17, part 3, 275–76.

Buddhist Reflections in a Prophetic Key #5

1. Byakuren Judith Ragir, "Yasodhara's Path," in *The Hidden Lamp: Stories from Twenty-Five Centuries of Awakened Women*, ed. Zenshin Florence Caplow and Reigetsu Susan Moon (Boston, MA: Wisdom, 2013), 149.

2. Ragir, "Yasodhara's Path," 147–48.

3. B. R. Ambedkar, *The Buddha and His Dhamma: A Critical Edition*, ed. Aakash Singh Rathore and Ajay Verma (New Delhi: Oxford University Press, 2011), xxix.

4. Ambedkar, *Buddha and His Dhamma*, 17–21.

5. Ambedkar, *Buddha and His Dhamma*, 22–24.

6. Ambedkar, *Buddha and His Dhamma*, 41.

7. "Putin's Apocalyptic Goals," *Commonweal*, March 15, 2022, accessed at https://www.commonwealmagazine.org/putins-apocalyptic-goals.

Chapter Six

1. John Winthrop, "A Modell of Christian Charity," in *God's New Israel: Religious Interpretations of American Destiny*, ed. Conrad Cherry (Englewood Cliffs, NJ: Prentice-Hall, 1971), 42–43.

2. Cornel West, *Black Prophetic Fire*, ed. Christa Buschendorf (Boston, MA: Beacon Press, 2014), 5.

3. Gustavo Gutiérrez, *Theology of Liberation* (Maryknoll, NY: Orbis Books, 1988), 5–12. We will examine this method in more detail in chapter 9.

4. angel Kyodo williams et al., *Radical Dharma: Talking Race, Love and Liberation* (Berkeley, CA: North Atlantic Books, 2016), 167.

5. williams et al., *Radical Dharma*, xxv, 81.

6. Michael Wiggelsworth, "God's Controversy with New England," in *God's New Israel: Religious Interpretations of American Destiny*, ed. Conrad Cherry (Englewood Cliffs, NJ: Prentice-Hall, 1971), 54. Winthrop's sermon and Wiggelsworth's poem are classic expressions of the earliest versions of the American jeremiad. This does not alter the fact that they are deeply problematic in several ways. First, there was nothing new about New England. Peoples had lived and thrived there for millennia. Second, Winthrop believes that the land was given by God to the Puritans who sought to possess it. By contrast, the natives did not see land as something that could be possessed. They learned by bitter experience that deeds were not pacts that formed a sharing relationship. Deeds conferred exclusive ownership. Third, the England part of "New England" implied a whole culture that was to be replicated in a "new" world, including gender roles, farming methods, child rearing practices, and the like. And, fourth, the divine mission was spelled out in their sacred Book. They did not have anything essential to learn from the native inhabitants. This delusion hid a multitude of evils, including collective greed in land speculation and the ideological justification that natives had not "improved' the land. For the view of the native peoples, see Lisa Brooks, *Our Beloved Kin: A New History of King Philip's War* (New Haven, CT: Yale University Press, 2018).

7. Sacvan Bercovitch, *The American Jeremiad* (Madison, WI: University of Wisconsin Press, 1978), 9, 62.

8. Bercovitch, *American Jeremiad*, 23.

9. Bercovitch, *American Jeremiad*, 61.

10. Herman Melville as cited in Bercovitch, *American Jeremiad*, 176–77.

11. Manisha Sinha, *The Slave's Cause: A History of Abolition* (New Haven, CT: Yale University Press, 2016), 77, 95.

12. Cathleen Kaveny, *Prophecy without Contempt: Religious Discourse in the Public Square* (Cambridge, MA: Harvard University Press, 2016), 179–81, 184, 225, 229.

13. Walter Rauschenbusch, *Christianity Social Crisis in the 21st Century: The Classic That Woke up the Church*, ed. Paul B. Raushenbush (New York: Harper One, 2007), 225, 228–29.

14. Kaveny, *Prophecy without Contempt*, 228–30, 248, 252, 347.

15. Daniel Berrigan, *Exodus: Let My People Go* (Eugene, OR: Cascade Books, 2008), 47, 49, 69.

16. Kaveny, *Prophecy without Contempt*, 9, 376–90, 396, 419–20.

17. Kaveny, *Prophecy without Contempt*, 248, 331–32, 420–21.

18. Martin Luther King Jr., "A Time to Break Silence," in *A Testament of Hope: The Essential Writings and Speeches of Martin Luther King Jr.*, ed. James M. Washington (San Francisco, CA: HarperSanFrancisco, 1986), 231–44.

19. Berrigan, *Exodus*, 69; Kaveny, *Prophecy without Contempt*, 356, 359.

20. Kaveny, *Prophecy without Contempt*, 351–53.

21. Abraham Lincoln, "Second Inaugural, Address," in *God's New Israel: Religious Interpretations of American Destiny*, ed. Conrad Cherry (Englewood Cliffs, NJ: Prentice-Hall, 1971), 195–96.

22. Kaveny, *Prophecy without Contempt*, 370, 372, 414.

23. Kaveny, *Prophecy without Contempt*, 419.

24. Cornel West, *Keeping Faith: Philosophy and Race in America* (New York: Routledge, 1993), xii.

25. David Howard-Pitney, *The African American Jeremiad: Appeals for Justice in America*, rev. ed. (Philadelphia, PA: Temple University Press, 2005), 10–11, 13, 18.

26. John Lewis as cited in Jonathan Rieder, *The Word of the Lord Is upon Me: The Righteous Performance of Martin Luther King Jr.* (Cambridge, MA: Harvard University Press, 2008), 193–94.

27. Gary S. Selby, *Martin Luther King and the Rhetoric of Freedom: The Exodus Narrative in America's Struggle for Civil Rights* (Waco, TX: Baylor University Press, 2008), 157–60, 168–71.

28. Willie Harrell Jr., "A Call to Consciousness and Action: Mapping the African American Jeremiad," *Canadian Review of American Studies* 36, no. 2 (Summer 2006): 157–60.

29. Jesmyn Ward, ed., *The Fire This Time: A New Generation Speaks about Race* (New York: Scribner, 2016).

30. David Walker as cited in Cornel West, *Prophecy Deliverance: An Afro-American Revolutionary Christianity* (Philadelphia, PA: Westminster Press, 1982), 102.

31. David Walker as cited in Harrell, "Consciousness and Action," 157.

32. Herbert Robinson-Marbury, *Pillars of Clouds and Fire: The Politics of Exodus in African American Biblical Interpretation* (New York: New York University Press, 2015), 13–14, 33–41.

33. David W. Blight, *Frederick Douglass: Prophet of Freedom* (New York: Simon and Schuster, 2018), 38–39, 157, 228–229.

34. Nathaniel Rodgers as cited in Blight, *Frederick Douglass*, 102–3.

35. Frederick Douglass, "The Meaning of the Fourth of July for the Negro," July 5, 1852, in *Frederick Douglass: Selected Speeches and Writings*, ed. Philip Foner (Chicago, IL: Lauren Hill Books, 1999), 188–205. All further references to this speech appear in parentheses in the text.

36. In ancient Israel, the "jubilee" was each fiftieth year, when debts were cancelled, all slaves were freed, and the expropriated land was returned to its original tillers. Whether or not it was ever implemented, it stood for a fundamental renewal of an egalitarian social contract.

37. Frederick Douglass, "The West Indies," in *Frederick Douglass: Selected Speeches and Writings*, 358–59.

38. Douglass, "West India Emancipation," 360–62.

39. West, *Black Prophetic Fire*, 140.

40. Ida B. Wells as cited in Howard-Pitney, *African American Jeremiad*, 75.

41. Howard-Pitney, *African American Jeremiad*, 77–79.

42. Ida B. Wells, "Lynching Our National Crime," National Negro Conference, May 31–June 1, 1909, 127, https://www.blackpast.org/african-american-history/1909-ida-b-wells-awful-slaughter/.

43. We will look at this distinction more deeply in chapter 10.

44. Kaveny, *Prophecy without Contempt*, 287–89, 312.

45. We will examine Dr. King's version of the three collective poisons—economic exploitation (greed), militarism (ill will), and racism (delusion)—in chapter 7.

46. Kaveny, *Prophecy without Contempt*, ix–x.

Chapter Seven

1. Martin Luther King, "The World House," in *Where Do We Go from Here? Chaos or Community* (New York: Harper and Row, 1967), 198–200.

2. Rabbi Abraham Heschel as cited in Cornel West, "Hope and Despair: Past and Present," in *To Shape a New World: Essays on the Political Philosophy of Martin Luther King, Jr.* ed. Tommie Shelby and Brandon M. Terry (Cambridge: Harvard University Press, 208), 329.

3. Willis Jenkins, "Christian Social Ethics after Bonhoeffer and King," in *Bonhoeffer and King: Their Legacies and Import for Christian Social Thought*, ed. Willis Jenkins and Jennifer M. McBride, Kindle Edition (Minneapolis, MN: Fortress Press, 2010).

4. As cited in Gary S. Selby, *Martin Luther King and the Rhetoric of Freedom* (Waco, TX: Baylor University Press, 2008), 52–53.

5. As cited in Selby, *Rhetoric of Freedom*, 8–11, 15.

6. As cited in Selby, *Rhetoric of Freedom*, 54–55.

7. Selby, *Rhetoric of Freedom*, 52, 56, 58–59. Social movements struggle over meaning. Their fights with others or with a hegemonic order take place over symbols as well as in the streets. Movements provide "interpretative frames" that are designed to reconfigure our perceptions of history, reality, and the moral order. They shape a collective identity and they do so, most of all, through narratives. "Narratives," Selby argues "make events in human experience meaningful by structuring them within temporal and causal sequences configuring the past in a way that explains

the present and predicts the future. They place events within a moral universe." Laden with memories of slave resistance, the Exodus narrative was ideally suited to frame Black lives and to be a counternarrative to those of white supremacy. Selby, *Rhetoric of Freedom*, 14, 43.

8. Nahum Ward-Lev, *The Liberating Path of the Hebrew Prophets: Then and Now* (Maryknoll, NY: Orbis Books, 2019); Selby, *Rhetoric of Freedom*, 156–60. This emphasis on the centrality of the Exodus narrative in King's role as Jeremiah and its and his rootedness in the Southern Black church, its rhetoric, idioms, and theology by no means detracts from his rich and complex intellectual formation. He was a student of the American Social Gospel tempered by the realism and the unflinching confrontation of evil of a Reinhold Niebuhr. He had read Marx and formed his own critical appropriation of Marx's thought, calling himself a Christian socialist. He was a proponent of a little-known philosophy called personalism. Dr. King also appropriated creatively what is called "America's civil religion," that is, the operative presence of sacred symbols, rituals, and values that erect a sacred canopy over the national community. He gradually became a student of Gandhi, developing a critical and creative appropriation of Gandhi's ideas and praxis. See Martin Luther King Jr., "Pilgrimage to Nonviolence," in *A Testament of Hope: The Essential Writings and Speeches of Martin Luther King, Jr.*, ed. James M. Washington (SanFrancisco, CA: HarperSanFrancisco, 1986), 35–40. See also Martin Luther King Jr., *Stride toward Freedom* (New York: Harper and Row, 1958), 72–88.

9. King, *Stride toward Freedom*, 114–15, This experience conforms to the archetype of the reluctant prophet that we saw in chapter 1.

10. Selby, *Rhetoric of Freedom*, 122–25.

11. To say that the prophetic persona exists only in relation is to acknowledge the hundreds of thousands who contributed in large and small ways to the civil rights revolution. That said, there are some caveats that we need to keep in mind when we draw upon the legacy of this prophet. First, as a man of his times, Dr. King and SCLC were infected by sexism and homophobia, particularly regarding his failure to find a leadership position for Ella Baker and Bayard Rustin to further expand their immense contributions to the movement. Cornel West, *Black Prophetic Fire*, ed. Christa Buschendorf (Boston, MA: Beacon Press, 2014), 91–92, 105–6. Second, charismatic leadership comes with some real liabilities, including overreliance on one vulnerable and limited human being. Even apart from his assassination, Dr. King was being ground down by the constant pressures of his national prominence. Third, we need to listen to Thich Nhat Hanh when he says that Maitreya, the Buddha of the future, will come not as an individual but as a community. Thich Nhat Hanh, "Go as a Sangha," in *Friends on the Path: Living Spiritual Communities*, ed. Jack Lawlor (Berkeley, CA: Parallax Press, 2002), 17. We cannot wait for an Engaged Buddhist with Dr. King's synthetic genius and rhetorical brilliance to lead us through the wilderness.

12. Martin Luther King Jr., "A Letter from Birmingham City Jail," in *A Testament of Hope: The Essential Writings and Speeches of Martin Luther King Jr.*, ed.

James M. Washington (San Francisco, CA: HarperSanFrancisco, 1986), 289–302. Further references to the letter appear in parentheses in the text.

13. Jonathan Rieder, *Gospel of Freedom: Martin Luther King Jr.'s Letter from a Birmingham Jail and the Struggle that Changed the Nation* (New York: Bloomsbury Press, 2013), 4, 13; David J. Garrow, *Bearing the Cross: Martin Luther King, Jr., and the Southern Christian Leadership Conference* (New York: Perennial Classics, 1986), 225–30.

14. Garrow, *Bearing the Cross*, 240–43.

15. Rieder, *Gospel of Freedom*, 35–41.

16. Recognizing the letter as actually enfolding several genres opens a window on King's hybrid vision. Jonathan Rieder, *The Word of the Lord Is upon Me: The Righteous Performance of Martin Luther* King, Jr. (Cambridge, MA: Harvard University Press, 2008), 105.

17. Rieder, *Gospel of Freedom*, 49–51.

18. Rieder, *Gospel of Freedom*, 52, 57–58.

19. King also criticizes laws as unjust that are not democratically created, that apply to only one group not all, and that are good on their face but are applied to suppress dissent. Martin Luther King Jr., "Letter from Birmingham City Jail," 294. These "procedural" stipulations also make more specific how the I-Thou relationship gets institutionalized. Everyone's voice in creating a just social order must be heard; the core principles of a society must in principle be universalizable, and good means must not be used to reach unjust ends.

20. Rieder, *Gospel of Freedom*, 75–76.

21. In the case of the Birmingham campaign, it was not Dr. King's ordeal in jail nor was it his masterful letter that turned the tide but the children. Desperate for more bodies to defy Sheriff O'Connor, the movement allowed teenagers to march, and more than a thousand did so. Rieder, *Gospel of Freedom*, 114–16. When the sheriff turned his dogs and fire hoses on the young people, a nation became outraged. Garrow, *Bearing the Cross*, 247–51.

22. Martin Luther King Jr., "A Time to Break Silence," in *A Testament of Hope: The Essential Writings and Speeches of Martin Luther King Jr.*, ed. James M. Washington (San Francisco, CA: HarperSanFrancisco, 1986), 231–44. Further references to "A Time to Break Silence" appear in parentheses in the text.

23. Reider, *Word of the Lord*, 261.

24. Garrow, *Bearing the Cross*, 552.

25. Martin Luther King Jr. as cited in Johnathon Eig, *King: A Life* (New York: Farrar Straus and Giroux, 2023), 516.

26. Elsewhere in this speech he identifies the three as racism, militarism, and poverty, poverty being the flipside of collective greed/economic exploitation. King, "A Time to Break Silence," 242.

27. Martin Luther King Jr. as cited in Garrow, *Bearing the Cross*, 553.

28. Martin Luther King Jr. as cited in Garrow, *Bearing the Cross*, 554.

29. Martin Luther King Jr. as cited in Garrow, *Bearing the Cross*, 563.

30. All references are to the original publication of King's *Where Do We Go from Here?*. See also King, "World House," 617–33. Further references to the "World House" appear in parentheses in the text.

31. For a comparison of King's understanding of interdependence with Buddhist interpretations, see Roy Money, "A Network of Mutuality: Martin Luther King, Jr., on Interdependence and Ethics," in *In an Inescapable Network of Mutuality: Martin Luther King, Jr., and the Globalization of an Ethical Ideal*, ed. Lewis V. Baldwin and Paul R. Dekar (Eugene, OR: Cascade Books, 2013), 217–31.

32. Cornel West, "Introduction," in *The Radical King*, ed. Cornel West (Boston, MA: Beacon Press, 2016), xv.

33. This appears to be changing with a new generation of Engaged Buddhists. Larry Yang, *Awakening Together: The Spiritual Practice of Inclusivity and Community* (Somersville, MA: Wisdom, 2017). For an overview, see Ann Gleig, *American Dharma: Buddhism Beyond Modernity* (New Haven, CT: Yale University Press, 2019).

34. Martin Luther King Jr., "A Testament of Hope," in *A Testament of Hope: The Essential Writings and Speeches of Martin Luther King Jr.*, ed. James M. Washington (San Francisco, CA: HarperSanFrancisco, 1986), 328.

Buddhist Reflections in a Prophetic Key #6

1. Lt. Col. William A. Boekel to Col. Karl Bendetsen, Western Defense Command, as cited in Duncan Ryuken Williams, *American Sutra: A Story of Faith and Freedom in the Second World War* (Cambridge, MA: Harvard University Press, 2019), 76.

2. *Los Angeles Times* editorial, February, 1942.

3. Misao Yumibe as cited in Williams, *American Sutra*, 122–23.

4. I use the term "concentration camps" deliberately as designating the forced imprisonment without due process of law of an entire class of people not for any crime but purely because they are of a certain race, ethnicity, gender, sexual orientation, or religion.

5. Williams, *American Sutra*, 43.

6. Williams, *American Sutra*, 86.

7. Williams, *American Sutra*, 16–22, 46–47, 106–8, 116.

8. Williams, *American Sutra*, 229–33.

Chapter Eight

1. Thich Nhat Hanh, The Art of Power (New York: HarperCollins, 2007), 15.

2. Reinhold Niebuhr, Moral Man and Immoral Society (New York: Charles Scribner's Sons, 1932), xii–xv.

3. David Cortright, *Gandhi and Beyond: Nonviolence for a New Political Age*, 2nd ed. (Boulder, CO: Paradigm, 2009), 191–92.

4. B. R. Ambedlkar as cited in Christophe Jaffrelot, *Dr. Ambedkar and Untouchability* (New York: Columbia University Press, 2005), 91.

5. My analysis in this chapter has been greatly aided by an article by Sallie B. King, "Buddhism, Nonviolence and Power," *Journal of Buddhist Ethics* 16 (2009): 103–35. Koans generally involve an encounter between a disciple and her teacher. They challenge conventional wisdom. They are to be lived and breathed. Prophetic wisdom offers its own twist on the encounter with a Zen teacher. We examined such a twist in the case of the old woman's encounter with Zhaozhou. See above "Buddhist Reflections in a Prophetic Key #1: Cries of the Crows: A Buddhist Take on the Prophetic Voice," 31–32.

6. Hannah Arendt, *On Violence* (New York: Harcourt Brace, 1970), 52–53.

7. Arendt, *On Violence*, 56.

8. Arendt, *On Violence*, 82.

9. Arendt, *On Violence*, 44, 52–54.

10. Arendt, *On Violence*, 40, 56.

11. Gene Sharp, *Waging Nonviolent Struggle* (Boston, MA: Porter Sargent, 2005), 28.

12. Gene Sharp, *The Politics of Nonviolent Action*, part 1, *Power and Struggle* (Manchester, NH: Porter Sargent, 1973), 12.

13. Sharp offers a pragmatic justification for nonviolent action that does not depend upon a spiritual transformation of the activists into committed pacifists, nor does it depend on converting the opponent: "Nonviolent struggle is identified by what people do, not by what they believe." Sharp, *Waging Nonviolent Struggle*, 14, 15, 19.

14. James M. Jasper, *The Art of Moral Protest* (Chicago, IL: University of Chicago Press, 1997), 78.

15. Daniel Berrigan, *Isaiah: Spirit of Courage, Gift of Tears* (Minneapolis, MN: Fortress Press, 1996),75.

16. Charles R. Strain, *The Prophet and the Bodhisattva: Daniel Berrigan, Thich Nhat Hanh, and the Ethics of Peace and Justice* (Eugene, OR: Wipf and Stock, 2014), 108–12.

17. Jasper, *Art of Moral Protest*, 14–15.

18. In his famous autobiographical essay "Pilgrimage to Nonviolence," written after the successful conclusion of the Montgomery bus boycott, King drew upon the deepest sources of wisdom in his Christian tradition to elaborate the meaning of "agape." He defines agape as "redemptive goodwill." By enduring "unmerited suffering" while remaining steadfast in their purpose, the nonviolent resisters employed a lever more powerful than reason alone to persuade their opponents to change their hearts and minds. Martin Luther King Jr., *Stride toward Freedom: The Montgomery Story* (New York: Harper and Row, 1958), 84–88. Buddhists committed to ending suffer-

ing rightfully balk at this seeming adulation of the redemptive power of unmerited suffering. However, Buddhists can affirm agape defined as unconditional recognition of the other and the refusal to retaliate, to repay hate with hate, violence with violence. In this sense agape is a powerful lever for breaking the cycle of violence.

19. M. L. King, *Stride toward Freedom*, 88; Martin Luther King Jr., *The Radical King*, ed. Cornel West (Boston, MA: Beacon Press, 2015), 50–53.

20. Brandon M. Terry, "Requiem for a Dream: The Problem-Space of Black Power," in *To Shape a New World: Essays on the Political Philosophy of Martin Luther King Jr.*, ed. Tommie Shelby and Brandon M. Terry (Cambridge, MA: Harvard University Press, 2018), 305.

21. Martin Luther King Jr., "My Trip to the Land of Gandhi," in *A Testament of Hope: The Essential Writings and Speeches of Martin Luther King Jr.*, ed. James M. Washington (San Francisco, CA: HarperSanFrancisco, 1986), 25–26.

22. Martin Luther King Jr., "Pilgrimage to Nonviolence," in *A Testament of Hope: The Essential Writings and Speeches of Martin Luther King Jr.*, ed. James M. Washington (San Francisco, CA: HarperSanFrancisco, 1986), 39.

23. Terry, "Requiem for a Dream," 305.

24. Martin Luther King Jr., *Where Do We Go from Here: Chaos or Community?* (New York: Bantam Books, 1968), 27, 38–41.

25. M. L. King, *Where Do We Go from Here?* 42–44.

26. John Makransky, "Confronting the 'Sin' out of Love for the 'Sinner': Fierce Compassion as a Force for Social Change," *Buddhist-Christian Studies* 36 (2016): 87–96. Movements for political change when faced with a recalcitrant opponent frequently engage in dualistic thinking and become imprisoned in their own ideological rigidity. I can't count the number of demonstrations that I have been a part of that succumbed to dualistic chanting. Fierce compassion is hard to come by.

27. M. L. King, *Where Do We Go from Here*, 106.

28. Martin Luther King Jr., "All Labor Has Dignity," in *The Radical King*, ed. Cornel West (Boston, MA: Beacon Press, 2015), 250–51.

29. Martin Luther King Jr., "The Trumpet of Conscience," in *A Testament of Hope: The Essential Writings and Speeches of Martin Luther King Jr.*, ed. James M. Washington (San Francisco, CA: HarperSanFrancisco, 1986), 650.

30. Sallie King, *Being Benevolence: The Social Ethics of Engaged Buddhism* (Honolulu: University of Hawaii Press, 2005), 213–14.

31. S. King, *Being Benevolence*, 209–10.

32. Thich Nhat Hanh, *Calming the Fearful Mind: A Zen Response to Terrorism* (Berkeley, CA: Parallax Press, 2005), 101.

33. As cited in S. King, *Being Benevolence*, 221.

34. As cited in S. King, *Being Benevolence*, 218. Distributive justice focuses on the goods necessary for surviving and thriving. Who is entitled to what and how will it be delivered? Do basic rights include social and economic rights? Dis-

tributive justice is extolled in several discourses attributed to the Buddha. In one a king ignores the advice of the king who ruled before him and fails to distribute his wealth. As a result, poverty becomes rife and with it a cascade of social suffering: "From the growth of poverty, theft increased. From the increase of theft, the use of weapons increased. From the increased use of weapons, the taking of life increased, lying increased, divisive speech increased and sexual misconduct increased—and on account of this, people's life span decreased and their beauty decreased." See Digha Nikaya 26 in Bhikku Bodhi, ed., *The Buddha's Teachings on Social and Communal Harmony* (Somerville, MA: Wisdom, 2016), 189–91.

35. George Bond, *Buddhism at Work: Community Development, Social Empowerment and the Sarvodaya Movement* (Bloomfield, CT: Kumarian Press, 2004), 17.

36. S. King, *Being Benevolence*, 206.

37. Strain, *Prophet and Bodhisattva*, 193–95. See also Daniel Levine, *Popular Voices in Latin American Catholicism* (Princeton, NJ: Princeton University Press, 1992), 317–21, 335–44.

38. Nhat Hanh, *Calming the Fearful Mind*, 85.

39. Nhat Hanh, "Ahimsa," in *Love in Action: Writings on Nonviolent Social Change* (Berkeley, CA: Parallax Press, 1993), 66, 71.

40. Nhat Hanh, "Ahimsa," 65–71.

41. Strain, *Prophet and Bodhisattva*, 113–15, 193–201.

42. Traveling in America in 1831–32, the French aristocrat Alexis de Tocqueville was the first to take note of the proliferation of voluntary associations as a hallmark of a democratic society and to grasp their special sort of power. "Americans of all ages, all stations of life, and all types of disposition are forever forming associations," he argued. "As soon as several Americans have conceived of a sentiment or an idea that they want to produce before the world, they seek each other out, and when found, they unite. Thenceforth they are no longer isolated individuals, but a power conspicuous from the distance whose actions serve as an example; when it speaks men listen." Alexis de Tocqueville, *Democracy in America*, ed. J. P. Mayer (Garden City, NY: Doubleday, 1969), 513–16.

43. The classic study of the role of TANs in creating social change is Margaret E. Keck and Kathryn Sikkink, *Activists beyond Borders: Advocacy Networks in International Politics* (Ithaca, NY: Cornell University Press, 1998); see also Strain, *Prophet and Bodhisattva*, 194–96. On the Landmine TAN, see Jody Williams, Stephen D. Goose, and Mary Wareham, eds., *Banning Landmines: Disarmament, Citizen Diplomacy, and Human Security* (Lanham, MD: Rowman and Littlefield, 2008).

44. Thich Nhat Hanh, *Interbeing: Fourteen Guidelines for Engaged Buddhism*, 3rd ed. (Berkeley, CA: Parallax Press, 1998), 17–21.

45. Nhat Hanh, *Interbeing*, 41–42.

46. Nhat Hanh, *Interbeing*, 43.

47. Nhat Hanh, *Interbeing*, 47–48.

48. Nhat Hanh, *Interbeing*, 49.

49. On a more personal level, Thich Nhat Hanh urges us to "stay close to oppressed people, to work with them to secure their right to freedom from exploitation." Nhat Hanh, *Interbeing*, 50–51. This "staying close" to people who are oppressed strikes me as a crucial spiritual practice for those of us who live comfortable, cocooned lives.

50. Nhat Hanh, *Interbeing*, 43–44.

51. Martin Luther King Jr., "Letter from Birmingham Jail," in *A Testament of Hope: The Essential Writings and Speeches of Martin Luther King Jr.*, ed. James M. Washington (San Francisco, CA: HarperSanFrancisco, 1986), 290–92.

52. Thich Nhat Hanh did not entirely dismiss acts of nonviolent resistance. In fact, he praised the Vietnamese peace seekers who placed their family altars in the middle of the road and sat in to halt the tanks sent to crush nonviolent demonstrations. Publishing antiwar poetry, developing peace proposals, and engaging in hunger strikes were some of the forms that nonviolent action took. "Some people," Thich Nhat Hanh says, "were critical saying the [Vietnamese protesters] used religion for political purposes, but I do not agree. They were using their most potent spiritual force to directly confront violence. This was not a political act, it was an act of love." Nhat Hanh, *Love in Action*, 40–41. Unfortunately, this comment seems to accept the dichotomy between spiritual and political actions that a fusion of love, power, and justice seeks to overcome.

53. See, for example, David Loy, *Money, Sex, War, Karma: Notes for a Buddhist Revolution* (Boston, MA: Wisdom, 2008), 143–44.

54. I have been aided in my formulations of these principles by David Loy, *Money, Sex, War Karma*, 139–52; and David W. Chappell, "Buddhist Peace Principles," in *Buddhist Peacework: Creating Cultures of Peace*, ed. David W. Chappell (Boston, MA: Wisdom, 1999): 199–231.

55. Nhat Hanh, *Interbeing*, 23–29.

Chapter Nine

1. Cornel West, *Prophetic Thought in Postmodern Times* (Monroe, ME: Common Courage Press, 1993), 4.

2. Paulo Freire, *Pedagogy of the Oppressed* (New York: Herder and Herder, 1971), 75–76.

3. Gary Snyder, *Earth Household* (New York: New Directions, 1969), 90, 92.

4. David Loy, *The Great Awakening: A Buddhist Social Theory* (Boston, MA: Wisdom, 2003), 18, 75.

5. Michael Walzer, *Exodus and Revolution* (New York: Basic Books, 1985).

6. Karl Marx, "Theses on Feuerbach," in *The Writings of the Young Marx on Philosophy and Society*, ed. Lloyd Easton and Kurt Guddat (Garden City, NY: Dou-

bleday, 1967), 402. For a nuanced discussion of Marx's contribution, see Clodovis Boff, *Theology and Praxis: Epistemological Foundations* (Maryknoll, NY: Orbis Books, 1987), 13–14, 197–98.

7. Richard Bernstein, *Praxis and Action: Contemporary Philosophies of Human Activity* (Philadelphia: University of Pennsylvania Press, 1971), ix–xx.

8. David Tracy, *Blessed Rage for Order: The New Pluralism in Theology* (New York: Seabury, 1975), 243.

9. Clodovis Boff provides the fullest treatment of this understanding of praxis. Boff, *Theology and Praxis*, xxi–xxii, 4–8, 206–20, 229–32.

10. John Makransky, "What Christian Liberation Theology and Buddhism Need to Learn from Each Other," *Buddhist Christian Studies* 34 (2014): 12–21.

11. Gustavo Gutiérrez, *Theology of Liberation* (Maryknoll, NY: Orbis, 1973), 5, 9–12.

12. Hannah Arendt, *The Human Condition* (Garden City, NY: Doubleday, 1959), 15–61.

13. James Jasper, *The Art of Moral Protest* (Chicago, IL: University of Chicago Press, 1997), 112–13, 159–61.

14. George Bond, *Buddhism at Work: Community Development, Social Empowerment, and the Sarvodaya Movement* (Bloomfield CT: Kumarian, 2004); Joanna Macy, *World as Lover, World as Self*, 1st ed. (Berkeley CA: Parallax Press, 1991), 125–52.

15. Macy, *World as Lover*, 132, 136–38; Bond, *Buddhism at Work*, 10, 14–16, 49. Beyond this symbolic constitution of a new vision of integral human development, Sarvodaya combines basic strategies for community organizing with Gandhian methods of nonviolence and village-based self-reliance to build its own form of praxis. Macy, *World as Lover*, 145–51; Bond, *Buddhism at Work*, 8–10, 103–8.

16. Gutiérrez, *Theology of Liberation*, 9–10.

17. Brian Victoria, *Zen at War* (New York: Weatherhill, 1997).

18. Victoria, *Zen at War*, ix–xi.

19. Iida Toin as cited in Victoria, *Zen at War*, 101–2.

20. Okubo Koichi as cited in Victoria, *Zen at War*, 103.

21. D. T. Suzuki as cited in Victoria, *Zen at War*, 108–10.

22. Uchiyama Gudo as cited in Victoria, *Zen at War*, 41.

23. Victoria, *Zen at War*, 42–44.

24. Seno Giro as cited in Victoria, *Zen at War*, 67–68.

25. Victoria, *Zen at War*, 71.

26. Victoria, *Zen at War*, 70–73.

27. Victoria, *Zen at War*, 192–93.

28. Boff, *Theology and Praxis*, 5–8, 222–23.

29. David Loy, *Lack and Transcendence: The Problem of Death and Life in Psychotherapy, Existentialism, and Buddhism* (Somerville, MA: Wisdom, 2018), 25–27, 30–31, 86–87; Loy, *Great Awakening*, 9, 22–23, 35, 172; David Loy, *Money, Sex, War, Karma* (Boston, MA: Wisdom, 2008), 15–23.

30. Loy, *Lack and Transcendence*, 31.
31. Loy, *Great Awakening*, 20–23; Loy, *Money, Sex, War, Karma*, 87–88.
32. David Loy, *A Buddhist History of the West: Studies in Lack* (Albany, NY: SUNY Press 2002), 122, 151–52.
33. Loy, *Money, Sex, War, Karma*, 88–89, 93.
34. Raymond Geuss, *The Idea of a Critical Theory: Habermas and the Frankfurt School* (Cambridge: Cambridge University Press, 1981), 2–3.
35. David Loy, *Ecodharma: Buddhist Teachings for the Ecological Crisis* (Somerville, MA: Wisdom, 2018), 61.
36. Thich Nhat Hanh, *Interbeing: Fourteen Guidelines for Engaged Buddhism*, 3rd ed. (Berkeley, CA: Parallax Press, 1998), 23–29.
37. Loy, *Money, Sex, War, Karma*, 97–102.
38. Ken Jones, *The New Social Face of Buddhism: A Call to Action* (Boston, MA: Wisdom, 2003), 59. The *Samyutta Nikāya* is one collection of discourses attributed to the Buddha that are part of the Pali canon.
39. Jones, *New Social Face of Buddhism*, 53–57, 59–60.
40. Ken Jones, "Beyond Us and Them," in *Mindful Politics: A Buddhist Guide to Making the World a Better Place*, ed. Melvin McLeod (Somerville, MA: Wisdom, 2006), 165–69.
41. Loy, *Ecodharma*, 48.
42. Loy, *Great Awakening*, 87.
43. Marx, "Theses on Feuerbach," 402.
44. Karl Marx, "Economic and Philosophical Manuscripts," in *The Writings of the Young Marx on Philosophy and Society*, ed. Lloyd D. Easton and Kurt H. Guddat (Garden City, NY: Doubleday, 1967), 283–301; Bernstein, *Praxis and Action*, 44–45, 48, 306–7.
45. Bertell Ollman, *Alienation: Marx's Concept of Man in Capitalist Society* (London: Cambridge University Press, 1971), 27–42.
46. Marx, "Theses on Feuerbach," 401.
47. Sulak Sivaraksa, *Seeds of Peace* (Berkeley, CA: Parallax Press, 1992); Sulak Sivaraksa, *Conflict, Culture, Change: Engaged Buddhism in a Globalizing World* (Boston, MA: Wisdom, 2003); Stephanie Kaza, ed., *Hooked: Buddhist Writings on Greed, Desire, and the Urge to Consume* (Boston, MA: Shambhala, 2005); Melvin McLeod, ed., *Mindful Politics: A Buddhist Guide to Making the World a Better Place* (Boston, MA: Wisdom, 2006).
48. Ivan Petrella, *The Future of Liberation Theology* (London: SCM Press, 2006), ix, 3.
49. José Míguez Bonino as cited in Petrella, *Future of Liberation Theology*, 11–12.
50. Petrella, *Future of Liberation Theology*, 4; Ivan Petrella, "Liberation Theology: A Programmatic Statement," in *Latin American Liberation Theology: The New Generation*, ed. Ivan Petrella (Maryknoll NY: Orbis Books, 2005), 149–54.
51. Bernstein, *Praxis and Action*, x.

52. A. T. Ariyaratne, *Schumacher Lectures on Buddhist Economics* (Ratmalana, Sri Lanka: Sarvodaya Vishva Lekha, 1999), 21, 23, 30–32; Bond, *Buddhism at Work*, 17.
53. Ariyaratne, *Schumacher Lectures*, 25–28, 33–36, 51–52, 54–55, 60.
54. Ariyaratne, *Schumacher Lectures*, 28; Bond, *Buddhism at Work*, 87–88.
55. Thich Nhat Hanh, *The World We Have: A Buddhist Approach to Peace and Ecology* (Berkeley, CA: Parallax Press, 2008); cf. Loy, *Ecodharma*.
56. Susan M. Darlington, *The Ordination of a Tree: The Thai Buddhist Environmental Movement* (Albany, NY: Suny Press, 2012); Charles R. Strain, "Reinventing Buddhist Practices to Meet the Challenge of Climate Change," *Contemporary Buddhism* 17, no. 1 (May, 2016): 140–43.
57. Sallie King, "The Small Engage the Powerful: An American Buddhist-Liberation Theology-Quaker Trialogue," *Buddhist Christian Studies* 39 (2019): 105–6.

Chapter Ten

1. Rev. angel Kyodo Williams, and Lama Rod Owens, with Jasmine Syedullah, *Radical Dharma: Talking Race, Love, and Liberation* (Berkeley, CA: North Atlantic Books, 2016), 133.
2. James Baldwin, "My Dungeon Shook," in *James Baldwin: Collected Essays*, ed. Toni Morrison (New York: The Library of America, 1998), 294.
3. Thich Nhat Hanh, *Being Peace* (Berkeley, CA: Parallax Press, 2005), 52.
4. Chenxing Han, *Be the Refuge: Raising the Voices of Asian American Buddhists* (Berkeley, CA: North Atlantic Books, 2021), 8.
5. James Baldwin, "American Dream American Negro," in *James Baldwin: Collected Essays*, ed. Toni Morrison (New York: The Library of America, 1998), 714.
6. James Baldwin, "White Man's Guilt," in *James Baldwin: Collected Essays*, ed. Toni Morrison (New York: The Library of America, 1998), 723.
7. Bernie Glassman, *Bearing Witness: A Zen Master's Lessons in Making Peace* (New York: Bell Tower, 1998), xiv, 66–73.
8. This chapter reflects loosely the elements of a theory of praxis outlined in chapter 9. A full-fledged theory would require the contributions of many Engaged Buddhist thinkers, listening to and discussing the project with numerous sanghas and, most of all, with communities seeking justice for themselves and others.
9. George M. Fredrickson, *Racism: A Short History* (Princeton, NJ: Princeton University Press, 2002), 9.
10. Fania E. Davis, *Race and Restorative Justice: Black Lives, Healing, and Social Transformation* (New York: Good Books, 2019), 33–34.
11. Fredrickson, *Racism*, 5–6, 9.
12. Davis, *Racism and Restorative Justice*, 33.
13. Fredrickson, *Racism*, 6.
14. Davis, *Racism and Restorative Justice*, 32.

15. Jan Willis, *Dreaming Me: Black, Baptist, and Buddhist—One Woman's Spiritual Journey* (Somerville, MA: Wisdom, 2008), 59–61.

16. Emily Cohen, "Across Generations: Interview with Jan Willis," *Journal of Feminist Studies in Religion* 33, no. 2 (2017): 127–37.

17. Martin Luther King Jr., "Loving Your Enemies," in *The Radical King*, ed. Cornel West (Boston, MA: Beacon Press, 2015), 59.

18. Willis, *Dreaming Me*, 140, 167.

19. Willis, *Dreaming Me*, 208–10; Jan Willis, "Buddhism and Race: An African American Baptist-Buddhist Perspective," in *Buddhist Women on the Edge: Contemporary Perspectives from the Western Frontier*, ed. Marianne Dresser (Berkeley, CA: North Atlantic Books. 1996), 81–91.

20. Willis, "Buddhism and Race," 88.

21. Jan Willis, "Why We Can't Breathe," *Lion's Roar*, December 7, 2014, https://www/lionsroar.com/cant-breathe.

22. Jan Willis, "We Cry Out for Justice," *Lion's Roar*, May 29, 2020, https://www/lionsroar.com/cry-justice.

23. Helen Tworkov, "Many Is More," *Tricycle: the Buddhist Review* (Winter 1991), accessed at https://tricycle.org/magazine/many-more. "Racism at its deepest levels," argued Rick Fields, "is the power to define which is always the paramount power in a racist society. It is hardly surprising that it is white Buddhists who are busy doing the defining. Nor is it surprising that they are defining it in their own image." "Ethnic" Buddhists, even those who have been here for five generations, are seen as weighted down by "cultural baggage. "It's just like church" is the often disdainful attitude of these converts toward their fellow Buddhists. Rick Fields, "Divided Dharma: White Buddhists Ethnic Buddhists, and Racism," in *The Faces of Buddhism in America*, ed. Charles Prebish and Kenneth Tanaka (Berkeley: University of California Press, 1998), 200, 203.

24. Han, *Be the Refuge*, 22–23; see also 287–88n2.

25. Han, *Be the Refuge*, 212.

26. Rhonda Magee, *The Inner Work of Racial Justice: Healing Ourselves and Transforming Our Communities through Mindfulness* (New York: Tarcher Perigee, 2019), 146–47.

27. Magee, *Inner Work*, 329.

28. Magee, *Inner Work*, 31–33.

29. For examples, see Magee, *Inner Work*, 72–73, 91–92, 100–101, 196–99, 278–80.

30. Magee, *Inner Work*, 261–63.

31. Magee, *Inner Work*, 168, 274–76.

32. Magee, *Inner Work*, 24–25, 182.

33. Magee, *Inner Work*, 153.

34. Magee, *Inner Work*, 24, 187.

35. Claudia Rankine, "The Condition of Black Life Is One of Mourning," in *The Fire This Time: A New Generation Speaks about Race*, ed. Jesmyn Ward (New York: Scribner, 2016), 147–48.

36. Rankine, "Condition of Black Life,"150.

37. Nahum Ward-Lev, *The Liberating Path of the Hebrew Prophets: Then and Now* (Maryknoll, NY: Orbis Books, 2019), 160.

38. Thich Nhat Hanh, *Calming the Fearful Mind: A Zen Response to Terrorism* (Berkeley, CA: Parallax Press, 2005), 85.

39. Larry Yang, *Awakening Together: The Spiritual Practice of Inclusivity and Community* (Somerville, MA: Wisdom, 2017), 166, 233.

40. Yang, *Awakening Together*, 55.

41. Joseph Goldstein as cited in Ann Gleig, *American Dharma: Buddhism beyond Modernity* (New Haven, CT: Yale University Press, 2019), 166.

42. Yang, *Awakening Together*, 45–46, 94.

43. Yang, *Awakening Together*, 59, 62–63, 68–69.

44. williams, Owens, and Syedullah, *Radical Dharma*, 108.

45. williams, Owens, and Syedullah, *Radical Dharma*, 192.

46. williams, Owens, and Syedullah, *Radical Dharma*, xxi–xxii.

47. williams, Owens, and Syedullah, *Radical Dharma*, 194, 196–97.

48. williams, Owens, and Syedullah, *Radical Dharma*, xvi–xxvii.

49. williams, Owens, and Syedullah, *Radical Dharma*, 167, 193.

50. williams, Owens, and Syedullah, *Radical Dharma*, xxii, 42.

51. williams, Owens, and Syedullah, *Radical Dharma*, 102.

52. williams, Owens, and Syedullah, *Radical Dharma*, 95, 167–68.

53. williams, Owens, and Syedullah, *Radical Dharma*, 174–75.

54. williams, Owens, and Syedullah, *Radical Dharma*, xxiv–xxv.

55. It is well known that in the early canon the Buddha sees caste designations as conventions. Genuine worth is determined not by birth but by actions. It has not been emphasized that he also rejected any physical signs as determinative of one's worth as a human being: "Not by the hairs on the head,/ not by the ears or eyes;/ not by the mouth or nose, not by the lips or brows." He then proceeds to mention all body parts, none of which says anything about essential worth (*Majjhima Nikāya* 98). This should be read as a clear rejection of racial designations. See Bhikkhu Bodhi, ed., *The Buddha's Teachings on Social and Communal Harmony* (Somerville, MA: Wisdom, 2016), 182–84.

56. Isabel Wilkerson, *Caste: The Origins of Our Discontents* (New York: Random House, 2020), 15–16.

57. Wilkerson, *Caste*, 104.

58. Wilkerson, *Caste*, 105–8.

59. Wilkerson, *Caste*, 106.

60. Wilkerson, *Caste*, 109–14.

61. Wilkerson, *Caste*, 111–12.
62. Wilkerson, *Caste*, 115–30.
63. On the role of such primitive emotions in shaping behaviors and politics, see Martha Nussbaum, *Hiding from Humanity: Disgust, Shame, and the Law* (Princeton, NJ: Princeton University Press, 2004); and Martha Nussbaum, *Monarchy of Fear: A Philosopher Looks at Our Political Crisis* (New York: Simon and Schuster, 2018).
64. Wilkerson, *Caste*, 131–40.
65. Wilkerson, *Caste*, 141–50.
66. Nussbaum, *Hiding from Humanity*, 217.
67. Nussbaum, *Hiding from Humanity*, 217–21, 234.
68. Wilkerson, *Caste*, 151–58.
69. Edward E. Baptist, *The Half Has Never Been Told: Slavery and the Making of American Capitalism* (New York: Basic Books, 2014).
70. Wilkerson, *Caste*, 150–64.
71. Magee, *Inner Work*, 204–6.
72. Wilkerson, *Caste*, 382. See Noel Ignatieff, *How the Irish Became White* (New York: Routledge, 1995).
73. Michelle Alexander, *The New Jim Crow: Mass Incarceration in the Age of Colorblindness*, rev. ed. (New York: The New Press, 2011), 13.
74. Alexander, *New Jim Crow*, 72, 184–85.
75. Alexander, *New Jim Crow*, 52, 55–57, 60, 74–77, 185–86, 215–16, 231.
76. Alexander, *New Jim Crow*, 94–95, 141–43. For an ethnographic treatment of this life sentence, see Reuben Jonathan Miller, *Halfway Home: Race, Punishment, and the After Life of Mass Incarceration* (New York: Little, Brown, 2021).
77. Judith Tannenbaum as cited in Sallie King, "Elements of Engaged Buddhist Ethical Theory," in *Destroying Mara Forever: Essays on Buddhist Ethics Essays in Honor of Damien Keown*, ed. John Powers and Charles Prebish (Ithaca, NY: Snow Lion, 2009), 196.
78. For a defense from a Buddhist standpoint of retributive justice, see Peter Harvey, "Buddhist Perspectives on Crime and Punishment," in *Destroying Mara Forever: Essays on Buddhist Ethics in Honor of Damien Keown*, ed. John Powers and Charles Prebish (Ithaca, NY: Snow Lion, 2009), 47–66.
79. Howard Zehr, *The Little Book of Restorative Justice*, rev. ed. (New York: Good Books, 2015), 48.
80. Tony Marshall, "Restorative Justice: An Overview," in *A Restorative Justice Reader: Texts, Sources, Content*, ed. Gerry Johnstone (Portland, OR: Willan, 2003), 33.
81. Marshall, "Restorative Justice," 28.
82. Daniel Van Ness, "Creating Restorative Justice Systems," in *A Restorative Justice Reader: Texts. Sources, Content*, ed. Gerry Johnstone (Portland, OR: Willan, 2003), 271–73.
83. John Braithwaite, "Restorative Justice and a Better Future," in *A Restorative Justice Reader: Texts, Sources, Content*, ed. Gerry Johnstone (Portland, OR: Willan, 2003), 87, 89.

84. Zehr, *Restorative Justice*, 30.

85. Zehr, *Restorative Justice*, 60–69. John Braithwaite provides a lengthy overview of studies that evaluate the success of these programs. John Braithwaite, "Does Restorative Justice Work?" in *A Restorative Justice Reader: Texts, Sources, Content*, ed. Gerry Johnstone (Portland, OR: Willan, 2003), 320–52.

86. Danielle Sered, *Until We Reckon: Violence, Mass Incarceration, and a Road to Repair* (New York: The New Press, 2019), 51–53.

87. Sered, *Until We Reckon*, 9.

88. Sered, *Until We Reckon*, 15.

89. Sered, *Until We Reckon*, 5–6.

90. Sered, *Until We Reckon*, 14.

91. Sered, *Until We Reckon*, 100.

92. Common Justice accentuates human agency, so it does not talk about "victims" of crimes but about "survivors." Likewise, it talks about "responsible parties," not "criminals" or "offenders."

93. Sered, *Until We Reckon*, 22–27.

94. Sered, *Until We Reckon*, 96–124.

95. Sered, *Until We Reckon*, 144–46.

96. As cited in Sered, *Until We Reckon*, 146.

97. Daniel Van Ness and Karen Heetderks Strong, *Restoring Justice*, 2nd ed.(Cincinnati, OH: Anderson, 2002), 113–20.

98. Sered, *Until We Reckon*, 154.

99. Mariame Kaba, *We Do This until We Free Us: Abolitionist Organizing and Transforming Justice*, ed. Tamara Nopper (Chicago, IL: Haymarket Books, 2021), 77, 141.

100. Kaba, *We Do This*, 4, 13, 18–21, 24–25, 96.

Conclusion

1. Joanna Macy, "Afterword," in *A Wild Love for the World: Joanna Macy and the Work of Our Time*, ed. Stephanie Kaza (Boulder, CO: Shambhala, 2020), 358.

2. Bhikku Bodhi, ed., *The Buddha's Teachings on Social and Communal Harmony* (Somerville, MA: Wisdom 2016), 189–92.

3. Walter Brueggemann, *The Prophetic Imagination*, 2nd ed. (Minneapolis, MN: Fortress Press, 2001), 65.

4. Christopher S. Queen, "Introduction," in *Engaged Buddhism in the West*, ed. Christopher S. Queen (Somerville, MA: Wisdom, 2000), 1.

5. Back from the Brink is a campaign started by the Union of Concerned Scientists. Its five goals are: pursue global elimination, renounce first use, end sole authority of the president, end hair-trigger alert, and cancel enhanced weapons funding. Preventnuclearwar.org, accessed November 12, 2023, https//preventnuclearwar.org.

6. Martin Luther King Jr., "A Time to Break Silence," in *A Testament of Hope: The Essential Writings and Speeches of Martin Luther King Jr.*, ed. James M. Washington (San Francisco, CA: HarperSanFrancisco, 1986), 240–43.

7. Thich Nhat Hanh, *Opening the Heart of the Cosmos: Insights on the Lotus Sutra* (Berkeley, CA: Parallax Press, 2003), 80–81.

Works Cited

Alexander, Michelle. *The New Jim Crow: Mass Incarceration in the Age of Colorblindness*. Rev. ed. New York: The New Press, 2011.
Ambedkar, B. R. *Annihilation of Caste: The Annotated Critical Edition*. Edited by S. Anand. New York: Verso, 2016.
———. "Brahma Is Not Dharma. What Good Is Brahma?" In *Dr. Ambedkar and Democracy*, edited by Christophe Jaffrelot and Narender Kumar, 245–51. New Delhi: Oxford University Press, 2018.
———. *The Buddha and His Dhamma: A Critical Edition*. Edited by Aakash Singh Rathore and Ajay Verma. New Delhi: Oxford University Press, 2011.
———. "The Buddha Dhamma Will Be the Saviour of the World." In *Dr. B. R. Babasaheb Ambedkar Writings and Speeches*, edited by Hari Narake, Dr. M. L. Kasare, N. G. Kamble, and Ashok Godghate, 17, part 3, 524–45. Mumbai, India: Ambedkar Source Material Publication Committee, Higher Education Department, Government of Maharashtra, 2003.
———. "Buddha or Karl Marx." In *The Essential Writings of B. R. Ambedkar*, edited by Valerian Rodrigues, 173–88. New Delhi: Oxford University Press. 2002.
———. "Buddha or Karl Marx." In *Dr. Babasaheb Ambedkar Writings and Speeches*, edited by Hari Narake, Dr. M. L. Kasare, N. G. Kamble, and Ashok Godghate, 17, part 3, 549–558. Mumbai, India: Ambedkar Source Material Publication Committee, Higher Education Department, Government of Maharashtra, 2003.
———. "Buddhism Paved the Way for Democracy and Socialistic Patterns of Society." In *Dr. B. R. Babasaheb Ambedkar Writings and Speeches*, edited by Hari Narake, Dr. M. L. Kasare, N. G. Kamble, and Ashok Godghate, 17, part 3, 404–409. Mumbai, India: Ambedkar Source Material Publication Committee, Higher Education Department, Government of Maharashtra, 2003.
———. "Conversion Is Necessary for Your Emancipation." In *Dr. B. R. Babasaheb Ambedkar Writings and Speeches*, edited by Hari Narake, Dr. M. L. Kasare, N. G. Kamble, and Ashok Godghate, 17, part 3, 107–112. Mumbai, India: Ambedkar Source Material Publication Committee, Higher Education Department, Government of Maharashtra, 2003.

———. "Educate, Agitate, Organize, Have Faith and Lose No Hope." In *Dr. B. R. Babasaheb Ambedkar Writings and Speeches,* edited by Hari Narake, Dr. M. L. Kasare, N. G. Kamble, and Ashok Godghate, 17, part 3, 275–276. Mumbai, India: Ambedkar Source Material Publication Committee, Higher Education Department, Government of Maharashtra, 2003.

———. "Prospects of Democracy in India." In *Dr. Ambedkar and Democracy,* edited by Christophe Jaffrelot and Narender Kumar, 240–44. New Delhi: Oxford University Press, 2018.

———. "Unfortunately, I Was Born Hindu Untouchable but I Will Not Die a Hindu." In *Dr. B. R. Babasaheb Ambedkar Writings and Speeches,* edited by Hari Narake, Dr. M. L. Kasare, N. G. Kamble, and Ashok Godghate, 17, part 3, 94–99. Mumbai, India: Ambedkar Source Material Publication Committee, Higher Education Department, Government of Maharashtra, 2003.

———. *What Congress and Gandhi Have Done to the Untouchables.* Bombay: Thacher, 1945.

———. "What Way Emancipation?" In *Dr. B. R. Babasaheb Ambedkar Writings and Speeches,* edited by Hari Narake, Dr. M. L. Kasare, N. G. Kamble, and Ashok Godghate, 17, part 3, 113–47. Mumbai, India: Ambedkar Source Material Publication Committee, Higher Education Department, Government of Maharashtra, 2003.

Analayo, Bhikku. "Confronting Racism with Mindfulness." *Mindfulness* 11 (2020): 2283–97.

Anand, S. "A Note on the Poona Pact." In B. R. Ambedkar, *The Annihilation of Caste: The Annotated Critical Edition,* edited by S. Anand, 361–68. New York: Verso, 2016.

Arendt, Hannah. *The Human Condition.* Garden City, NY: Doubleday, 1959.

———. *On Violence.* New York: Harcourt Brace, 1970.

Ariyaratne, A. T. *Schumacher Lectures on Buddhist Economics.* Ratmalana, Sri Lanka: Vishva Lekha, 1999.

Baldwin, James. "The American Dream and the American Negro." In *James Baldwin: Collected Essays,* edited by Toni Morrison, 714–19. New York: The Library of America, 1998.

———. "My Dungeon Shook." In *James Baldwin: Collected Essays,* edited by Toni Morrison, 291–95. New York: The Library of America, 1998.

———. "The White Man's Guilt." In *James Baldwin: Collected Essays,* edited by Toni Morrison, 722–27. New York: The Library of America, 1998.

Baptist, Edward E. *The Half Has Never Been Told: Slavery and the Making of American Capitalism.* New York: Basic Books, 2014.

Behl, Aditya. "The Buddhist Renaissance in Modern India: Dr. B. R. Ambedkar and the Untouchables." *India International Centre Quarterly* 17, no. 2 (1990): 83–99.

Bercovitch, Sacvan. *The American Jeremiad.* Madison: University of Wisconsin Press, 1978.

Bernstein, Richard. *Praxis and Action: Contemporary Philosophies of Human Activity.* Philadelphia: University of Pennsylvania Press, 1971.
Berreman, Gerald. *Caste and Other Inequities: Essays on Inequality.* New Delhi: Ved Prakash Vatuk Folklore Institute, 1979.
Berrigan, Daniel, S. J. *Exodus: Let My People Go.* Eugene, OR: Cascade Books, 2008.
———. *Isaiah: Spirit of Courage, Gift of Tears.* Minneapolis, MN: Fortress Press, 1996.
———. *No God but One.* Grand Rapids, MI: William B. Eerdmans, 2009.
Blight, David W. *Frederick Douglass: Prophet of Freedom.* New York: Simon and Schuster, 2018.
Bodhi, Bhikku, ed. *The Buddha's Teachings on Social and Communal Harmony.* Somerville, MA: Wisdom, 2016.
Boff, Clodovis. *Theology and Praxis: Epistemological Foundations.* Maryknoll, NY: Orbis Books, 1987.
Bond, George. *Buddhism at Work: Community Development, Social Empowerment and the Sarvodaya Movement.* Bloomfield, CT: Kumarian Press, 2004.
Braithwaite, John. "Does Restorative Justice Work?" In *A Restorative Justice Reader: Texts, Sources, Content,* edited by Gerry Johnstone, 320–52. Portland, OR: Willan, 2003.
———. "Restorative Justice and a Better Future." In *A Restorative Justice Reader: Texts, Sources, Content,* edited by Gerry Johnstone, 83–97. Portland, OR: Willan, 2003.
Brooks, Lisa. *Our Beloved Kin: A New History of King Philip's War.* New Haven: Yale University Press, 2018.
Brown, Donna Lynn. "Beyond Queen and King: Democratizing 'Engaged Buddhism.'" *Journal of Buddhist Ethics* 30 (2023): 7–58.
Brueggemann, Walter. *The Prophetic Imagination.* 2nd ed. Minneapolis, MN: Augsburg Fortress Press, 2001.
———. *Reality, Grief, Hope: Three Urgent Prophetic Tasks.* Grand Rapids, MI: William B. Eerdmans, 2014.
Butler, Judith. *The Force of Nonviolence: An Ethico-Political Bind.* New York: Verso, 2020.
Caplow, Zenshin Florence, and Reigetsu Susan Moon, eds. *The Hidden Lamp: Stories from Twenty-Five Centuries of Awakened Women.* Boston, MA: Wisdom, 2013.
Chan Khong, Sr. *Learning True Love.* Berkeley, CA: Parallax Press, 2007.
Chappell, David W. "Buddhist Peace Principles." In *Buddhist Peacework: Creating Cultures of Peace,* edited by David W. Chappell, 199–231. Boston, MA: Wisdom, 1999.
Claassens, L. Juliana. "God and Violence in the Prophets." In *The Oxford Handbook of the Prophets,* edited by Carolyn J. Sharp, 334–59. New York: Oxford University Press, 2016.
———. *Mourner, Mother, Midwife: Reimagining God's Delivering Presence in the Old Testament.* Louisville, KY: Westminster John Knox Press. 2012.
Cobb, John A. Jr. *Beyond Dialogue: Toward a Mutual Transformation of Christianity and Buddhism.* Minneapolis, MN: Fortress Press, 1982.

Cohen, Emily. "Across Generations: Interview with Jan Willis." *Journal of Feminist Studies in Religion* 33, no. 2 (2017): 127–37.
Cortright, David. *Gandhi and Beyond: Nonviolence for a New Political Age.* 2nd ed. Boulder, CO: Paradigm, 2009.
Darlington, Susan M. *The Ordination of a Tree: The Thai Buddhist Environmental Movement.* Albany, NY: SUNY Press, 2012.
Davidson, Steed Vernyl. "Postcolonial Readings of the Prophets." In *The Oxford Handbook of the Prophets,* edited by Carolyn J. Sharp, 507–26. New York: Oxford University Press, 2016.
Davis, Fania E. *Race and Restorative Justice: Black Lives, Healing, and Social Transformation.* New York: Good Books, 2019.
Devall, Bill, and George Sessions. *Deep Ecology.* Salt Lake City, UT: Gibbs M. Smith, 1985.
Douglass, Frederick. "The Meaning of July Fourth for the Negro" (July 5, 1852). In *Frederick Douglass: Selected Speeches and Writings,* edited by Philip Foner, 188–205. Chicago, IL: Lauren Hill Books, 1999.
———. "The West India Emancipation." In *Frederick Douglass: Selected Speeches and Writings,* edited by Philip Foner, 358–68. Chicago, IL: Lauren Hill Books, 1999.
Eig, Jonathon. *King: A Life.* New York: Farrar Straus and Giroux, 2023.
Falk, Nancy Auer. "Rita Gross as Colleague and Collaborator." *Buddhist-Christian Studies* 31 (2011): 63–67.
Farmer, Paul. "An Anthropology of Structural Violence." In *Partner to the Poor: A Paul Farmer Reader,* edited by Haun Saussy, 350–75. Berkeley: University of California Press, 2010.
———. *Pathologies of Power: Health, Human Rights, and the New War on the Poor.* Berkeley: University of California Press, 2005.
Fields, Rick. "Divided Dharma: White Buddhists, Ethnic Buddhists, and Racism." In *The Faces of Buddhism in America,* edited by Charles Prebish and Kenneth Tanaka, 196–206. Berkeley: University of California Press, 1998.
Fiske, Adele, and Christoph Emmrich. "The Use of Buddhist Scripture in B. R. Ambedkar's *The Buddha and His Dhamma.*" In *Reconstructing the World: B. R. Ambedkar and Buddhism in India,* edited by Surendra Jondhale and Johannes Beltz, 97–119. New Delhi: Oxford University Press, 2004.
Fredrickson, George M. *Racism: A Short History.* Princeton, NJ: Princeton University Press, 2002.
Freire, Paulo. *Pedagogy of the Oppressed.* New York: Herder and Herder, 1971.
Gafney, Wilda C. *Daughters of Miriam: Women Prophets in Ancient Israel.* Minneapolis, MN: Fortress Press, 2008.
Garrow, David J. *Bearing the Cross: Martin Luther King, Jr., and the Southern Christian Leadership Conference.* New York: Perennial Classics, 1986.
Galtung, Johan. "Violence, Peace and Peace Research." *Journal of Peace Research* 6, no. 3 (1969): 167–91.

Geuss, Raymond. *The Idea of a Critical Theory: Habermas and the Frankfurt School.* Cambridge: Cambridge University Press, 1981.
Glassman, Bernie. *Bearing Witness: A Zen Master's Lessons in Making Peace.* New York: Bell Tower, 1998.
Gleig, Ann. *American Dharma: Buddhism beyond Modernity.* New Haven, CT: Yale University Press, 2019.
Green, Barbara. "Genre Criticism." In *The Oxford Handbook of the Prophets*, edited by Carolyn J. Sharp, 258–76. New York: Oxford University Press, 2016.
Gross, Rita. *Buddhism after Patriarchy.* Albany, NY: SUNY Press, 1993.
———. "Buddhism and Feminism: Toward Their Mutual Transformation, Part 1." *Eastern Buddhist* 19, no. 1 (1986): 44–58.
———. "Buddhism and Feminism, Part 2." *Eastern Buddhist* 19, no. 2 (1986): 62–74.
———. *Buddhism beyond Gender: Liberation from Attachment to Identity.* Boulder, CO: Shambhala. 2018.
———. *A Garland of Feminist Reflections: Forty Years of Religious Exploration.* Berkeley: University of California Press, 2009.
———. "I Am Speechless." *Buddhist Christian Studies* 31 (2011): 97.
———. "Is the Glass Half-Empty or Half-Full? A Feminist Assessment of Buddhism at the Beginning of the Twenty-First Century." *Feminist Theology* 16, no. 3 (2008): 291–311.
———. *Soaring and Settling: Buddhist Perspectives on Contemporary Society and Religious Issues.* New York: Continuum, 1998.
———. "The Suffering of Sexism: Buddhist Perspectives and Experiences." *Buddhist Christian Studies* 34 (2014): 69–81.
Guha, Ramachandra. *Gandhi: The Years That Changed the World, 1914–1948.* New York: Alfred A. Knopf, 2018.
Gustafson, James. M. *Varieties of Moral Discourse: Prophetic, Narrative, Ethical, and Policy.* The Stob Lectures Endowment, 1988.
Gutiérrez, Gustavo. *Theology of Liberation.* Maryknoll, NY: Orbis, 1973.
Han, Chenxing. *Be the Refuge: Raising the Voices of Asian American Buddhists.* Berkeley, CA: North Atlantic Books, 2021.
Harrell, Willie, Jr. "A Call to Consciousness and Action: Mapping the African American Jeremiad." *Canadian Review of American Studies* 36, no. 2 (Summer 2006): 149–80.
Harvey, Peter. "Buddhist Perspectives on Crime and Punishment." In *Destroying Mara Forever: Essays on Buddhist Ethics in Honor of Damien Keown*, edited by John Powers and Charles Prebish, 47–66. Ithaca, NY: Snow Lions, 2009.
Heschel, Abraham. *The Prophets.* New York: Harper and Row, 1962.
Holt, Else K. "The Prophet as Persona." In *The Oxford Handbook of the Prophets*, edited by Carolyn J. Sharp, 299–318. New York: Oxford University Press, 2016.
Howard-Pitney, David. *The African American Jeremiad: Appeals for Justice in America.* Rev. ed. Philadelphia, PA: Temple University Press, 2005.

Ignatiev, Noel. *How the Irish Became White*. New York: Routledge, 1995.
Jaffrelot, Christophe. *Dr. Ambedkar and Untouchability*. New York: Columbia University Press, 2005.
Jasper, James M. *The Art of Moral Protest*. Chicago, IL: University of Chicago Press, 1997.
Jassen, Alex P. "The Prophets in the Dead Sea Scrolls." In *The Oxford Handbook of the Prophets*, edited by Carolyn J. Sharp, 353–72. New York: Oxford University Press, 2016.
Jenkins, Willis. "Christian Social Ethics after Bonhoeffer and King." In *Bonhoeffer and King: Their Legacies and Import for Christian Social Thought*, edited by Willis Jenkins and Jennifer M. McBride, 4794–5104. Minneapolis, MN: Fortress Press, 2010. Kindle.
Jones, Ken. *Beyond Optimism: A Buddhist Political Ecology*. Oxford UK: John Carpenter, 1993.
———. "Beyond Us and Them." In *Mindful Politics: A Buddhist Guide to Making the World a Better Place*, edited by Melvin McLeod, 165–69. Somerville MA: Wisdom, 2006.
———. *The New Social Face of Buddhism: A Call to Action*. Boston, MA: Wisdom, 2003.
Kaba, Mariame. *We Do This until We Free Us: Abolitionist Organizing and Transforming Justice*, edited by Tamara Nopper. Chicago, IL: Haymarket Books, 2021.
Kadambi, Rajeev. "Ambedkar's Framing of the 'Political' within Ethical Practice." *Studies in Indian Politics* 4, no. 2 (2016): 143–58.
Kaveny, Cathleen. *Prophecy without Contempt: Religious Discourse in the Public Square*. Cambridge, MA: Harvard University Press, 2016.
Kaza, Stephanie, ed. *Hooked: Buddhist Writings on Greed, Desire, and the Urge to Consume*. Boston, MA: Shambhala, 2005.
Keck, Margaret E., and Kathryn Sikkink. *Activists beyond Borders: Advocacy Networks in International Politics*. Ithaca, NY: Cornell University Press, 1998.
King, Martin Luther Jr. "All Labor Has Dignity." In *The Radical King*, edited by Cornel West, 245–51. Boston, MA: Beacon Press, 2015.
———. "The American Dream." In *A Testament of Hope: The Essential Writings and Speeches of Martin Luther King, Jr.*, edited by James M. Washington, 208–16. San Francisco, CA: HarperSanFrancisco, 1986.
———. "Letter from Birmingham City Jail." In *A Testament of Hope: The Essential Writings and Speeches of Martin Luther King, Jr.*, edited by James M. Washington, 289–302. San Francisco, CA: HarperSanFrancisco, 1986.
———. "Loving Your Enemies." In *The Radical King*, edited by Cornel West, 55–64. Boston, MA: Beacon Press, 2015.
———. "My Jewish Brother." In *The Radical King*, edited by Cornel West, 101–3. Boston, MA: Beacon Press, 2015.

———. "My Trip to the Land of Gandhi." In *A Testament of Hope: The Essential Writings and Speeches of Martin Luther King, Jr.,* edited by James M. Washington, 23–30. San Francisco, CA: HarperSanFrancisco, 1986.

———. "Pilgrimage to Nonviolence." In *A Testament of Hope: The Essential Writings and Speeches of Martin Luther King, Jr.,* edited by James M. Washington, 35–40. San Francisco, CA: HarperSanFrancisco, 1986.

———. *Stride toward Freedom: The Montgomery Story.* New York: Harper and Row, 1958.

———. "A Testament of Hope." In *A Testament of Hope: The Essential Writings and Speeches of Martin Luther King, Jr.,* edited by James M. Washington, 313–28. San Francisco, CA: HarperSanFrancisco, 1986.

———. "A Time to Break Silence." In *A Testament of Hope: The Essential Writings and Speeches of Martin Luther King, Jr.,* edited by James M. Washington, 231–44. San Francisco, CA: HarperSanFrancisco, 1986.

———. "The Trumpet of Conscience." In *A Testament of Hope: The Essential Writings and Speeches of Martin Luther King, Jr.,* edited by James M. Washington, 634–53. San Francisco, CA: HarperSanFrancisco, 1986.

———. "The World House." In *Where Do We Go from Here: Chaos or Community?,* 195–223. New York: Harper and Row, 1967.

King, Sallie B. *Being Benevolence: The Social Ethics of Engaged Buddhism.* Honolulu: University of Hawaii Press, 2005.

———. *Buddha Nature.* Albany: State University of New York Press, 1991.

———. "Buddhism, Nonviolence and Power." *Journal of Buddhist Ethics* 16 (2009): 103–35.

———. "Elements of Engaged Buddhist Ethical Theory." In *Destroying Mara Forever: Essays on Buddhist Ethics in Honor of Damien Keown,* edited by John Powers and Charles Prebish, 187–203. Ithaca, NY: Snow Lion, 2009.

———. "Right Speech Is Not Always Gentile: The Buddha's Authorization of Sharp Criticism, Its Rationale, Limits, and Possible Applications." *Journal of Buddhists Ethics* 24 (2017): 347–67.

———. "The Small Engage the Powerful: An American Buddhist-Liberation Theology-Quaker Trialogue." *Buddhist Christian Studies* 39 (2019): 103–14.

———. *Socially Engaged Buddhism.* Honolulu: University of Hawaii Press, 2009.

———. "Thich Nhat Hanh and the Unified Buddhist Church." In *Engaged Buddhism: Buddhist Liberation Movements in Asia,* edited by Sallie B. King and Christopher S. Queen, 321–63. Albany, NY: SUNY Press, 1996.

———. "Through the Eyes of Auschwitz and the Killing Fields: Mutual Learning between Engaged Buddhism and Liberation Theology." *Buddhist Christian Studies* 36 (2016): 55–67.

Klein, Naomi. *This Changes Everything: Capitalism vs. the Climate.* New York: Simon and Schuster, 2014.

Knitter, Paul. *Without Buddha I Could Not Be a Christian*. Oxford: One World, 2009.

Kolbert, Elizabeth. *The Sixth Extinction: An Unnatural History*. New York: Henry Holt, 2014.

Korten, David C. *The Great Turning: From Empire to Earth Community*. Bloomfield, CT: Kumarian Press, 2006.

Kosicki, Piotr. "Putin's Apocalyptic Goals." *Commonweal*, March 15, 2022. Accessed at https://www.commonwealmagazine.org/putins-apocalyptic-goals.

Kumar, Aishwary. *Radical Equality: Ambedkar, Gandhi, and the Risk of Democracy*. Stanford, CA: Stanford University Press, 2015.

Laity, Sr. Annabel. Foreword to *My Master's Robe: Memories of a Novice Monk*, by Thich Nhat Hanh, ix–xiv. Berkeley, CA: Parallax Press, 2002.

Leclerc, Thomas. *Yahweh Is Exalted in Justice: Solidarity and Conflict in Isaiah*. Minneapolis, MN: Fortress Press, 2008.

Leighton, Taigen Dan. "Being Time and Deep Time." In *A Wild Love for the World: Joanna Macy and the Work of Our Time*, edited by Stephanie Kaza, 226–35. Boulder, CO: Shambhala, 2020.

———. *Faces of Compassion: Classic Bodhisattva Archetypes and Their Modern Expression*. Boston, MA: Wisdom, 2003.

Lertzmann, Renee. "Researching Psychic Dimensions to Ecological Degradation: Notes from the Field." *Psychoanalysis, Culture and Society* 17, no. 1 (2012): 92–101.

Levine, Daniel. *Popular Voices in Latin American Catholicism*. Princeton, NJ: Princeton University Press, 1992.

Lifton, Robert Jay. *Death in Life: Survivors of Hiroshima*. New York: Random House, 1967.

Lifton, Robert Jay, and Richard Falk. *Indefensible Weapons: The Political and Psychological Case against Nuclearism*. New York: Random House, 1982.

Lincoln, Abraham. "Second Inaugural Address." In *God's New Israel: Religious Interpretations of American Destiny*, edited by Conrad Cherry, 195–96. Englewood Cliffs, NJ: Prentice-Hall, 1971.

Loy, David. *A Buddhist History of the West: Studies in Lack*. Albany, NY: SUNY Press, 2002.

———. *Ecodharma: Buddhist Teachings for the Ecological Crisis*. Somerville, MA: Wisdom, 2018.

———. *The Great Awakening: A Buddhist Social Theory*. Boston, MA: Wisdom, 2003.

———. "Healing Justice: A Buddhist Perspective." In *The Spiritual Roots of Restorative Justice*, edited by Michael L. Hadley, 81–97. Albany, NY: SUNY Press, 2012.

———. *Lack and Transcendence: The Problem of Death and Life in Psychotherapy, Existentialism, and Buddhism*. Somerville MA: Wisdom, 2018.

———. *Money, Sex, War, Karma: Notes for a Buddhist Revolution*. Boston, MA: Wisdom, 2008.

Macy, Joanna. "Afterword." In *A Wild Love for the World: Joanna Macy and the Work of Our Time*, edited by Stephanie Kaza, 357–61. Boulder, CO: Shambhala, 2020.

---. *Despair and Personal Power in the Nuclear Age.* Philadelphia, PA: New Society, 1983.

---. *Mutual Causality in Buddhism and Systems Theory.* Albany: State University of New York Press, 1991.

---. "Our Life as Gaia." In *Thinking Like a Mountain: Towards a Council of All Beings,* edited by John Seed, Joanna Macy, Pat Fleming, and Arne Naess, 57–65. Philadelphia, PA: New Society, 1988.

---. "The Presence of the Future Beings." In *A Wild Love for the World: Joanna Macy and the Work of Our Time,* edited by Stephanie Kaza, 221–25. Boulder, CO: Shambhala, 2020.

---. *Widening Circles: A Memoir.* Gabriola Island, BC: New Society, 2000.

---. *World as Lover, World as Self.* Berkeley, CA: Parallax Press, 1991.

---. *World as Lover, World as Self.* 2nd ed. Berkeley, CA: Parallax Press, 2007.

Macy, Joanna, and Chris Johnstone. *Active Hope: How to Face the Mess We Are in without Going Crazy.* Novato, CA: New World Library, 2012.

Macy, Joanna, and Molly Young Brown, *Coming Back to Life: Practices to Reconnect Our Lives, Our World.* Gabriola Island, BC: New Society, 1988.

Magee, Rhonda. *The Inner Work of Racial Justice: Healing Ourselves and Transforming Our Communities through Mindfulness.* New York: Tarcher Perigee, 2019.

Maier, Christl M. "Feminist Interpretation of the Prophets." In *The Oxford Handbook of the Prophets,* edited by Carolyn J. Sharp, 467–82. New York: Oxford University Press, 2016.

Makransky, John. "A Buddhist Critique of and Learning from Christian Liberation Theology." *Theological Studies* 75 (2014): 635–57.

---. "Confronting the 'Sin' Out of Love for the 'Sinner': Fierce Compassion as a Force for Social Change." *Buddhist-Christian Studies* 36 (2016): 87–96.

---. "What Christian Liberation Theology and Buddhism Need to Learn from Each Other." *Buddhist-Christian Studies* 34 (2014): 117–34.

Marko, Eva Myonen. "Ziyong's Earth." In *The Hidden Lamp: Stories from Twenty-Five Centuries of Awakened Women,* edited by Florence Caplow and Susan Moon, 241–43. Boston, MA: Wisdom, 2013.

Marshall, Tony. "Restorative Justice: An Overview." In *A Restorative Justice Reader: Texts, Sources, Content,* edited by Gerry Johnstone, 28–45. Portland, OR: Willan, 2003.

Marx, Karl. "Economic and Philosophical Manuscripts." In *The Writings of the Young Marx on Philosophy and Society,* edited by Lloyd D. Easton and Kurt H. Guddat, 283–301. Garden City, NY: Doubleday, 1967.

---. "Theses on Feuerbach." In *The Writings of the Young Marx on Philosophy and Society,* edited by Lloyd Easton and Kurt Guddat, 400–402. Garden City, NY: Doubleday, 1967.

McCann, Dennis, and Charles Strain. *Polity and Praxis: A Program for an American Practical Theology.* Minneapolis, MN: Winston, 1985. Repr., Lanham, MD: University Press of America, 1990.

McLeod, Melvin, ed. *Mindful Politics: A Buddhist Guide to Making the World a Better Place.* Somerville MA: Wisdom, 2006.

McMahon, David L. *The Making of Buddhist Modernism.* New York: Oxford University Press, 2008.

Merton, Thomas. "Foreword." In *Vietnam: Lotus in a Seas of Fire,* by Thich Nhat Hanh, vii–x. New York: Hill and Wang, 1967.

Miller, Reuben Jonathan. *Halfway Home: Race, Punishment, and the After Life of Mass Incarceration.* New York: Little, Brown, 2021.

Money, Roy. "A Network of Mutuality: Martin Luther King, Jr. on Interdependence and Ethics." In *An Inescapable Network of Mutuality: Martin Luther King, Jr., and the Globalization of an Ethical Ideal,* edited by Lewis V. Baldwin and Paul R. Dekar, 217–231. Eugene, OR: Cascade Books, 2013.

Naess, Arnie. "The Deep Ecology Movement: Some Philosophical Aspects." In *Environmental Ethics: An Anthology,* edited by Andrea Light and Homes Rolston III, 262–74. Malden, MA: Blackwell, 2003.

Nagaraj, D. R. *The Flaming Feet and Other Essays: The Dalit Movement in India,* Rev. ed. Calcutta: Seagull Books, 2010.

Nepstad, Sharon Erickson. *Religion and War Resistance in the Plowshares Movement.* New York: Cambridge University Press, 2008.

Nhat Hanh, Thich. "Ahimsa." In *Love in Action: Writings on Nonviolent Social Change,* 65–71. Berkeley, CA: Parallax Press, 1993.

———. *The Art of Power.* New York: HarperCollins, 2007.

———. *Being Peace.* Berkeley, CA: Parallax Press, 2005.

———. *Call Me by My True Names: The Collected Poems of Thich Nhat Hanh.* Berkeley, CA: Parallax Press, 1993.

———. *Calming the Fearful Mind: A Zen Response to Terrorism.* Berkeley, CA: Parallax Press, 2005.

———. *Fragrant Palm Leaves.* New York: Riverhead Books, 1968.

———. "Go as a Sangha." In *Friends on the Path: Living Spiritual Communities,* edited by Jack Lawlor, 17–48. Berkeley, CA: Parallax Press, 2002.

———. *Interbeing: Fourteen Guidelines for Engaged Buddhism.* 3rd ed. Berkeley, CA: Parallax Press, 1998.

———. *Living Buddha, Living Christ.* New York: Riverhead Books, 1995.

———. *Love in Action: Writings on Nonviolent Social Change.* Berkeley, CA: Parallax Press, 1993.

———. *My Master's Robe: Memories of a Novice Monk.* Berkeley, CA: Parallax Press, 2002.

———. *Opening the Heart of the Cosmos: Insights on the Lotus Sutra.* Berkeley, CA: Parallax Press, 2003.

———. *Peace Is Every Step.* New York: Bantam Books 1992.

———. *Vietnam: Lotus in a Sea of Fire.* New York: Hill and Wang, 1967.

———. *The World We Have: A Buddhist Approach to Peace and Ecology*. Berkeley, CA: Parallax Press, 2008.

Nhat Hanh, Thich, and Daniel Berrigan. *The Raft Is Not the Shore*. Maryknoll, NY: Orbis Books, 2001.

Nicolsen, Shierry Weber. *The Love of Nature and the End of the World*. Cambridge, MA: MIT Press, 2002.

Niebuhr, Reinhold. *Moral Man and Immoral Society*. New York: Charles Scribner's Sons, 1932.

Nieman, Susan. *Learning from the Germans: Race and the Memory of Evil*. New York: Farrar Straus and Giroux, 2019.

Nixon, Rob. *Slow Violence and the Environmentalism of the Poor*. Cambridge, MA: Harvard University Press, 2011.

Nussbaum, Martha. *Hiding from Humanity: Disgust, Shame, and the Law*. Princeton, NJ: Princeton University Press, 2004.

———. *The Monarchy of Fear: A Philosopher Looks at Our Political Crisis*. New York: Simon and Schuster, 2018.

O'Brien, Julia M. *Challenging Prophetic Metaphor: Theology and Ideology in the Prophets*. Louisville, KY: Westminster John Knox Press, 2008.

———. "Metaphorization and Other Tropes in the Prophets." In *The Oxford Handbook of the Prophets*, edited by Carolyn J. Sharp, 241–57. New York: Oxford University Press, 2016.

O'Connor, Kathleen. *Lamentations and the Tears of the World*. Maryknoll, NY: Orbis Books, 2002.

———. "Terror All Around: Confusion as Meaning Making." In *Jeremiah (Dis)placed: New Directions in Writing/Reading Jeremiah*, edited by A. R. Pete Diamond and Louis Stulman, 67–79. New York: T&T Clark, 2011.

Odin, Steve. "The Japanese Concept of Nature in Relation to the Environmental Ethics and Conservation Aesthetics of Aldo Leopold." In *Buddhism and Ecology: The Interconnection of Dharma and Deeds*, edited by Mary Evelyn Tucker and Duncan Ryuken Williams, 89–109. Cambridge, MA: Harvard University Press, 1997.

Ohnuma, Reiko. "Mother-Love and Mother-Grief: South Asian Buddhist Variations on a Theme." *Journal of Feminist Studies in Religion* 23, no. 1 (2007): 95–116.

Ollman, Bertell. *Alienation: Marx's Concept of Man in Capitalist Society*. London: Cambridge University Press, 1971.

Petrella, Ivan. *The Future of Liberation Theology*. London: SCM Press, 2006.

———. "Liberation Theology: A Programmatic Statement." In *Latin American Liberation Theology: The New Generation*, edited by Ivan Petrella, 149–54. Maryknoll NY: Orbis Books, 2005.

Queen, Christopher. "Ambedkar's Dhamma: Sources and Method in the Construction of Engaged Buddhism." In *Reconstructing the World: B. R. Ambedkar and*

Buddhism in India, edited by Surendra Jondhale and Johannes Beltz, 132–50. New Delhi: Oxford University Press, 2004.

———. "The Dharma of Natural Systems." In *A Wild Love for the World: Joanna Macy and the Work of Our Time,* edited by Stephanie Kaza, 165–73. Boulder, CO: Shambhala, 2020.

———. "Dr. Ambedkar and the Hermeneutics of Buddhist Liberation." In *Engaged Buddhism: Buddhist Liberation Movements in Asia,* edited by Christopher S. Queen and Sallie B. King, 45–71. Albany: State University of New York Press, 1996.

———. "Introduction: A New Buddhism." In *Engaged Buddhism in the West,* edited by Christopher Queen, 1–31. Boston, MA: Wisdom, 2000.

Ragir, Byakuren Judith. "Yasodhara's Path." In *The Hidden Lamp: Stories from Twenty-Five Centuries of Awakened Women,* edited by Zenshin Florence Caplow and Reigetsu Susan Moon, 147–49. Boston, MA: Wisdom, 2013.

Rankine, Claudia. "The Condition of Black Life Is One of Mourning." In *The Fire This Time: A New Generation Speaks about Race,* edited by Jesmyn Ward, 145–55. New York: Scribner, 2016.

Rauschenbusch, Walter. *Christianity and the Social Crisis in the 21st Century: The Classic That Woke up the Church,* edited by Paul B. Raushenbush. New York: Harper One, 2007.

Regan, Julie. "The Soaring and (Final) Settling of Rita Gross, 1943–2015." *Journal of Feminist Studies in Religion* 32, no. 2 (2016): 5–10.

Rieder, Jonathan. *Gospel of Freedom: Martin Luther King, Jr.'s Letter from a Birmingham Jail and the Struggle That Changed the Nation.* New York: Bloomsbury Press, 2013.

———. *The Word of the Lord Is upon Me: The Righteous Performance of Martin Luther King, Jr.* Cambridge, MA: Harvard University Press, 2008.

Robinson-Marbury, Herbert. *Pillars of Clouds and Fire: The Politics of Exodus in African American Biblical Interpretation.* New York: New York University Press, 2015.

Roy, Arundhati. "Introduction: The Doctor and the Saint." In B. R. Ambedkar, *The Annihilation of Caste: The Annotated Critical Edition,* edited by S. Anand, 17–179. London: Verso, 2016.

Selby, Gary S. *Martin Luther King and the Rhetoric of Freedom: The Exodus Narrative in America's Struggle for Civil Rights.* Waco, TX: Baylor University Press, 2008.

Sered, Danielle. *Until We Reckon: Violence, Mass Incarceration, and a Road to Repair.* New York: The New Press, 2019.

Sharp, Gene. *The Politics of Nonviolent Action.* Part 1, *Power and Struggle.* Manchester, NH: Porter Sargent, 1973.

———. *Waging Nonviolent Struggle.* Boston, MA: Porter Sargent, 2005.

Simmer-Brown, Judith. Introduction to *Buddhism beyond Gender: Liberation from Attachment to Identity,* by Rita Gross, ix–xvii. Boulder, CO: Shambhala. 2018.

———. "Rita Gross's Contribution to Contemporary Western Tibetan Buddhism." *Buddhist Christian Studies* 31 (2011): 69–74.
Sinha, Manisha. *The Slave's Cause: A History of Abolition*. New Haven, CT: Yale University Press, 2016.
Sivaraksa, Sulak. *Conflict, Culture, Change: Engaged Buddhism in a Globalizing World*. Boston, MA: Wisdom, 2003.
———. *Seeds of Peace*. Berkeley, CA: Parallax, 1992.
Snyder, Gary. *Earth Household*. New York: New Directions, 1969.
Solnit, Rebecca. *Hope in the Dark*. New York: Nation Books, 2006.
———. "How Buddhism Has Changed the West for the Better." *Guardian*, February 8, 2022.
Strain, Charles R. "Borrowing a Prophetic Voice, Actualizing the Prophetic Dimension: Rita Gross and Engaged Buddhism." *Journal of Buddhist Ethics* 25 (2018): 1–30.
———. "Engaged Buddhist Practice and Ecological Ethics." *Worldviews* 20 (2016): 189–210.
———. "Is a Buddhist Praxis Possible?" *Journal of Buddhist Ethics* 25 (2018): 71–97.
———. *The Prophet and the Bodhisattva: Daniel Berrigan, Thich Nhat Hanh, and the Ethics of Peace and Justice*. Eugene, OR: Wipf and Stock, 2014.
———. "Reinventing Buddhist Practices to Meet the Challenge of Climate Change," *Contemporary Buddhism* 17, no. 1 (May 2016): 138–56.
Stroud, Scott R. "Force, Nonviolence and Communication in the Pragmatism of Bhimrao Ambedkar." *Journal of Speculative Philosophy* 32, no. 1 (2018): 112–30.
———. "The Rhetoric of Conversion as Emancipatory Strategy in India: Bhimrao Ambedkar, Pragmatism, and the Turn to Buddhism." *Rhetorica* 35, no. 3 (2017): 314–45.
Stulman, Louis. *Jeremiah*. Abingdon Old Testament Commentaries. Nashville, TN: Abingdon Press, 2005.
———. "Prophetic Words and Acts as Survival Literature." In *The Oxford Handbook of the Prophets,* edited by Carolyn J. Sharp, 310–33. New York: Oxford University Press, 2016.
Stulman, Louis, and Hyun Chul Paul Kim. *You Are My People*. Nashville, TN: Abingdon Press, 2010.
Sullivan, Kathleen. "The Journey of a Nuclear Guardian." In *A Wild Love for the World: Joanna Macy and the Work of Our Time,* edited by Stephanie Kaza, 261–73. Boulder, CO: Shambhala, 2020.
Sunim, Chi Kwang. "Old Woman, Zhaozhou and the Tiger." In *The Hidden Lamp: Stories from Twenty-Five Centuries of Awakened Women,* edited by Florence Caplow and Susan Moon, 135–37. Boston, MA: Wisdom, 2013.
Swearer, Donald K. "Bimba's Lament." In *Buddhism in Practice,* edited by Donald S. Lopez, 541–52. Princeton, NJ: Princeton University Press, 1995.
Sweeney, Marvin A. *The Prophetic Literature*. Nashville, TN: Abingdon Press, 2005.

Terry, Brandon M. "Requiem for a Dream: The Problem-Space of Black Power." In *To Shape a New World: Essays on the Political Philosophy of Martin Luther King, Jr.*, edited by Tommie Shelby and Brandon M. Terry, 290–324. Cambridge, MA: Harvard University Press, 2018.

Therīgāthā: Poems of the First Buddhist Women. Translated by Charles Hallisey. Cambridge, MA: Harvard University Press, 2015.

Tobey, Kristen. *Plowshares: Protest, Performance, and Religious Identity in the Nuclear Age*. University Park: Pennsylvania State Press, 2016.

Tocqueville, Alexis de. *Democracy in America*, edited by J. P. Mayer. Garden City, NY: Doubleday, 1969.

Tracy, David. *The Analogical Imagination*. New York: Crossroad, 1981.

———. *Blessed Rage for Order: The New Pluralism in Theology*. New York: Seabury, 1975.

Tworkov, Helen. "Many Is More." *Tricycle: The Buddhist Review* (Winter 1991). Accessed at https://tricycle.org/magazine/many-more.

Van Ness, Daniel. "Creating Restorative Justice Systems." In *A Restorative Justice Reader: Texts Sources, Content*, edited by Gerry Johnstone, 270–79. Portland, OR: Willan, 2003.

Van Ness, Daniel, and Karen Heetderks Strong. *Restoring Justice*. 2nd ed. Cincinnati, OH: Anderson, 2002.

Victoria, Brian. *Zen at War*. New York: Weatherhill, 1997.

Walters, Jonathan S. "Gotami's Story." In *Buddhism in Practice*, edited by Donald S. Lopez, Jr., 113–38. Princeton, NJ: Princeton University Press, 1995.

Walzer, Michael. *Exodus and Revolution*. New York: Basic Books, 1985.

———. *In God's Shadow: Politics in the Hebrew Bible*. New Haven, CT: Yale University Press, 2012.

———. *The Paradox of Liberation: Secular Revolutions and Religious Counterrevolutions*. New Haven, CT: Yale University Press. 2015.

———. *Revolution of the Saints: A Study in the Origins of Radical Politics*. New York: Atheneum, 1969.

———. *Spheres of Justice: A Defense of Pluralism and Equality*. New York: Basic Books, 1983.

Ward-Lev, Nahum. *The Liberating Path of the Hebrew Prophets, Then and Now*. Maryknoll, NY: Orbis Books, 2019.

Wells, Ida B. "Lynching Our National Crime." National Negro Conference, May 31–June 1, 1909. Available at https://www.blackpast.org/african-american-history/1909-ida-b-wells-awful-slaughter/.

West, Cornel. *Black Prophetic Fire*. Edited by Christa Buschendorf. Boston, MA: Beacon Press, 2014.

———. "Hope and Despair: Past and Present." In *To Shape a New World: Essays on the Political Philosophy of Martin Luther King, Jr.*, edited by Tommie Shelby and Brandon M. Terry, 325–37. Cambridge, MA: Harvard University Press, 2018.

———. *Keeping Faith: Philosophy and Race in America.* New York: Routledge, 1993.

———. *Prophecy Deliverance: An Afro-American Revolutionary Christianity.* Philadelphia, PA: Westminster Press, 1982.

———. *Prophetic Thought in Postmodern Times.* Monroe, ME: Common Courage Press, 1993.

Wigglesworth, Michael. "God's Controversy with New England." In *God's New Israel: Religious Interpretations of American Destiny,* edited by Conrad Cherry, 44–54. Englewood Cliffs, NJ: Prentice-Hall, 1971.

Wilkerson, Isabel. *Caste: The Origins of Our Discontents.* New York: Random House, 2020.

williams, angel Kyodo, and Lama Rod Owens, with Jasmine Syedullah. *Radical Dharma: Talking Race, Love, and Liberation.* Berkeley, CA: North Atlantic Books, 2016.

Williams, Duncan Ryuken. *American Sutra: A Story of Faith and Freedom in the Second World War.* Cambridge, MA: Harvard University Press, 2019.

Williams, Jody, Stephen D. Goose, and Mary Wareham, eds. *Banning Landmines: Disarmament, Citizen Diplomacy, and Human Security.* Lanham, MD: Rowman and Littlefield, 2008.

Willis, Jan. "Buddhism and Race: An African American Baptist-Buddhist Perspective." In *Buddhist Women on the Edge: Contemporary Perspectives from the Western Frontier,* edited by Marianne Dresser, 81–91. Berkeley, CA: North Atlantic Books. 1996.

———. *Dreaming Me: Black, Baptist, and Buddhist—One Woman's Spiritual Journey.* Somerville, MA: Wisdom, 2008.

———. "We Cry Out for Justice." *Lion's Roar,* May 29, 2020. Accessed at https://www/lionsroar.com/cry-justice. e https://www/lionsroar.com/cry-justice.

———. "Why We Can't Breathe." *Lion's Roar,* December 7, 2014. Accessed at https://www/lionsroar.com/cant-breathe.

Winthrop, John. "A Modell of Christian Charity." In *God's New Israel: Religious Interpretations of American Destiny,* edited by Conrad Cherry, 39–43. Englewood Cliffs, NJ: Prentice-Hall, 1971.

Yang, Larry. *Awakening Together: The Spiritual Practice of Inclusivity and Community.* Somerville, MA: Wisdom, 2017.

Yee, Gail A. "Materialist Analysis of the Prophets." In *The Oxford Handbook of the Prophets,* edited by Carolyn J. Sharp, 491–506. New York: Oxford University Press, 2016.

Zehr, Howard. *The Little Book of Restorative Justice.* Rev. ed. New York: Good Books, 2015.

———. "Retributive Justice, Restorative Justice." In *A Restorative Justice Reader: Texts, Sources, Content,* edited by Gerry Johnstone, 69–82. Portland, OR: Willan, 2003.

Zelliot, Eleanor. *From Untouchable to Dalit: Essays on the Ambedkar Movement.* New Delhi: Manohar, 2001.

Zulick, Margaret. "The Agon of Jeremiah or the Dialogic Invention of Prophetic Ethos." *Quarterly Journal of Speech* 78, no. 2 (May 1992): 125–48.

———. "The Normative, the Proper and the Sublime: Notes on the Use of Figure and Emotion in Prophetic Argument." *Argumentation* 12 (1998): 481–92.

Index

Abolitionist movement, 114, 117
  Slavery as original sin, 124
Agape, 151–52, 161
  Defined, 15
  As love in action, 152, 247–48n.18
Ahimsa (non-harming), 157
Alexander, Michelle
  Bird Cage, 200–204, 213
  Mass Incarceration as new Jim Crow, 201–203
Alienation, 172–73, 177–78
Ambedkar, B. R., 8, 87–107
  Annihilation of Caste, 93–95
  Buddha's leave taking, alternate version, 174
  Buddhism's importance for the emergence of a democratic society, 239n.42
  Burning *Manusmriti*, 92
  Caste, 8, as irredeemable, 93
  Comparison with King's, Birmingham Jail letter, 94–95
  Criteria for selecting Buddhism, 96–97
  On Dalits liberation, 92
  On democracy, 92, 94–96
  Early life, 88–89, 155
  Four Noble Truths, revision of, 96–99
  And Gandhi, 87–88, 90–92
  On liberty, equality and maitri, 95–96, 155
  And Marxism, 99–100
  Mass conversion to Buddhism, 87–88, 96, 100–101
  And Navayana, 88
  Religion's role in destroying caste, 204
  And Round Table Conferences, 91–92
  Satyagraha campaigns, 89–90
  On social revolution; social versus political tyranny, 94
  Struggle as spiritual, 103
  Summary of similarities with Hebrew prophets, 101–103
  Use of skillful means, 148, 158, 215
  On Vedas, 213
  Worse than Jim Crow, 88–89
  See Dewey
Amos (prophet), 21–23, 80, 133, 136
Aquinas, Thomas, 131
Arendt, Hannah
  On power as action in concert, 148–49
Ariyaratne, A. T., 179
Avalokiteshvara (bodhisattva), 57–58, 232 n.36

Baker, Ella, 244n.11

275

Baldwin, James, 185–87
Beat Generation, 143
Beaver Lake Cree Nation
   Bearing witness with, 85
Becker, Ernst, 172–73
Boeckel, William, 142
Beloved Community, 157
Bercovitch, Sacvan, 113–14
Berrigan, Daniel SJ, 60–61, 115–16, 150
   Critique of *Exodus*, 115–16
Birmingham as apartheid, 129
   King's Passion in, 130
Birmingham Jail, Letter from, 129–32
   Charges of clergy listed, 130
   On creating a crisis by bringing underlying violence to surface, 131
   Critique of white moderates and of southern white churches, 132
   Forms of oppression, 131
   Letter genre and basic equality, 130
   Negative peace, 160
   On nonviolence as four steps disciplined practice, 130–31
   On just versus unjust laws, 131, 245n.19
Black church, 136, 156, 193–94
Black Lives Matter (campaign), 168, 201
Black Power, 147–48, 152
Blight, David, 119
Bodhicitta, 48, 230 n.5
Bodhisattva Path, 215
Boff, Clodovis, 172
Bonino, José Míguez, 178–79
Brown v. Board of Education, 128, 130
Brueggemann, Walter
   On grief, 25
   On hope, 26
   On prophetic critique of royal consciousness, 23–24
   On prophetic imagination, 26, 214–15
Buber, Martin, 131
Buddha
   Ambedkar revision of Gautama's Leave taking, 97–98, 105–107
   Problem of conflict at all levels of society, 105–107
   Reluctance to admit women but changed his mind, 38
   Turning the wheel, 80
Buddha Nature (tathagatagarbha), 40, 45, 125, 208, 210 212
   All are capable of transformation, 204
   And critique of Patriarchal Buddhism, 126
   Defined, 229n.38
   And Socialism, 171–72
Buddhism
   Classical Buddhism sought world renunciation, 2, 39, 43
   Made of non-Buddhist elements, 50
   Mahayana, 40, 54, 171–72
   Navayana, 88, 99, 216
   See Engaged Buddhism; Patriarchal Buddhism; Tibetan Buddhism
Buddhist Dhamma/Dharma (teachings)
   Classical Buddhist teachings as androcentric, 38–40
   Radical dharma, 112
   See bodhicitta; Buddha Nature (Tathagatagarbha); dukkha; Eightfold Path; Emptiness; Four Noble Truths; Impermanence; karma, maitri; pratitya samutpada (Dependent coarising); Right speech
Buddhist Peace fellowship, 216
Buddhist reflections in a prophetic key, 10
Business as Usual, 80

Caste, 88–89; 255n.55
  Ambedkar's metaphor for, 89
  American system, *see* Wilkerson
  As "graded inequality," 93–94
  Indian system, 240n.58
  Purity/pollution frame, 89
  Racial caste system, 197–200, 202–203, 210
  And social boycott, 94
  As structural violence, 94
  See Ambedkar *Annihilation of Caste*
Chandramani, Bhikku, 100
Chan Khong, Sr., 51
Chinese Exclusion Act, 142
Choegyal Rinpoche, 70
Christian Realism, 136
Churches
  Southern Black and civil rights movements, 156
City upon a Hill, 8
  As cautionary image, 112
Civil religion, American, 136
Civil rights movement, 156, 210
  See Birmingham Jail, letter
  See Nonviolence
Claassens, Juliana
  God as Mother versus God as Divine Warrior, 20–21
ColorInsight (practices), 192, 200, 216
Common Justice (NGO), 206–208
Compassion, 2, 25, 39, 41, 44, 48, 56–58, 62–63, 66–67, 102–103, 159, 161, 166, 170, 191–92, 194, 204, 209, 214
  Bodhisattva ethic of, 36
  Fierce, 153, 158, 163
  Is not enough, 147, 162, 189
  And justice, 37, 125, 156
  Lincoln's, 116
  Shambhala Warriors, 69–70, 81–82
Congress Party, 95
Cortright, David, 147–48

Council of All Beings (exercise), 77, 216
Countervailing institutions, 157–58, 160, 162

Dalai Lama, 154–55
Dalits (Untouchables), 236–37n.3
Davis, Fania, 187–88
Dead Sea Scrolls, 18
"Death on the Seashore" (sermon), 128–29
Deaths, stupid, 48
Deep ecology
  And intrinsic value of other species' lives, 76–77
  And systems thinking, 76
Deep time, 79
Dependent coarising, 3, 40, 72–74, 81, 136, 177
  Dr. King on, 135
  See Pratītya samutpāda
"Despair and Empowerment" (workshop), 74
  Acknowledges grief, 75
  Elicits "negative" emotions, 7, 70–71, 75, 81
  See Novozybkov, 84
Deuteronomic theology, 19, 21, 25–26, 224n.22
Dewey, John, 90, 92, 95, 100, 178
Dhammapada
  And Dr. King, 189
Diem, Ngo Dinh, 51
"Don't Shoot Your Brother" (campaign), 55
Douglass, Frederick, 119–22, 124, 215
  Early life, 11
  On failure of Christian churches, 121
  Meaning of Fourth of July to the Negro, 119–22
  On saving principles of the Republic, 120–21

278 | Index

Douglass, Frederick *(continued)*
   West Indies as authentic city on the hill, 122
Dukkha
   Collective, 4–5, 221n.15
   Defined, 221n.15
   Psychological/existential, 39
   See alienation
   See social misery

East Bay Meditation Center, 193–94
Egypt, world is not all, 181
Eightfold Path, 30, 98, 101, 160
   Ambedkar's reversal of customary roles, 98
   King's practice of nonviolence similar to, 137
   Sarvodaya's version, 169
Emptiness, 173
   Defined, 228n.36
   Means no fixed gender traits, 40
Engaged Buddhism
   And American Jeremiad, 124–25
   And Buddhist Peace Fellowship, 181
   Defined, 2
   Dismantling mass incarceration as historical project for, 203–209
   Dr. King's contributions to and challenges to, 137–38, 151
   Family resemblance to prophetic traits, 6
   Generational change, 5
   And ideology critique, 175–76, 182
   Models of engaged religious communities, 181
   Needs a critical social theory, 166
   And nonviolence, 148
   Principles to guide Buddhist engagement, 161–62
   And prophetic ethos, 3
   Types of engagement, 219–20n.5
   Versus racism, 148, 186

Exodus
   As frame for American Jeremiad, 113, 243–44n.7
   As ongoing journey, 23, 28
   And radical politics, 27
   Reenacted, 118, 129
   As subversive memory, 22–23
Ezekiel (prophet), 18, 217

Falk, Nancy, 34–35
Feminism, 2
   Indigenous Buddhist, 34, 41–42
   And prophetic voice, 35
   Search for alternative social order, 46
   Theological method of, 42
Floyd, George, 189
Four Noble Truth, 154, 160
   Ambedkar on, 98
   Gross and, 35
   Sarvodaya's version of, 169
Fourteen Mindfulness Trainings, 52
   Comparison with King's nonviolence steps, 160
   First three as ideology solvent, 175
   Putting tenth training into practice, 159–60
Frederickson, George
   Definition of race, 187–88
Freire, Paulo, 165

Gandhi, Mohandas, 88, 94, 102
   On caste and Dalits, 92
   Confrontation with Ambedkar, 91–92
   Rejects Dalits' satyagraha campaign, 90
Garner, Eric, 189
Garrison, William Lloyd, 119, 121
Gender
   Fixed roles as prison, 37
   Gender equality normative for all Buddhists, 40

Roles a product of causes and conditions, 40
Geuss, Raymond, 174
Giro, Seno, 171
Glassman, Bernie
  At Auschwitz-Birkenau, 83
  Don't know mind, 186
  See Zen Peacemaker Order
Goldstein, Joseph, 194
Great Turning (Macy), 80, 215
  Three kinds of action, 80
Great Unraveling, 80
Grief, practice of, 24–26
  Gross leaning into, 43, 215
  Mourning as act of resistance, 191–92
  See Kisa Gotami
  See Jeremiah
Gross, Rita, 2, 6–7, 33–46
  On anger, 43–44
  As boundary crosser, 2
  Critique of Patriarchal Buddhism, 36, 38–41
  Critique of Patriarchal Buddhism as fulfillment of bodhisattva vows, 44
  Early life, 34–35
  Experience of trauma and longing, 37
  On Four Noble Truths, 35
  And indigenous Buddhist feminism, 34
  And practice of grief, 43–44
  And prophetic method, 19, 34, 36, 38
  Summary of borrowings, 45–46
  Takes permission to use prophetic voice, 2
  See Patriarchal Buddhism
Guido, Uchiyama
  On Buddha Nature and Socialism, 171

Gutiérrez, Gustavo, 112, 169

Hastings, James, 97
Harrell, Willie, 118
Heschel, Abraham Rabbi, 8, 127, 138
  On the Divine pathos, 25
  On the monstrosity of injustice, 5
Historical project, 183
  Defined, 178–80
  Ending mass incarceration as possible historical project, 203–204
Hope, practice of
  Active hope, 78
  Buddhists skepticism about, 61, 71, 78
  Flight from the present moment, 61, 46, 78, 82
  And Hebrew prophets, 210
  Jeremiah's new covenant, 26
  See Solnit
Hosea (prophet), 20

Ideology critique, 19, 97, 172
  Mindfulness trainings as ideology solvent, 174–76
Imamuro, Ryo Rev., 190
Impermanence, 2
Interbeing, 76
Isaiah (prophet), 14–15, 18, 20–22, 121, 136, 150, 154, 210
Israel, Northern Kingdom of, 15

Japanese Americans
  Placed in concentration camps, 141–43, 190
  Preserving Buddhism, 142–43
  Racism towards, 141–42
Jaspers, James, 150–51
Jat-Pat Todak Mandal, 93
Jenkins, Willis, 127

Jeremiad
    African American, 117–23
    American, 8, 111–16
    Buddhist objections to, 124
    Dueling Jeremiads and moral balkanization, 115
    European, 113–14
    As skillful means, 124–25
    See moral chemotherapy
Jeremiah (prophet), 4–5, 14, 17, 22, 25–28, 45–46, 55–56, 59, 61, 80, 115, 133–34, 136–37, 186, 189, 214–15, 150
    On grief, 24–25
    On hope, 215
    And keeners, 5, 25
    And a new Exodus, 23, 213
    And prophetic stream, 23
    Sentenced to death, 217
    Versus Hananiah, 176
    Voice of, 211
    Wears yoke, 15
Joel (prophet), 20
Jones, Ken, 175
    On antithetical bonding, 176, 182
Jubilee, 121, 243n.36
Judah, Southern Kingdom of, 15
Justice
    Distributive justice, 154–55, 248–49 n.34
    Engaged Buddhists ambivalence towards, 154–55
    Hebrew prophets and, 21–22
    Restorative justice, 125, 204–209, 213
    Retribution as Incompatible with Buddhist teachings, 19, 154, 204–205, 233n.6
    Retributive justice, 19, 125, 154, 204–206, 214

Kaba, Mariame, 210

Kalama Sutta, 96
Kairos, 129
Karma
    Engaged Buddhists rejection of traditional interpretation of, 98
Kaveny, Cathleen, 176
    Critique of prophets' Oracles to the Nations, 116
    Lincoln and King standard for Jeremiads, 116, 124–25
    On moral chemotherapy, 19, 32, 115, 125–26, 244n.11
    See moral chemotherapy
Kim, Hyun Chul Paul, 15
King, Martin Luther Jr., 127–39
    Agony of prophet, 134
    As America's Jeremiah, 8–9, 136
    Collective version of Three poisons, 134
    And *Dhammapada*, 152
    Fierce urgency of now, 134
    Hagiography, 127–28, 136
    New turning of the wheel, 135
    Nonviolence vs. co-annihilation, 134
    On Love and Power, 135, 152–53
    Opposition to war in Vietnam, 132–34
    As reluctant prophet, 14, 129
    On Rip van Winkle and revolution, 127, 135, 215
    On spiritual death, 217
    World House, 135
    See Agape
    See Birmingham Jail, Letter from
    See Black Power
King, Sallie B.
    Definition of Engaged Buddhism, 2
    Moral obligation to speak forcefully, 32
    On "Please Call Me by My True Names," 66–67

Kisa Gotami, 47–48
Knitter, Paul, 3
Koan, 247n.5

Lamentations, Book of, 25–26
   Challenges Deuteronomic theology, 25
Lewis, John, 118
Liberation, 4
   Critique of, 53
   Of each requires liberation of all, 40
   Outer requires inner, 5
   As worldwide movement, 128
Liberation theology, 47, 166–68
   As contextual, 112, 169
   New generation, of 178
Lifton, Robert Jay, 73, 79, 136, 193, 217
   See also psychic numbing
Lincoln, Abraham
   Second inaugural speech as gold standard, 116
Love
   Discourse on, 195–96
   And fierce compassion, 195–96
   And Justice and power, 147–63
   See Agape; Bodhicitta; Maitri (loving-kindness)
Loy, David, 166, 176–77, 182
   On collective dukkha, 173
   On institutionalized ego, 173
   On lack, 172–74
   On weapons of mass deception, 175, 213

Macy, Joanna, 1, 69–85, 125, 136, 211
   Contributions to prophetic wisdom, 70–71
   And key religious experiences, 71, 73
   And open systems, 72–74
   Shambhala Warriors (myth), 69–70
   See also Despair and Empowerment workshops
   See Council of All Beings
   See deep ecology/deep time
   See Great Turniing
   See systems
   See Work that Reconnects
Magee, Rhonda
   Inner Work for Racial Justice, 180, 191–94, 200, 216
   STOP, 191
   See ColorInsight
Mahars, 88–89, 100–101
Maitreya (Buddha of the future), 61–62, 210, 216, 244n.11
Maitri, 92, 100
   And liberty and equality, 94–95
Makransky, John, 167–68
Manusmriti
   Ambedkar's burning of, 90, 158, 168
Marx, Karl, 92
   Theses on Feuerbach, 166, 177
Mass Incarceration
   Dismantling of as possible historical project for Engaged Buddhists, 203–204
   As new Jim Crow, 202–203
Melville, Herman
   On Exodus, 114
Merton, Thomas
   On Vietnam war, 53
Micah (prophet), 22
Misogyny, 20
Mobley, Mami Till, 192–93
Moral chemotherapy, 19–20, 28, 56, 63, 115, 125, 188, 203, 207, 215, 218
Moral discourse types of, 222–23n.6
Moses (prophet), 10, 211
   Puritans reenact final sermon of, 112

Mother love/mother's grief, 47–48

NAACP, 128, 156–57
Ness, Arne, 76
Nhat Chi Mai, 57–58
   Self-immolation, 57
Nhat Hanh, Thich, 49–66, 181, 185–86, 218
   Buddhism made of non-Buddhists elements, 4
   Buddhist peace delegation/Third way, 52–54
   Comparison with the Hebrew prophets, 7, 55, 62–63
   Exile and community building, 52, 60–61, 156–57
   Life and influence, 2–3, 50
   "Please Call Me by My True Names," 65–67, 232n.40
   Poems banned by both sides, 51
   On power, 147–48, 250n.52
   On war in Vietnam, 49
   See Fourteen Mindfulness Trainings
   See Order of Interbeing (Tiep Hien)
Nibbana/Nirvana
   Ambedkar on, 98, 101
Niebuhr, Reinhold, 147–48, 151, 157
Nonviolence, 3, 130–31, 133, 137, 147–63, 151
   As hallmark of Engaged Buddhism, 9
   Never pure, 162
   And pragmatism, 149
   And principles for action, 161–62
   As requiring disobedience, 149
   See Birmingham Jail, Letter from
Novozybkov, 84

O'Brien, Julia M.
   Metaphors and frame, 20
Ohnuma, Reiko, 47–48
Oppression, 40, 122
   Of Dalits, 92
   Defined, 4–5
   And Egypt, 27
   And entrenched power, 157
   Shifting forms of racial, 201
   As systemic, 81
   World wide movements in opposition to, 128
   See liberation
Owens, Lama Ron, 194–96
   On fierce love, 195–96
Order of Interbeing, 159, 175
   Formation of, 52, 59
   See Fourteen Mindfulness Trainings

Pajapati (Gotami), 33–34
Patriarchal Buddhism, 14, 19, 35, 40, 43, 126, 138, 212
   As justice issue for all Buddhists, 45
Patriarchy
   And Buddhism, 39
   As historical not biological, 39
   As oppressive, 39–40
   As systemic, 126
Personalist philosophy, 131
Petrella, Ivan
   On the idea of a historical project, 178–79
   See Bonino, Jose Miguez
Postracial society, 201
Power, 147–48
   Arendt and, 148–49
   Cortright and, 147–48
   Love and, 150–54
   Nhat Hanh and, 147, 231n.26
Pratītya samutpāda (Dependent coarising), 72
   Defined, 221n.13
   See dependent coarising
Praxis, 166–83
   Critical reflection on, 112
   Critical social theory, 172
   Defined, 167–68
   Historically situated, 169–72

Ideology critique, 174–76
Strategic action, 178–80
Summary of components, 181–83
Symbolically constituted, 168–69
See Alienation
See Loy, David
Present moment, 61
Prophets, Hebrew, 13–29
Confront collective trauma, 24–25
Contemporary scholarship on, 14, 222n.3
M. L. King on, 13
And power politics, 148–50
Read signs of times, 6
Prophetic texts
As classics, 17–18
As polyphonic texts, 16–17
Require ethical interpretation, 20
Prophets, characteristic traits of
Alternative narrative, 16
Call for action, 16
Call for justice by, 16, 21–22
Critique of royal consciousness by, 213
Ideology critique by, 16–17
Practice of grief by, 16
Practice of hope by, 16
Reluctant, 14, 222n.4
Subversive memory of, 16–17
Summary of, 28–29, 212–13
See Amos; Ezekiel; Hosea; Isaiah; Jeremiah; Joel; Micah
Prophetic action, 150
Prophetic dimension, 36–37
Prophetic Ethos, 3
As spiritual practice, 21, 230n.49
Prophetic imagination, 26–27
Prophetic method, 19
Prophetic persona, 14, 129
Prophetic Voice of, 13–15, 31, 212
And symbolic actions, 15, 31–32
Prophetic wisdom, 10; 221–22n.21

Psychic numbing, 73
Collective, 73–74, 136
And prophets of Exile, 75
See Lifton, Robert Jay
Puritans
World transforming mission of, 113–14, 117
See Winthrop, John and Wiggelsworth, Michael

Quang Duc, Thich
Self-immolation 55
Queen, Christopher, 2, 88, 97–98
On Ambedkar's revision of Buddhist teachings, 98
On Navayana, 215
Qumran community, 18, 212
And Pesharim and expanded prophetic narratives, 18

Race/racism, 9–10, 185–210 187–88
Defined, 187–88
Needs moral chemotherapy, 188
Racial caste system, 197–200, 202–203, 210
Racial Justice, inner work for
STOP (exercise), 191
See Rhonda Magee
Rankine, Claudia
Mourning as resistance, 192–93
Rauschenberg, Walter, 114–15
Religious experience
Nontheistic, 42
And transcendence and immanence, 42–43
Re-membering, 61
Right Speech
Criteria for, 31–32
Roy, Arundhati, 89, 91–92, 94
Royal consciousness, 23–24
And Hindu caste system, 93
Ruether, Walter, 153
Rustin, Bayard, 244n.11

Sarvodaya movement (Sri Lanka), 155
  Historical project of, 179–80
Satyagraha (truth force), 101, 103, 158, 198
  Gandhi's rejection Dalits' campaigns, 90–91
Sered, Danielle
  On Restorative Justice, 206–209
Shambhala Warriors, 68–70
  Similarities to Hebrew prophets, 70
Sharp, Gene
  Nonviolence as expression of power, 149
Sivaraksa, Sulak, 155, 178
Slow violence, 84–85
Snyder, Gary, 165–66
Social Gospel, Christian, 97, 114–15
  And Dr. King, 136
Social misery, 100, 165–66, 172, 182–83
  See collective dukkha
Social revolution
  And compassion, 165–66
  And maitri, 100
Social theory, critical, 9
Social tyranny
  Worse than political tyranny, 94
Solnit, Rebecca, 2–3, 78
  On hope, 27–28
Spiritual death, 28, 43, 116, 122
Structural violence, 1–5, 36, 48, 94, 137, 148, 152–53, 155, 162, 174, 178
  And caste system, 94
  Defined, 220n.6
Stulman, Louis, 15–17, 20, 24–25
Suzuki, D. T. and Japanese imperialism, 170–71
Syedullah, Jasmine
  On radical dharma, 194–96
Systemic injustice, 2, 5, 48, 116, 124, 137, 203

Systems
  And Great Turning, 80
  Theory of, 71–74, 76–77, 172, 175
  See Caste
  See racial caste system

Thai environmental monks, 181–82
Therigatha
  As counter narrative, 41, 48
Three poisons, 44, 98
  Collective, 125, 134, 137
Thubten Yeshe, Lam, 189
Tibetan Buddhism, 35, 70, 189
Till, Emmett, 192–93
Tocqueville, Alexis de, 158, 249n.42
Tracy, David, 17, 167
Transnational Advocacy Networks (TANS), 158
Turning the Wheel, 128, 135, 137
Tworkov, Helen, 190

Van Volde, Elizabeth, 19
Victoria, Brian, 170–72, 182
Vedas, 93

Walker, David, 118–19
Walzer, Michael, 22–23
  On Exodus and hope, 27, 117
War
  Buddha vs. Augustine, 107
  As ecological catastrophe, 56
  Inner bombs waiting to explode, 58
  As metastatic cancer, 59
  Requires a new Engaged Buddhism, 50
  See Nhat Hanh, Thich
Ward, Jesmyn, 118
Ward-Lev, Nahum Rabbi, 150–51, 166, 192
  On Exodus as ongoing, 22–23
Washington, Booker T., 122
Wells, Ida B., 122–23, 215

West, Cornel, 165–66
　On Black prophetic fire, 111, 114
　On the radical King, 128
White supremacy, 117–18, 123, 129, 136, 188, 192, 199, 218
　Exodus as counter narrative to, 118
Wigglesworth, Michael, 113
Wilkerson, Isabel
　On eight pillars of caste, 196–200
　Engaged Buddhism's resources for dealing with the caste pillars of pollution and stigmatization, 198–200
williams, angel Kyodo, 112, 185
　And radical dharma, 194–96
Willis, Jan, 188–89, 213
Winthrop, John, 111
Work that Reconnects
　Acknowledging pain for the world, 76
　Spiral process of, 78
World Renunciation, 2, 39, 43

Yang, Larry, 193–94
Yasodhara (Buddha's wife), 41–42, 105–106
YHWH
　And grief, 25
　And preferential option for widow, orphan and alien, 28
　As prosecutor, judge and executioner, 18
　As transcendent, 24
Yumibe, Misao, 141–42
Youth League for Revitalizing Buddhism *See* Seno Giro

Zehr, Howard, 205–206
Zen Peacemaker Order, 181
　Three tenets of, 83
Zen priests support for Japanese imperialism, 161
Zhaozhou and the old woman, 31
Ziyong, 32
Zulick, Margaret, 17

www.ingramcontent.com/pod-product-compliance
Lightning Source LLC
Chambersburg PA
CBHW020640230426
43665CB00008B/251